The E

Dying, De

John R Ling

Day One

© Day One Publications 2002
First printed 2002

All Scripture quotations are from The New International Version © 1973,1978,1984, International Bible Society. Published by Hodder and Stoughton.

British Library Cataloguing in Publication Data available
ISBN 1 903087 30 9

Published by Day One Publications
3 Epsom Business Park, Kiln Lane, Epsom, Surrey KT17 1JF.
01372 728 300 FAX 01372 722 400
email—sales@dayone.co.uk
web site—www.dayone.co.uk
North American—e-mail—sales@dayonebookstore.com
North American web site—www.dayonebookstore.com

Designed by Steve Devane and printed by CPD

For
Simeon, Benjamin and Anna.

Contents

Contents

Contents

Contents

Contents

Contents

Contents

Contents

Contents

Acknowledgements

A book may have one author, but it is never the work of just one person. I have many to thank for helping me with this volume.

First, there are my chums, from the Citizenship Committee of the Fellowship of Independent Evangelical Churches, who initially thought that I could, and moreover, should, write this book. Second, there are the early influences that informed and structured my thinking about bioethical issues. Foremost among these were the late Francis Schaeffer and C Everett Koop with their project, *Whatever Happened to the Human Race?*, which, in the late 1970s, awakened me to the horrors of euthanasia, together with those of abortion and infanticide. Third, there are my many friends and co-belligerents from the pro-life charity, LIFE and its specialist grouping, Evangelicals for LIFE. Fourth, there are those friends and family, who have spurred me on by enquiring about this book's progress. Fifth, there is Sergey Rakhmaninov, or, at least, his four soothing piano concertos and three stirring symphonies, which have helped me concentrate on this project, hour after hour. The recordings by the BBC National Orchestra of Wales on Nimbus Records are a real snip at just £25 for six CDs! Finally, there is my wife, Wendy, who has again been a real helpmeet in this venture. She has not only kept control of relevant press cuttings, articles, letters and photocopies for the last twenty years, but she has also generously given me the time and space to complete this work.

Dear Reader,

It may seem impertinent, even rude, at the very beginning of a book, to cause you alarm, but I have some disturbing news for you. Let me tell you straight. Hopefully, you are sitting down. Ready? Here it is—*you are going to die.*

Most of us have already had some brushes with death—we have fallen off ladders, been in car accidents, and so on—but the real thing, the big one, your very own finale, is coming. When it will happen, I cannot be sure, but I think it will be sooner than most of you imagine. It is already a few minutes nearer than when you first picked up this book.

Death is that most certain of certainties. Axiomatically, life is so uncertain. It is so fragile. Now we inhale, then exhale, inhale, exhale, but it will not continue like this, will it? It will come to a halt. It will finish. Your breathing, heartbeat, brain, and then your entire life, will come to a stop. As the title of this book suggests, you and I are already living on the edge of life.

This certainty and proximity of death should unsettle us. They should also cause us to ask the fundamental question that underlies this book— *am I ready to die?* If not, then it would be wise to start thinking about dying and death, and even to begin making some preparations to face them. This book has been written to help you do exactly that.

Preface

When I began writing this book, it was to be a straightforward examination of just the one issue, euthanasia. To tell the truth, the partly-written manuscript grew to be so irksome that I hid it away in a box for several months and instead wrote an easier and more heartening book entitled, *Responding to the Culture of Death—A Primer of Bioethical Issues*. Then I realized that a book about euthanasia alone was bound to be dreary because the subject is skewed. What it needed was to be balanced by the topics of dying and death. These may not seem like jolly corrective themes, but believe me, they are. So, I broadened my original remit and have now written about these three edge-of-life topics, together with some of the other bioethical issues that surround them.

Throughout, I have had three simple aims. First, I want to persuade you that thinking about dying and death is not only prudent, but also beneficial. Such contemplations need not be morbid or depressing. In fact, I expect the outcome to be quite the opposite. With death in view, we are much more likely to live well. 'My people live well and die well.' That boast, or something pretty similar, has often been attributed to John Wesley, that remarkable eighteenth-century Christian leader. Strangely, I can find no evidence, anywhere, that he actually said or wrote it, but no matter, because it remains a grand and fitting epitaph for every Christian. All Christians should aim for a good life *and* a good death. Thinking about dying and death will turn us into realists. We will realize what little time we have left—the clock is ticking and its ratchet goes only one way. That thought alone should provoke us to become more useful people, and it should preserve us from idleness and triviality. *Carpe diem* should be our motto. For the non-Christian and the Christian alike, the end of this life is coming into view, fast. Are you prepared for your last lap? When Christians see that finishing tape, they should want to run faster and better (Hebrews 12:1–3). For the non-Christian, there must be hesitation, serious doubt, and some stark questions to ponder. That is my number one aim, to get you to think about, understand, and prepare for dying and death.

My second aim is to persuade you of the horrors of modern-day euthanasia. Euthanasia is like a wretched spanner in the works. The fact that people out there might want to kill you and me before our natural end, the fact that some doctors are willing to do the dirty deed, and the fact that some politicians and other influential decision-makers approve of such a course of action, is alarming. Euthanasia should make us all uneasy. Most Christians, indeed, most morally-sensitive people, feel that they should be opposed to euthanasia, but they are usually none too sure why—they have not yet thought sufficiently seriously about the issue. Euthanasia is wrong, above all, because it is counter to a proper understanding of the dignity and value of human life, and because it distrusts the providence of God. Supporters of euthanasia argue in its favour mainly on the grounds of so-called compassion and personal autonomy—these people are gravely mistaken and misguided. Aim number two is therefore to help you unravel and understand modern-day euthanasia and several other of its associated topics.

Whenever a family member or a friend is dying, and death becomes imminent, all kinds of new problems and complex burdens arise. And when you and I are dying, we too will create similar difficulties and become the cause of stress and strain for our loved ones. These problems will need solving and these burdens will need bearing. Usually, it is not easy. At these crucial times, what we, and they, will need are not anodyne instructions or lukewarm platitudes, but 'principled compassion'. This is the proper PC, namely, the sort of care and caring that is deeply rooted within the ethical framework of the Bible. This is another of the enduring themes of this book. That you will become genuinely convinced of the need to give, and one day, to receive, this principled compassion is my aim number three.

We all want to live well and die well. Therefore we all need a deep, deep understanding of both living and dying. The raw truth is that we need a practical theology of living *and* of dying. The latter is a particularly scarce item. Overall, this book seeks to begin to redress that dearth. If reading it helps anyone perform these two great tasks of living and dying any better, then my labours will have been well rewarded.

John R Ling
Aberystwyth
January 2002

Introduction

'But in this world nothing can be said to be certain, except death and taxes.'

In a book with a title like this one, I knew it would be tricky to avoid quoting this droll adage. In the end, obviously, I could not resist. However, I want to put a somewhat different spin on it from Benjamin Franklin's eighteenth-century original. While taxes and death remain unavoidable, my contention is that nowadays taxes are being used *for* death. That is, more and more countries are adopting public policies that are putting to death their very own citizens, and we are all paying for this human slaughter with our taxes. Abortion, infanticide and euthanasia are costing us dear. And the cost is not just financial, it is also psychological, medical, social and bioethical. In truth, the three issues of abortion, infanticide, and latterly, euthanasia are ripping us all apart.

1.1 Three issues—one mindset

There seem to be no limits to the cruelty inflicted on humans by humans. Indeed, much of our history can be viewed as a catalogue of cruelty *by* the human race *towards* the human race—men, women and children. And we are not talking here about the cruelties of war, or famine, or political strife, or personal animosity. No—there is this other, far more remarkable, category of human cruelty.

It is one of the curious, even bizarre, features of our so-called civilized, educated, wealthy and sophisticated societies that we insist on, and persist in, deliberately putting to death our own defenceless, young offspring. And currently, we do it to millions and millions each year. This is a human cruelty above all others. It is spearheaded by the practice of abortion and then, by default, infanticide. And now, our world is displaying an increasing enthusiasm for hastening the death of its more elderly citizens, by euthanasia.

Euthanasia is undeniably linked to these two already well-established, life-ending practices. To be sure, it comes from the same mindset, the same songsheet, as abortion and infanticide. Others have used a different, perhaps more striking, analogy. They have likened this lethal trio to a row of three upended dominoes—when the first practice is initially tolerated, then sanctioned and finally legalized, it topples over and inexorably knocks over the second, and then the third. This is the 'domino theory' applied to bioethics. Abortion leads to infanticide leads to euthanasia. And so it has come to pass, not just in theory, but also in earnest practice.

1.2 Abortion—the number one issue

Abortion was the number one bioethical issue of the twentieth century— euthanasia is set to collect the same accolade for the twenty-first. History is full of lessons and warnings, so a brief examination of some of the events that precipitated changes in abortion law, and some of the features that have developed in the aftermath of legalized abortion, can be salutary, yet instructive.

For centuries, legal safeguards for the unborn child had been enshrined in several Acts of Parliament. Calls for changes to these protective laws had been isolated and muted until the 1930s, when some concerted and strident voices started to be raised. This pro-abortion rhetoric came initially from just a few propagandists, especially from members of the Abortion Law Reform Association (ALRA), and it was largely countered by those from within the medical, political and legal establishments. Then, some illegal abortions were revealed. Next, a few hard cases were placarded. Finally, one or two lawsuits ensued. It was all shrewd publicity. The notion that 'hard cases make bad law' was conveniently forgotten. These various colliding elements, foisted on a largely uninformed, but by now, anxious public, by a vocal, well-organized and well-heeled minority, culminated in the 1967 Abortion Act—arguably the most cruel and discriminatory piece of legislation ever to appear on our Statute Book.

What was legalized, or, at least, declared to be no longer 'unlawful', in Great Britain in 1967, spread across the USA in 1973, and subsequently has become the norm in almost every country. This legalization of abortion has profoundly changed our world, forever, and entirely for the worse. It has wrecked the medical profession in both its ethics and practice. The supposed beneficiaries, namely, pregnant women, have been damaged physically, and especially psychologically. It has helped undermine marriage. It has abrogated the protective role of fathers. It has distorted family life and increased grief, guilt and remorse among its members. It has subverted deep relationships between men, women and children. It has brought uncertainty to born children and grandparents. It has confounded adoption. It has reintroduced eugenics. It has hardened our compassion towards the weak. It has upset our demographic balance. More could be added to this blacklist, but these are enough. The aftermath of legalized abortion certainly makes for a breathtaking compendium of personal tragedy and social decline. One cruel law, written on just three-and-a-half sides of official Parliamentary paper, ushered in the practice of a cruel medicine, the ramifications of which have affected, and infected, us all. Pre-eminently, this advent of easy, legal abortion has changed our view of unborn human life. What was once protected by law and described by adjectives such as, 'unique', 'precious' and 'inviolable', is now legally vulnerable and regarded in many quarters as 'cheap', 'insignificant' and 'disposable'. The irrefutable evidence to support such seemingly-audacious statements is found among the tens of millions of abortions that are carried out each year, worldwide. The vast, vast majority of these are performed on preborn children who are both completely normal and entirely healthy—can this practice be anything other than savage medicine?

1.3 Infanticide—the go-between issue

The abortion domino has well and truly fallen, and it has knocked over the next one—infanticide is now part of our scheme of things. Uncounted and untold thousands, even millions, of newborn children are deliberately killed every year. Infanticide stands, or rather, falls, as the inevitable intermediary between abortion and euthanasia. Unlike abortion, infanticide is still widely unlawful, but like abortion that does not stop it being widely practised. It is linked to abortion because one kills the *un*born child, and the other kills the *new*born child. It is linked to euthanasia because it is in reality, *neonatal* euthanasia. Truly, it is the go-between issue.

Abortion and infanticide are two horrible examples of medical practices that have thrived under such frivolous euphemisms as, 'freedom of choice' and 'a woman's right to choose'. To choose what? To destroy her own offspring, her own unborn, or newborn, child? When abortion and infanticide are put together with the more recent practice of human embryo experimentation, they demonstrate how entirely comprehensive our medicalized destruction of human life has become during the first part of the age spectrum. Indeed, early human life itself has become trivialized.

But why stop there? What about life at the other end of the age spectrum? If a six-month-old unborn child, who is sentient and viable, can be legally killed, just because his mother so chooses, and a kicking and whimpering child, who just happens to display some disability six hours after birth, can also suffer the same outcome, then why cannot a six-year-old child, or, most poignantly in the context of this book, a sixty-six-year-old man, be killed? After all, they too can be inconvenient and unwanted by their relatives, unproductive and costly for society. Just what is the logic of our current prohibition on euthanasia? Surely, it cannot be medical squeamishness? Surely, it cannot be anything as philosophically flimsy as an age-related barrier? Surely, sauce for the little gosling can also be sauce for that old goose and gander? What holds us back from a wholesale purging of our old people's homes and hospital wards? Just think, for one moment, of the financial savings that such a policy would bring to the National Health Service. Consider the benefits that euthanasia would bring in terms of sparing scarce medical resources, preserving personal peace and reducing emotional turmoil. Can you see how near the surface the implementation of a public policy of euthanasia must be in the minds of some? Such a move would also bring about a neat and tidy symmetry. The legalization of euthanasia for the elderly would complete our control of *all* human life. We already have abortion for the unborn, and infanticide for the newborn. Euthanasia for the elderly would allow us to regard *any*, and even *all*, human life as worthless, futile and expendable.

1.4 Euthanasia—the current issue

Euthanasia is one of the central issues of this book. It may be difficult to believe, but once upon a time, euthanasia was a wonderful word. It originally referred to what everybody wanted, 'a good, happy death'. Then, during the nineteenth century, the meaning of the word was changed so that it became associated with putting people to death before their natural end. Now, modern-day, twenty-first century euthanasia has become a decidedly ugly word.

Despite this somewhat confusing etymology, euthanasia, that is, the deliberate killing of people prematurely, has been practised, albeit probably sporadically, and in smallish numbers, from ancient times. Now, at the beginning of the third millennium, it has mushroomed into one of the most controversial issues of medical ethics and practice. So it is not a new issue. Nor is it a simple issue. Euthanasia is enmeshed with several other topics as complex and diverse as dying and death, autonomy, eugenics, permanent vegetative state, ageing, and the like. Furthermore, the same long and winding process that preceded the legalization of abortion has already begun with respect to euthanasia, and the outcome looks similarly bleak, and almost as inevitable.

The great social experiment of euthanasia must never be allowed to be conducted. There are good reasons, derived from the precedents of abortion and infanticide, to believe that legalized euthanasia, even of the voluntary variety, will launch an ethical disintegration and an additional dimension of dehumanization within society that we have not yet even dared to consider. It will distort our bioethical perceptions to such an extent that once legalized it will be prescribed for those who are neither dying, nor able to give their consent. Furthermore, we would be wholly naive to assume that any law permitting euthanasia will not produce widespread, inhumane abuses. The poor and the vulnerable will be further marginalized. Care for the elderly will inevitably decline. 'Why waste time and money on them?', will become the popular cry. Human life will be further demeaned. We must never allow all this to happen. Herein is one of the challenges of this book—will you be part of the problem, or part of the solution?

1.5 The approach of other books
Of all the books about euthanasia published during the last two decades, any listing of the most influential would have to include *The End of Life—*

Euthanasia and Morality, by James Rachels (1986), *Should the Baby Live?*, by Helga Kuhse and Peter Singer (1986), and *An Intelligent Person's Guide to Ethics*, by Mary Warnock (1998).

It is intriguing to note that all of these pro-euthanasia authors, and many others too, begin their books by describing one or two exceptionally difficult human cases. They would, I am sure, say that they were simply 'setting the scene'. Nevertheless, it is reminiscent of the tactics used by members of ALRA as part of their scare-mongering strategy to liberalize abortion law during the last century. I would contend that the selection, by these authors, of such emotionally-charged examples are designed to confuse genuinely-inquiring readers in order to win them over to the author's viewpoint. Furthermore, this approach demonstrates just how muddled these moral philosophers are. They all have got it the wrong way round—they have put the cartload of examples before the ethical horse. For them, the hard cases become the centre of focus. Such an approach inevitably gives rise to their beloved 'situation ethics', whereby the particular case, rather than the search for an underlying general principle, takes centre stage and determines the ethic as well as the ensuing action. Their back-to-front arguments are from the particular to the general— welcome to the topsy-turvy world of modern moral philosophy! And, since these authors' worldviews are, without exception, secular humanistic and utilitarian, their recommended practical responses are, naturally, unprincipled and pragmatic. After all, that is what situation ethics is all about. And whatever you do, don't mention 'absolutes'—they all despise them. Of course they do. For them, the only absolute is that there are no absolutes!

1.6 The approach of this book

This book begins quite differently. Part 1 begins, not with individual cases, but with foundational principles—plain, universal principles, derived from the Bible. Once these ethical principles have been laid down, the primary issues will be bolted on in Part 2. This is the proper way to build, be it a house, or an ethical worldview—foundations first, then the superstructure. And because the threat and awfulness of euthanasia cannot be grasped adequately without a decent understanding of dying and death, it is these three grand topics that become interwoven and highlighted throughout all the Parts of this book. To ensure that the primary issues of Part 2 cannot be dismissed as merely abstract concepts, some traumatic, ground-breaking case studies are examined in Part 3. Next, a whole raft of other secondary, but related, bioethical issues are explained in Part 4. Then, and as important as any other portion of this book, Part 5 contains some practical, pro-life responses to these issues. Part 6 is the coda. An adequate appreciation of edge-of-life issues requires some historical background, some contemporary quotations, some ethical perspective, some unsentimental analysis, and some up-to-date information—these too are included throughout the following pages.

But to begin at the beginning, these issues will be considered within the ethical warp and weft of biblical truth. This is no antediluvian, anti-intellectual, quasi-religious cop-out. Indeed, it is quite the reverse, for two very good reasons. First, the Bible declares itself to be true (John 17:17; 2 Timothy 3:16). This means that the information it conveys is inerrant, and the standards it sets are absolute. In other words, we are here dealing with unconditional, non-negotiable, true, truths. The Bible therefore provides us with the real basis for discussing, for example, who we are as human beings, and how we should live, individually, in families, and in society—both before men and before God. This is immensely liberating—it releases us from the bondage and uncertainty of the shifting relativism of society's current mindset, namely, secular humanism.

Second, the Bible makes far greater demands upon those who follow its teaching than does any man-made system of ethics. It compels us, for instance, not just to care for our families, and help our friends, but, revolutionarily, it commands us to love our enemies (Luke 6:27). The normal Christian life is one of cross-bearing and denial of self (Matthew 16:24). The Scriptures' portrayal of the good life is one of service, giving of our time, energy and talents for the benefit of others. In the context of this book, it means that we are to uphold and promote the utmost respect for all human life. We are to defend, protect and cherish all men, women and children. Such a valiant enterprise will be neither effortless, nor trouble-free. Legalizing and giving in to euthanasia, that is the real cop-out, the easy evasion, the secular humanist's dodge, the utilitarian's fudge.

Opposing euthanasia will never be the simple or comfortable option. There are some rather clever people out there who are bent on legalizing euthanasia—some of them are the most engaging people you will ever meet, and sometimes their arguments sound so plausible. Countering them will be demanding. Many of them are from the political and medical establishments and they often have high media profiles, as well as friends in high places. Therefore, we need to be sure of our principles and the veracity of our cause. Yet, however clever their pro-euthanasia arguments and tactics are, it is profoundly reassuring to know that there are objective truths upon which we can construct and sustain an entirely robust anti-euthanasia stance. And in the final analysis, euthanasia will be defeated because ordinary people, like you and me (no, not *like* you and me, but *actually* you and me), not only knew, but also acted upon, these truths.

This is the Bible's two-fold configuration for all aspects of Christian living. First, the truths, the doctrines, the statutes, the precepts, the principles are presented. These are the credenda—things to be believed. Second, comes the call to think, to speak, and to live those very truths. These are the agenda—things to be done. So it must be for those who are mandated to care for all those made in the image of God, and who are therefore implacably opposed to euthanasia. First, principles. Second, action. This is the overall pattern of this book. First, the ethical bedrock is assembled, and upon this, all the major and minor edge-of-life issues are examined and judged. Second, the answers and practical responses to these issues are developed and applied. Together, the credenda and agenda generate that greatest of all responses, principled compassion.

1.7 This book is for all

But this book is not just for Christians, it is aimed at a much wider readership—all the living. Whatever your mindset or worldview, dying, death and euthanasia are issues that you will be forced to confront. And they will require answers from you. So where will you find a solid ethical grounding, a sure philosophical base, upon which you can build a secure bioethical superstructure to provide those answers? Currently, the predominant driving force behind ethics, and particularly medical ethics, is secular humanism. This is a man-made, man-centred, shifting utilitarianism—it believes that whatever action produces the greatest good for the greatest number of people must be true. But just look at what this mindset has produced. Its fruit are a bunch of horrors including abortion-on-demand, destructive experimentation on human embryos, infanticide, and now, euthanasia. Medicine's once-proud ethics and practices have come to this miserable end—its modern mantra has become, 'killing the patient can be OK'.

Of course, medical personnel are at the sharp end of these fatal practices. Nevertheless, this book is *not* a vendetta, or some smug diatribe, against doctors and other healthcare professionals—all of us are, to some extent, blameworthy. Nevertheless, doctors and their associates should know better than to participate in abortion, infanticide and euthanasia, but many of them have become little more than the unthinking pawns of society. They have become our social executioners—we have asked them to carry out these ghastly deeds, and they have complied, usually, it must be said, without much honourable resistance, or praiseworthy hesitation. Thus, one by one, healthcare professionals, and their previously-illustrious medical specialties, have fallen. Obstetrics and gynaecology have already been ruined by the practice of abortion. Paediatrics has become contaminated by infanticide. And now geriatrics is under siege from euthanasia. There is currently a widespread belief throughout the medical profession, and elsewhere, that some human beings are morally valueless, substandard non-persons who can, and even should, be put down. That is, they should be selected, and then culled by abortion, infanticide, or euthanasia.

So this book is not just for Christians, nor just for healthcare professionals. It is for all, because none can escape dying and death. Many of us have already had to face them, as it were, by proxy, usually with the loss of our parents, or elderly relatives. Such times are invariably difficult and we were probably surprised how unprepared and how emotionally affected we were, even when these events were anticipated. Such times will come again, and next time, hopefully, we will be more prepared and better able to cope. But dying and death have an additional and intensely personal edge to them—our own dying and death are not far away. Their inevitability and nearness should rattle us.

If dying and death are inescapable, and have always been challenging and tough, now there is this additional edge-of-life obstacle, euthanasia. Recent developments in medical ethics and practice confirm the increasing probability of our having to face such a predicament. It may be on behalf of an aged aunt, a father, a brother, or a wife, and eventually, on behalf of no one else, but ourself. And what will you think, and say, and do then? To be forewarned is to be forearmed. Now is the time to understand the issues, rehearse the arguments and formulate your responses—in the heat of the moment, at the hospital bedside, will generally be too late.

This book seeks to be a guidebook to the edge of life. It is *not* a comprehensive book, though it does seek to tackle the key issues and answer the main questions. It is *not* a medical textbook, though a little medical knowledge will be provided where necessary. It is *not* a counselling handbook, though communicating with others and seeking their advice and support is a recommended strategy. It is *not* an academic book, though it remains serious rather than lightweight, yet also warm-hearted rather than frosty. In addition, there is an intentional development of ideas and themes throughout its six Parts and it therefore makes most sense to read it from beginning to end. However, that will not be everyone's practice— many readers will want to dip into single chapters. To allow for this, most chapters have been written to be largely free-standing. This, of course, demands some repetition—please bear with it. On the other hand, who does not benefit from a little recapitulation now and again?

These edge-of-life issues will test us all to the full. How then will you think, speak, and act realistically and properly when confronted by them? Hopefully, this book will help. We can be very good at evading reality, avoiding the truth, and seeking to minimize our discomfort as we press on, searching for that life of personal peace and affluence. Getting to grips with these edge-of-life issues will shatter some of these pursuits. But it will also highlight the fundamentals of life and death. And this is the huge payoff from facing dying and death—it exchanges doubt, and fatuity for certainty and reality.

Whenever I walk through our local cemetery, I always pause by one grave. On it is inscribed this message for the living from Psalm 90:12, 'Teach us to number our days aright, that we may gain a heart of wisdom.' It will not be long before we will all be in a similar graveyard somewhere, scattered on the ground, or buried six feet under. For some people, death is the ultimate unknown and therefore frightening. For others, death itself holds little fear, but the process of dying can be a fearful prospect. The wise will therefore start now to number their days and begin to prepare for a good death, for what will be their 'true euthanasia'.

And the preparation starts here. In the realm of bioethics, we must learn how to walk before we can run, but, even before that, we must discover how to get up onto our bioethical feet and simply stand. Principles and themes from the Scriptures will enable us to do just that—so, look to the next page.

The Foundations

'Indeed, we are already witnessing the erosion of our idea of man as something splendid or divine, as a creature with freedom and dignity. And clearly, if we come to see ourselves as meat, then meat we shall become.'

Leon R Kass, (1972) *The Public Interest.*

Any book that deals with edge-of-life issues must deal with foundations—what is the basis, or source, of the author's, and thus the book's, ethical stance? The answers for this author and this book are the Judaeo-Christian doctrines and the Hippocratic oath. These were the very foundations of the ethics and practice of early medicine, and they remained so for about the next 2,500 years.

The importance of the Hippocratic oath may have diminished somewhat, but the Scriptures remain. To this day, they are the most powerful and pervasive ethical code the world has ever known—they still continue to turn the lives of men and women, and as a consequence, societies, upside down. Their influence upon civilization, especially in the West, means that they have structured so many aspects of our lives, including, of course, medicine. Their impact upon the latter has been undeniably profound and wholly beneficial, creating a culture of life. That is why they occupy a pre-eminent position in this Part—you cannot understand the development of the ethics and practice of medicine without understanding something of the Scriptures.

One of the major themes of this book is that modern medicine has gone wrong. It has forsaken its two-fold original foundation, and instead, it has substituted feeble philosophies and crumbly values, typified by secular humanism. The original, sure foundations produced a high view of human life and a wholesome medicine, practised within this so-called culture of life. These new, shifting foundations have resulted in a low view of human life and have turned much of medicine into a dubious endeavour, practised within a culture of death. To understand modern-day medicine and the threats posed by these edge-of-life issues, something of the rise and fall of the ethics of medicine must be grasped, hence their presentation in the second half of this Part.

Themes from the Scriptures

We can all agree that dying, death and euthanasia are fascinating but complex issues—after all, they have captivated and bewildered most people throughout most of history. To grasp them sufficiently is going to require some serious cerebral exercising and mental wrestling—at times, the going is going to get tough.

Above all, we will need wisdom, that all-too rare commodity, which transcends mere knowledge and experience, but which is the practical and prudent application of both. Common sense is good, but wisdom is far better. Where can we go to get such wisdom? The Bible despises the self-styled 'wisdom of this world', which is both man-centred and self-congratulatory—it calls it 'foolishness' (1 Corinthians 3:19). On the other hand, Christians are offered a double source of true wisdom, namely, the God of the Book, and the Book of God. First, there is the God of the Book. James 1:5 declares, 'If any of you lacks wisdom, he should ask God ...' Furthermore, this offer is backed up by the divine guarantee, namely, '... and it will be given ...' Christianity is rooted in this 'knowability' of the infinite, yet personal God. Because he may be enquired of, it follows that this infinite God may be personally known. As the verse starkly states, '... ask God ...' Second, there is the Book of God, the Scriptures, the Bible, the Word of God. This is also to be our wise guide, 'Your word is a lamp to my feet and a light for my path' (Psalms 119:105). And as it says of itself, 'All Scripture is God-breathed and is useful for teaching, rebuking, correcting and training in righteousness, so that the man of God may be thoroughly equipped for every good work' (2 Timothy 3:16). Transcendent wisdom, help from above, can be ours. What more could we want? What more could we need to tackle these edge-of-life issues?

Yet search this Book for the words 'euthanasia', or 'infanticide', or even 'suicide', and none of them will be found, anywhere. It may therefore be concluded that the Bible has nothing to say on these subjects. However, that would be wrong, quite wrong. The Book is not silent about such topics—relevant doctrines, concepts, precepts, and examples abound. Oh yes, the Bible has plenty to say about human life and death, its value, its purpose and its destiny. However, the Bible is not exhaustive—it does not tell us everything we might want to know. But it is sufficient—it does tell us everything that we need to know. In other words, because it is the true and eternal Word of God, it is sufficient in all matters of faith, doctrine and practice, for all believers, everywhere, throughout all ages. Therefore, the Scriptures, this amazing library of sixty-six books, which claim to be both supernatural and true, can provide the ground rules for both our understanding of, and our responding to, all aspects of human life and human death.

So contrary to the perhaps expected paucity of information about these issues, the Bible is actually stuffed with pertinent principles and germane guidance. The sheer quantity and quality of this biblical teaching produces a remarkable corpus from which can be developed the most rugged bioethical platform. It matters not whether we are dealing with abortion, gene therapy, infanticide, surrogacy, or more fittingly, dying, death and euthanasia, these biblical themes provide a robust foundation for our understanding of all these so-called life issues. In their magisterial book, *Principles of Biomedical Ethics* (1979), Beauchamp and Childress defined (p. 13) what they considered to be the four essential attributes of any decent ethical theory—it must be 'consistent and coherent', 'complete and comprehensive', moreover, 'simplicity is a virtue of theories', and finally, it must be 'complex enough to account for the whole range of moral experience.' Well, I can think of no more fitting description of the biblical scheme of ethics. The Bible is the veritable *vade-mecum* of these edge-of-life issues.

What follows is a brief, but adequate framework—readers can use it to splice in additional biblical passages. For a more detailed treatment of some of these scriptural topics, check out chapter 2 in *Responding to the Culture of Death—A Primer of Bioethical Issues*. Here, the discussion is directed specifically towards the issues surrounding dying, death and euthanasia. So, let the theology begin!

2.1 Human life is unique and special

The opening sentence of any book should be significant—every writer aims to make it trenchant and arresting. But none can compare with that of the Bible's. It opens with Genesis 1:1, the most staggering and sublime declaration, 'In the beginning God created the heavens and the earth.' Therefore, the universe exists and has meaning and form because it was created by this infinite, yet personal God. Herein is majesty, the awesome power of the Creator God. This is earth-shaking, epoch-making stuff. But there is more. The whole of the opening chapter of Genesis explains the unfolding order of creation, using the Hebrew word for 'created', *bara*, on three momentous occasions. First, in Genesis 1:1, God created something out of nothing, *ex nihilo*. Second, in Genesis 1:21, God created conscious life—the birds of the air, the fish of the sea, and the animals of the land. Third, and lastly, in Genesis 1:27, God created human beings, man and woman, '… in the image of God …'

So early in Genesis, and then throughout the rest of the Book, human beings are clearly different and distinct from every other created form of life. Human life is the pinnacle of God's creative endeavours. Men, and, of course, in the generic sense, women and children too, are made in the image of God. We alone bear the *imago Dei*. This is the most stunning of doctrines. It is the basis of human dignity and worth. We are not nothing. We have value. Human life is not pointless and empty. We have purpose and meaning. Why? Because we are made in the image of God. Hence, we are unique. Hence, we are special. This is indeed good news for the best of days, as well as for the worst of days. It is why we belong to God. Why? Because we are made in his image and likeness. We—men and women, boys and girls, young and old, disabled and 'normal', rich and poor, black and white, chic and scruffy—all are unique and special, and all have intrinsic value before their Creator.

This fact, that we are made in the image of God, is of primary importance. Misunderstand it, fail to grasp it, get it wrong and you will never, never make proper sense of life and death, or any bioethical issue, let alone euthanasia. How can we ever be compassionate and constructive in the face of dying and the death of a person, if we fail to understand the very purpose and value of that human life?

Now, this proposition, that human life is unique and special, runs counter to twenty-first century zeitgeist. Most people consider that men and women, including, of course, themselves, are of little, or even no, significance, that life has no meaning, that we are merely cogs in a mechanistic universe, that we are products of time and chance in an impersonal, meaningless universe. This type of thinking, this worldview, is not just wrong, it is also indescribably dismal. And it has devastating consequences. In the context of bioethical issues, it produces a low view of human life, in both thought and practice. Logically, we must say, of course, it does. If you and I are not made in the image of God, if we are not special, then the door is open to any practice and any abuse, including abortion and infanticide, but also pornography, human embryo destruction, paedophilia, and all kinds of other violence and evil, plus, of course, euthanasia. Then why are we so surprised that our televisions and newspapers report such dreadful occurrences every day? Christians, above all people, should understand why these atrocities occur. It is because the world has adopted a worldview that is out of kilter with its Creator, with the Scriptures, and therefore, with reality. Pushed to its ultimate conclusion, this worldview makes no distinction between kicking, or even chopping up, a chair, a little boy, or an old woman—after all, they are all composed of similar stuff, similar atoms and molecules, are they not? If a human being, young or old, can be judged, either by himself, or by others, to have a life so devoid of any intrinsic value and dignity that it is 'not worthy to be lived', then what can stand in the way of that person, or a doctor, or the State from killing that life?

Much of our society's confusion about edge-of-life issues can be exposed by raising some interrelated questions. For instance, how can we live properly, if we do not know who we are? How can we die properly, if we do not know how to live properly? If the end of man is annihilation, then why bother? Modern men and women are unable to answer these questions satisfactorily. Why? Because they refuse to acknowledge the Creator and Sustainer of life. Furthermore, they have rejected the Maker's handbook, and instead have turned to their own ways and trusted in their own understanding. Is it any wonder that we are in such a bioethical mess? Is a man who buys a car, throws the handbook in the dustbin, and then promiscuously decides to put water in the engine, petrol in the radiator, and oil in the fuel tank, a fool? Is the man who lives in dogged defiance of God and his instructions any more sensible? Psalm 53:1 confirms that, 'The fool says in his heart, "There is no God." They are corrupt, and their ways are vile; there is no-one who does good.' When we forget our origins and who we are, when we think that life is meaningless and that people are nothing, then we get into all sorts of dire philosophical predicaments and the only sure outcome is going to be bioethical mayhem. The recommended treatment for this sickness is a good dose of Genesis—that will undoubtedly put us on the road to intellectual recovery and bioethical fitness.

2.2 Human life begins at conception

Some may ask, why has this section about the *beginning* of human life been included here? Particularly here, in a book primarily about dying and death, the *end* of human life? What has it to do with euthanasia? The answer is—everything. Because if it can be demonstrated that the Bible regards any stage of human life, from conception to natural death, as trifling, or of no account, then we too can support practices like abortion, infanticide and euthanasia. But it does not—so we can not! However, you must not draw that conclusion before examining the evidence.

Our world is dreadfully confused about the beginning of human life. Metaphysicians consider it a virtue to be 'uncertain' and 'ambiguous' about such matters, moral philosophers want to witter on about 'personhood' or 'consciousness', scientists rummage around for 'primitive streaks', or 'ethically relevant characteristics', and bishops blether on about 'ensoulment' or 'the divine spark'. Others regard birth, or twenty-eight weeks, or viability, or fourteen days, or implantation as the decisive event at which human life begins. The very range of these indicators demonstrates just how arbitrary each of them really is. Suppose, for example, that fourteen days was the answer. What then is present a day before? Is it non-human life? What about an hour, or a minute before? Is it then human non-life? Can you see the philosophical, let alone the practical, problems produced by these options? None is sufficient to count as the defining moment, before which, there was something of no consequence, but after which, there is valuable human life. Can anyone say, without intellectually blushing, 'Before this or that developmental event, I was not, but after it, I was'? These, and a host of other ingenious beginning-of-life markers, are ethical red herrings. The truth is that for many, the real answer is simply too simple. These clever clogs would be out of a job if they could not carry on pondering and debating this great question. You encounter this sort of bioethical evasion in, for example, the infamous Warnock Report (1984), which unhelpfully concluded (p. 60) that, '… when life or personhood begin … are complex amalgams of factual and moral judgements …' But there is often a more sinister, ulterior motive lurking behind such bioethical dithering. Being vague allows doctors and scientists to kill deliberately and to experiment destructively with human life. And if you can remain uncertain about the beginning of human life, then you must, *ipso facto*, also be unsure of its value—such an agnostic stance empowers you to destroy human life, and, at the same time, continue in the self-delusion that you are acting entirely honourably. Dishonest, uncertain and negative are the words that spring to mind.

Thankfully, and by contrast, the Scriptures are honest, definite and positive. Now, there is no attempt here at crude proof-texting. The Bible is neither a textbook of embryology, nor of geriatrics. Nevertheless, the Scriptures possess a momentum and a compelling insistence that human life begins at conception, and ends at natural death (see section 2.4), both of which are determined by the sovereign God.

Throughout the Bible, conception is seen as a precious gift from God (Psalm 127:3–5). But there is much, much more to reflect upon. For example, the account of the lives of Esau and Jacob begins with their lives in the womb (Genesis 25:21–26). These were real babies, already real human lives in the womb of Rebekah. Indeed, in the foreknowledge of God, they were regarded then and there as the progenitors of two future nations.

This concept of the foreknowledge of God is especially noteworthy. Though it is beyond our full comprehension, the fact is that the Creator has known us even before we were conceived. Jeremiah 1:5 assures us that God knew us in pre-natal life. From God's viewpoint, we certainly have an identity at conception, but even before that, we each had a 'pre-history'. The same theme is found in Psalm 139:13–16, where David recalls how he was known by God throughout the time he was in his mother's womb, and even before that.

Earlier, in Psalm 51:5, the same King David adumbrates the cardinal doctrine of man as a sinner by both practice *and* nature. He admits that he was, from birth, a sinner, who practised sin. This is the obligatory, unavoidable practice of all newborns—they need no instruction in how to sin. But, we are sinners, first of all, not because we commit or practise sin, but, because it is in our very nature. Sin is in our constitution. Yet, this sinful nature was present, not just as the psalmist says, '... from birth ...', but '... from the time my mother conceived me.' Why is that? Because we are all descendants of our forebears, the fallen Adam and Eve. This sinful nature is ubiquitous, it has been passed down through all the generations of human beings—it is an integral part of the human condition. So we are sinners right from the time we entered the human race. And when was that? As soon as, like King David, '... my mother conceived me.'

Ever since our first parents had sexual intercourse and conceived Cain (Genesis 4:1), conception has been the universal start of every human life. Even the Lord Jesus Christ, when he was incarnated, that is, when he too entered the human race, was the product of conception (Matthew 1:20). Sure, his conception was different from ours in that he was conceived in the virgin Mary by the Holy Spirit. This enabled him to remain 'very God', but also to become 'very Man', to share our humanity, in every way, except without sinning. To accomplish this, his earthly life had to start like ours (Hebrews 2:17). Since his began at conception, so did ours!

Scripture and science agree that human life begins at conception, or what is also often known as fertilization. Implantation, or fourteen days, or viability, or twenty, or twenty-eight, weeks are simply events in a life already begun. We all began at conception when one sperm from our father fertilized one ovum from our mother to form one cell, technically known as a zygote. At that point, all the genetic material was present to make you. All that you needed from then on was nutrition and a safe environment. We all spent the first nine months or so of our lives inside our mothers. Thus, there is only one starting point of human life that is scripturally, scientifically, and philosophically satisfactory, and that is, conception.

Since human life begins at conception, that is the time from which it must be protected. But this is not the opinion generally held by the majority within our society. They have had their thinking shaped by secular humanism. Such a mindset is dangerous because it always cheapens human life. Perhaps above all, this low view of human life is demonstrated by the practice of abortion. It has been pro-abortionists who have mentally mugged us and convinced us that the human embryo, the fetus, and the unborn child are merely collections of cells, pieces of undifferentiated tissue, things of little consequence. Once the general public had swallowed these untruths, we were on the slippery slope to a low view of human life in *all* its stages, both in utero and ex utero. After all, if human life, in its early development, can be disposed of, then why not in its later stages too? If abortion can become acceptable and legal, then give me one good reason why infanticide and euthanasia cannot follow suit. Answers on a postcard please, to me, c/o Day One Publications.

2.3 Human life requires stewardship

The period between our conception and our death is what we call our earthly life, or what the Old Testament refers to as, '… the few days of life God has given …' (Ecclesiastes 5:18). It is that time span, which can be literally as short as a few days, or perhaps as long as ninety or more years. Do you ever wonder why God brought you into existence? I do. In some of my more introspective moments, I can be quite surprised that I am me, and not someone else, in a different place, at a different time. Then reality kicks back in and I remind myself that this is my providence—this is how God has decreed it for me. This, here and now, is my 'gracious gift of life' (1 Peter 3:7). Who can expound that magnificent phrase? It embraces the path of life (Psalm 16:11), the fountain (Psalm 36:9), the light (Psalm 56:13; John 8:12), the covenant (Malachi 2:5), the fragrance (2 Corinthians 2:16), the word (Philippians 2:16), the promise (2 Timothy 1:1), and the crown of life (James 1:12). And this gift is much more besides. It is in many ways mysterious, sometimes almost overwhelmingly perplexing, and yet, continually wondrous.

This biblical motif of the 'gift of life' is important for at least three reasons. First, a gift reminds us of grace. Our lives are demonstrations of God's grace—his goodness to undeserving men and women. You and I are living, breathing testimonies to God's grace (Romans 6:23). Second, a gift, especially one so great, deserves gratitude from the given to the Giver

(Psalm 139:14). Gratitude should characterize us—we should be people '...overflowing with thankfulness' (Colossians 2:7). Third, a gift from God must be valuable, so it deserves to be guarded and nurtured (Deuteronomy 30:19). We are to treasure what God has given us. In other words, we are to be good stewards of human life. This can be achieved in at least three practical ways. First, and foremost, it means that we are answerable to our Maker for the stewardship of our own life (Romans 14:12), second, we are to have a caring concern for the lives of those within our immediate family (1 Timothy 5:8), and third, we are to have a protective interest in the lives of our neighbours, and the wider human family—even the whole human race (Luke 10:30–37).

Christian stewardship has become a neglected concept, but it is a key feature in developing a biblical view of human life. It prevents us from slipping into the thinking of modern men and women, who reject the idea of 'stewardship' in favour of 'ownership'. 'It's my life, my body', is their autonomous cry. But we do not 'own' our lives. By creation, both Christians and non-Christians belong to God (Genesis 1:27). Moreover, by redemption, Christians are told categorically in 1 Corinthians 6:19–20 that, 'You are not your own; you were bought at a price.' The notion of self-ownership is dangerous because it encourages people to live lives of unfettered restraint, self-determination, and disregard for others. For example, it encourages a quest for rights, my rights. On the other hand, stewardship makes people circumspect, mindful of their Owner, and careful with what has been entrusted to them. It encourages a fulfilment of duties and care towards others. Most of all, good stewardship never involves the intentional return of the gift—grace is never to be shunned. Nor does it include the premature termination of the stewardship—stewardship of our lives is our lifelong privilege. Therefore, euthanasia, infanticide, abortion and suicide can never be regarded as the marks of good stewards.

So we are stewards, not owners, of this gift—this marvellous, fragile, unpredictable entity, called human life. It is the gift of God, for us to enjoy, both when the going is easy, and when it is tough. Even in the most difficult and miserable episodes of life, God attributes value, meaning and purpose to our lives. We, on the other hand, can be so contrary. The required correctives are found in the Scriptures. When life is tiring and tiresome, and we feel sorry for ourselves, God declares, '... my thoughts are not your thoughts, neither are your ways my ways' (Isaiah 55:8). When life is hard, almost too hard, and we fear that we are sinking, the Scriptures declare, 'No temptation has seized you except what is common to man. And God is faithful; he will not let you be tempted beyond what you can bear. But when you are tempted, he will also provide a way out so that you can stand up under it' (1 Corinthians 10:13).

We need to remind ourselves of 'our chief end', our abiding purpose, as the answer to question one in the Westminster Shorter Catechism (1648) so succinctly frames it, 'Man's chief end is to glorify God, and to enjoy him for ever.' Therefore, our little span is to be lived out in devotion to, and service of, God. 'The few days of life God has given ...' are our probation. We are preparing for an eternal life of peace, fulfilment, joy and rest. Life, now lived in the face of sin, is awkward and abnormal. We now experience, or know of, hardship and suffering, if not for ourselves, then certainly among our neighbours and friends. Christians live in the real world—we cannot always supply undemanding solutions, nor would we dare offer trite answers, and least of all, do we recommend blind optimism. Yet we believe that God is mindful of the weak and their suffering (Leviticus 19:14; Matthew 12:20), and that despite, at times, the seemingly-conflicting evidence around us, grace and mercy will eventually triumph (1 Corinthians 15:54–57), and that finally, our heavenly Father will take us home (John 14:1–4). That is the Christian perspective on human life. Bearing the *imago Dei* is not a cruel sentence imposed by a remote, austere being, but rather an adventure of stewardship, to be lived out with the Friend of sinners, day by day, and, not least, during its final days.

2.4 Human life ends in natural death

God is the Creator (Genesis 1:27) and Sustainer of human life (Psalm 54:4). Life is a gift (1 Peter 3:7) and God is the giver (1 Timothy 6:13). But God is also the Taker of human life. Our death, as well as our life, is in this God's hands (1 Samuel 2:6). It cannot be otherwise, or else he would not be a sovereign God, would he? As the psalmist asserts, with words of no more than two syllables, '... when you take away their breath, they die and return to the dust (Psalm 104:29). Similarly, Job affirms the sovereignty of God at life's end, 'Naked I came from my mother's womb, and naked I shall depart. The LORD gave and the LORD has taken away; may the name of the LORD be praised' (Job 1:21). The Lord Jesus Christ asked, 'Are not two sparrows sold for a penny? Yet not one of them will fall to the ground apart from the will of your Father ... So don't be afraid; you are worth more than many sparrows' (Matthew 10:29, 31). Thus, our death is in the hands of God, according to his will, at his timing, in his place. Would you want it any other way?

Therefore, to choose, or engineer, or bring about death, whether our own, or someone else's, without divine sanction, is to usurp God's prerogative. It is to challenge his providence. Such a biblical precept sticks in the craw of today's secular humanists. 'It's my life, and I will do as I please', they proudly announce. This is latter-day autonomy. And such autonomy lies at the root of much unrest and confusion when confronting these edge-of-life issues. *I Did It My Way* is not just the title of a Frank Sinatra record—it is the theme song of modern men and women. But all this is nothing new. Rebellion, defiance, autonomy, and self-centredness have always been human characteristics. These personality aberrations were at the heart of the big question in the Garden of Eden (Genesis 3:11)—who is to rule, the Creator or the created, God or man? With man striving to usurp the role of God and seeking to be in control, untimely death was bound to be the upshot. And so it was. Moreover, it still is. What is more, so it will be.

2.5 Innocent human life is not to be taken

The Cain and Abel narrative of Genesis 4:9–10 reveals how precious human life is in God's sight. The killing of animals was acceptable (Genesis 9:3), but the first murder, the killing of Abel, brought down anger from above. It was an offence to God, that one made in his image should be killed by another, 'Whoever sheds the blood of man, by man shall his blood be shed; for in the image of God has God made man' (Genesis 9:6). The Sixth Commandment (Exodus 20:13) can be applied here too, 'You shall not murder.' That is, you shall not deliberately take the life of another human being. Such an action violates God's holy law. The Bible is pro-life—we should be too.

Scripture does not forbid the taking of *all* human life, though beyond the remit of this book, it does contain limited sanctions for capital punishment and war. What the Scripture does forbid however is the taking of *all innocent* human life. The word 'innocent' in this context does not mean 'without sin', but 'without harm', denoting that no crime or offence has been committed. This theme, of the culpability of those who take innocent life, is expounded in both Isaiah 59:7 and Romans 3:15, 'Their feet rush into sin; they are swift to shed innocent blood. Their thoughts are evil thoughts; ruin and destruction mark their ways.' It was also part of Judas' confession, '"I have sinned," he said, "for I have betrayed innocent blood"' (Matthew 27:4). Therefore, innocent human beings are absolutely not to be killed deliberately, never, ever. Yet, this is exactly what is happening in so many areas of medicine and science as confirmed by abortion, infanticide, euthanasia, human embryo experimentation, and so on.

To squander or fritter this gift of life is an insult to its Giver and its Sustainer. The intrinsic value of a human life is God-given, not man-determined. To take innocent human life is not just unfair, or even merely unjust, it is a blatant, sinful offence against God.

2.6 All human life needs special care

These innocent lives are to be protected, not plundered. We are to have a special concern for the weak and vulnerable of society. These include the widow and the fatherless (James 1:27), but also those with disabilities, those who have no voice, those who cannot protect themselves, the unborn and the newborn, the elderly, and especially, the dying. Such people should be able to look to Christians, above all others, for love, protection, support and practical care (Zechariah 7:8–10).

We hear so much about euthanasia, besides abortion and infanticide, for the 'hard cases' and for 'difficult social reasons', in particular, when those in question are frail and disabled. Some Christians, plus a number of morally-sensitive people, unthinkingly hide behind these atypical cases and make them a wedge in order to justify their approval, albeit begrudgingly, of such practices.

What is to be our correct thinking here? The weak and disabled, whether young or old, are still human, still bearers of the *imago Dei*. They have been made that way by the sovereign God. Exodus 4:10–12 tells of God rebuking Moses for doubting this. We are just as bad. We tend not to regard disability from that divine perspective. Instead, we persist in that medieval, or old fishwife's, belief that the parents, the sufferer, or someone, anyone, must be to blame. Exactly this type of shabby thinking is recounted in John 9:1–3, where the biblical remedy can also be glimpsed. Such biblical correctives are further developed in Isaiah 35:5–6, which heralds one aspect of the great Christian hope, namely, that all such weaknesses and disabilities will disappear in the Great Day of the Lord.

The subject of handicap can easily condemn us. I know the word 'handicapped' is offensive to many, but I have deliberately employed it here, not least, because it is the term used in the 1967 Abortion Act and the 1990 Human Fertilisation and Embryology Act to justify the abortion of the disabled. That practice is far more offensive than any inappropriate word could ever be. Yet the irony is that while 'handicapped' can be politically incorrect in the caring situation, it remains politically correct in the aborting situation. This issue of disability can search us. It can confirm how far our feet have trespassed into the camp of the secular humanists. We have too often embraced their thought patterns and values and believed, like them, that this world is for only 'the big, the bright and the beautiful'. We have too often adopted the mores of the eugenicists and wished that the handicapped could be done away with. Just ponder the costs and efforts needed to care for them. Think about how embarrassing they can be. Consider how unproductive they are. If you have ever entertained such thoughts, shame on you!

And anyway, who of us is not weak and disabled? We should all be only too aware of our mental, physical, and certainly spiritual, disabilities. The truth is, we are all disabled, to some extent. To stigmatize some people as 'the disabled', while we consider ourselves to be 'the normal', and therefore somewhat superior, is to fall again into the eugenicist's trap. There are nothing but degrees of disability—you and I sit somewhere along that continuum. We too have special needs. And, if we can currently cope without too much help from others, then we should be thankful, but remember it will almost certainly not always be like this. Some day, perhaps quite soon, we too will need extra-special care.

Finally, the real antidote to our embarrassment about mental and physical disability, and especially towards those who are overtly affected, is found in Isaiah 52:14. Here is a prophetic account of the sufferings of the Saviour. Many readers will profess to follow and serve this One. How many of us would have turned away in awkward embarrassment if we had been there at the foot of the cross, gawping at the Lord Jesus Christ, who was so weak and grossly disfigured? We should go red in the face for adopting this world's lamentable customs and thoughts! Our response should be one of deep sorrow, and a determination to cultivate a more Christ-like attitude towards weak and needy people.

This sextet of themes, drawn from the Scriptures, provides the surest and firmest foundation for developing our thinking about edge-of-life issues. These themes will also encourage and enable us to frame proper responses. In addition, they will help us to understand and assist those facing dying, death and euthanasia. These, needless to say, include dying patients and their families, but also healthcare professionals, those at the frontline of medical practice. Some insight into the thinking and ethics of this latter group will prove invaluable. Therefore, the advance and, alas, the retreat of medical ethics are the subjects of the next chapter.

Medicine and ethics

In my earlier book, *Responding to the Culture of Death—A Primer of Bioethical Issues*, I maintained that Western medicine had lost its way because it had departed from its original, wholesome, ethical foundations. As a result, I argued, that many doctors, healthcare professionals and others, had become corrupted in both their ethical thinking and their medical practice. Furthermore, this corruption now manifests itself in everyday medical procedures such as abortion, infanticide, human embryo destruction, prenatal eugenic screening, and, of course, euthanasia. Nothing has changed my views, at least, not for the better. This sleazy type of medicine is still with us. And it is sleazy because it is built on frail and faulty medical ethics. So, what are they?

3.1 Medical ethics are for all
Medical ethics determine medical practice, that is, they are the rules of medicine, the guiding principles used by medical personnel in order to decide what to do, and what not to do. Many people consider that medicine is some sort of unassailable discipline, beyond the grasp of the mere layman. Indeed, such a gnostic view of medicine has been happily fostered by generations of arrogant doctors. Consequently, many people now have the wrong idea about its ethics. Three points should be noted.

First, medical ethics are not the preserve of the medical profession. Just because we have no medical qualifications does not mean that we cannot have an informed view about matters of medical ethics. Of course, we acknowledge that doctors have special technical skills, and that they know more clinical science than most of us, but they do not necessarily have any special ethical abilities—nor, it must be said, do we! To achieve such ethical insight we will have to crank up our minds. That does not mean that we will have to endure the rigours of a university degree in moral philosophy or medical ethics, nor, on the other hand, does it mean that we can somehow passively absorb the required information, by some sort of intellectual osmosis. If we want to be able to question our doctor sensibly about some course of action she is proposing for our aged relative, or if we want to sit down with our neighbour and, over a cup of coffee, present some sound advice about dying and death, or some arguments against euthanasia, then we are going to have to work at it. To be genuinely constructive and effective in such situations requires more than just mouthing some cheaply-garnered claptrap. You may never become a television or radio pundit, commenting on medical ethics, but you could well become a bioethically-informed person of inestimable usefulness within your family, your church and your community.

Second, medical ethics should never be relegated to a rarely-opened box, somewhere deep inside our brains. The ethics of medicine, like all other aspects of our thinking and behaviour, are cross-connected with the ethics of finance, sex, law, education, and so on. This is important to recognize because an individual's worldview should be well rounded. We should never become, or be accused of becoming, 'one-issue' people. Instead, striving to be knowledgeable and fully integrated is the route to developing a consistent and robust ethical stance across all of life's (and death's) issues. This is the way we will become strong and supportive men and women. It should certainly be the aim of every Christian—to be mature, with the mind of Christ (1 Corinthians 2:16), informed, by the Word of God (2 Timothy 3:16), and guided, by the Holy Spirit (John 16:13).

Third, many Christians, and other morally-sensitive people, are often fearful of taking a strong stand on any ethical issue. OK, it is not always easy to stand up and be counted. Sadly, such ethical cowardice is partly why our society is in such moral confusion and decay today. We have been hoodwinked into thinking that it is wrong to criticize people, their thinking, and their behaviour—we are told, it is simply, not nice, that it amounts to a nasty prejudice. 'Toleration' is the ethical buzzword for many, at least, that is, until you disagree with them! So, when a call comes to support a legal ban of some activity, such as euthanasia, we can become confused, and even confusing. Our opponents may further mesmerize us by arguing that morality can never be sanctioned by the force of law. That is, we should not be imposing our Christian convictions on our pluralistic society. This is hogwash. It displays a serious misunderstanding about the relationship between law and morality. The laws of our society reflect its citizens' sense of justice and equality and therefore they inevitably contain an ethical component. Hence, the key question in the area of protesting and law-making is not whether laws should, or should not, reflect an ethical worldview, but rather *which* ethical worldview should they reflect? We need to understand the myth of the ethically-neutral law. And we need to ask, why should the absolutes of the Judaeo-Christian worldview be excluded from the formulation of laws and from public policy debates? If Christians will not speak up, others certainly will.

In summary, do not fear medical ethics. After all, there is currently so much muddle and uncertainty about each and every aspect of ethics that we need to make our stand and have our say—Christians can bring clarity and certainty to our sad and perplexed world. If we make the effort to understand the issues and to communicate effectively and winsomely, some will undoubtedly listen. This is the way forward—we come to present a better way that will benefit not just the individual, but also the whole of society. Truly, medical ethics are for everyone—therefore, read on!

3.2 The origins of medical ethics

The origins of medical ethics are fascinating, and two-fold. From a moral perspective, they are pagan plus religious, and from a cultural perspective, they are Greek plus Hebrew. The earliest code of medical ethics can be traced back to the Greek physician, Hippocrates (perhaps 460–377 BC), who is generally regarded as the 'Father of Medicine'. He, or maybe others of like-mind, formulated the most enduring code of medical ethics, which has become known as the Hippocratic oath. For the last 2,500 years, its influence upon the world of professional medicine has been immeasurably beneficial. Basically, this oath outlined four principles of good medical practice. First, it recognized the need for the co-ordinated instruction and registration of doctors—the public was to be protected from quacks and charlatans. Second, the doctor was to be there for the benefit of his patients—to the best of his ability, he must do them good. This principle, commonly condensed to the maxim, 'do no patient any harm', is the most profound and durable feature of the oath. Third, the nature of the doctor-patient relationship was outlined—the doctor was never to take advantage of this relationship. Fourth, the practices of euthanasia, abortion and suicide were specifically and strictly forbidden—they were never to be a part of proper medicine. When these Hippocratic principles were first propounded, they were regarded as radical, and represented a new departure for ancient medicine. They were certainly in stark contrast to the cruelty and self-centredness practised by the various surrounding pagan cultures of the day.

Alongside, and intertwined with, this pagan Greek oath were the Judaeo-Christian doctrines. These have been undeniably pervasive in so many areas of human endeavour, but here the context is medicine. The Old and New Testaments regard conception, birth, maintenance of health, parenthood, family life, length of days, and death itself, as a partnership between God and man—the Creator and the created are inseparable collaborators in both life and death. The physical, mental and spiritual health of God's people are tokens of his blessing. The Bible can be viewed as a book of human welfare. It shows God as constantly caring and providing for his people. It shows him continually guiding and correcting them. It even features some early 'medicines' for their use in the form of oils, balms and wines, as well as sound nutritional, fitness and health guidance. But it has been its ethical contributions that have been incalculable. These are epitomized by the so-called Golden Rule of the New Testament, as spoken from the very lips of the Lord Jesus Christ, in Matthew 7:12, 'In everything, do to others what you would have them do to you.' This was deemed to be such essential teaching that it was paraphrased in both the Old and the New Testaments, in Leviticus 19:18 and in Matthew 22:39 as, 'Love your neighbour as yourself.' This is, according to Paul, in Romans 13:9, the summation of the law. It was foundational, but also revolutionary, to the good practice of early, wholesome medicine. Furthermore, the doctrines of creation and redemption, was well as the biblical understanding of life and death, imbued human life with its matchless, intrinsic value. These Judaeo-Christian doctrines present this wonderfully holistic, pro-life portrayal of human life, from womb to tomb. This is human life at its best and most complete. This biblical knowledge brought a transforming dynamic to Hippocratic-type medicine—the praiseworthy outcome was a safe and compassionate medicine. And because early medicine's ethics were noble and true, so was its practice. It established and sustained what can be called, the culture of life.

3.3 The origins of the culture of life

Christianity has never been afraid of medicine. Indeed, proper medicine owes the hugest debt to Christianity. The Judaeo-Christian doctrines have habitually been at odds with the ethos of the day, whether in first-century Greece, or twenty-first century Britain. As a consequence, they have consistently shaped Christian men and women into principled and compassionate rebels. Within the medical profession, they have produced real heroes. They encouraged the early doctors to display denial of self and compassion towards all those made in the image of God. Their successors have been the men and women who have maintained Christianity's non-negotiable ethics, and who have been inspired by the biblical emphasis on the importance of human beings, their spiritual, physical and mental well-being, as well as their need of relationships. Such men and women have been the heralds, instigators and maintainers of this culture of life.

The length, breadth and depth of this Christian goodness is delightfully captured by that great historian of ideas, William E H Lecky, in his famous *History of European Morals from Augustine to Charlemagne* (1913, vol. 2, p. 17), 'The first aspect in which Christianity presented itself to the world was as a declaration of the fraternity of men in Christ. Considered as immortal beings, destined for the extremes of happiness or of misery, and united to one another by a special community of redemption, the first and most manifest duty of a Christian man was to look upon his fellowmen as sacred beings, and from this notion grew up the eminently Christian idea of the sanctity of all human life.' Lecky continues (p. 20), 'Now, it was one of the most important services of Christianity, that besides quickening greatly our benevolent affections it definitely and dogmatically asserted the sinfulness of all destruction of human life as a matter of amusement, or of simple convenience, and thereby formed a new standard higher than any which then existed in the world.' And again (p. 34), 'This minute and scrupulous care for human life and human virtue in the humblest forms, in the slave, the gladiator, the savage, or the infant, was indeed wholly foreign to the genius of Paganism. It was produced by the Christian doctrine of the inestimable value of each immortal soul. It is the distinguishing and transcendent characteristic of every society into which the spirit of Christianity has passed.'

In other words, the Judaeo-Christian doctrines, combined with the Hippocratic oath, have, for the last two millennia and more, fostered a high view of human life. This ethic produced, and maintained, a medicine that in practice has been largely honourable, wholesome and beneficial. Such medicine has promoted this magnificent culture of life. This proper medicine has sometimes cured, often relieved, and always comforted. It has done us all good—for that we should be nothing but grateful.

3.4 The origins of the culture of death

The above description of proper medicine no longer rings true. How can medicine be 'honourable, wholesome and beneficial' when doctors and nurses are engaged in activities such as abortion, infanticide and euthanasia? These are practices that belong not the culture of life, but to the culture of death.

Originally, medical ethics and practice were centred in this culture of life. Sickness and disease were its enemies. Life was to be encouraged, and death was to be resisted. Nevertheless, it was always well understood that every patient would eventually die. Therefore the expected and accepted outcome of every life was natural death. But unnatural, premature death was something else—it was regarded as anathema. The doctor who hastened it, encouraged it, or caused it, was a charlatan, a disgrace to the profession, and not worthy of the title of healer and protector of human life. Deliberately killing patients, whether they were preborn or newborn, teenaged or middle-aged, elderly or dying, was never a part of proper medicine. Such practices were contrary to the Hippocratic guideline, 'do no patient any harm', as well as to the Christian dictum, 'Love your neighbour as yourself.'

Even so, it is not suggested that there was once a golden age when every single doctor and nurse believed and practised these precepts with all their hearts. But there was undoubtedly a time when these truths were the common ethical currency of medicine, and they were generally accepted and upheld by the vast majority of medical personnel and policy makers. And we should never forget that the outworkings of such basic Hippocratic and Christian teachings were a balm to patients. They produced a professional integrity, a respect for personal responsibility and freedom, and they engendered a caring ethos within the medical profession—in short, a culture of life. That is, I would argue, proper medicine—Hippocratic-type, God-honouring, principled, compassionate medicine.

3.5 How has medicine gone wrong?

Where then has modern medicine gone so awry? After more than twenty centuries of medical ethics producing medical practice of the highest calibre and the greatest respect for human life, why the modern collapse, why the practices of rampant abortion, cryptic infanticide, and now, poised euthanasia? How did it start out so well, yet finish up so badly? How did we exchange the culture of life for this culture of death?

In a nutshell, the two original pillars of medical ethics have been allowed, even encouraged, to crumble. They have both been rejected. First, there has been the rejection of medicine's traditional codes of ethics. These so-called 'core values' have sought to encapsulate the precepts, prohibitions and practices that would promote medical cohesion and integrity. They are, in other words, the benchmark of what is deemed to be good, medical practice. Nearly all medical students in the US, and something like half of those in the UK, still swear an oath, often the Hippocratic oath, or some variant of it, usually upon graduation. Indeed, there has been a recent resurgence of interest in medical ethics and codes of conduct. There have been several calls for a new version of the Hippocratic oath, as well as a greater ethical content in medical training. The British Medical Association (BMA) has recommended that all medical graduates should make a commitment to observe an ethical code. This is a laudable statement, but the question remains, what will be the content of that ethical code?

The Hippocratic oath was uncompromising in its stand against abortion, '... and especially I will not aid a woman to procure abortion', and euthanasia, 'I will give no deadly drug to any, though it be asked of me, nor will I counsel such ...' More recent oaths have echoed this. Perhaps the most famous of these was first published on 19 August 1947, in the aftermath of the war crimes' tribunal at Nuremberg. It was the Declaration of Geneva (adopted by the General Assembly of the World Medical Organization in 1948), which stated, 'I will maintain the utmost respect for human life from the time of conception, even under threat I will not use my medical knowledge contrary to the laws of humanity.' This hefty ethical statement was the recognized standard just two generations ago.

Subsequent codes of medical ethics and practice have become more ambiguous, more feeble, less protective. Just over twenty years ago, Tom Beauchamp and James Childress warned (p. 113) in their renowned 1979 book, *Principles of Biomedical Ethics* that, 'Rules against killing in a moral code are not isolated moral principles; they are threads in a fabric of rules that support respect for human life. The more threads we remove, the weaker the fabric becomes.' That is, weaker and weaker ethical codes have reflected, or perhaps even led, the great ethical downgrade of medicine with its consequent reduction in respect for human life. The unavoidable conclusion is, faulty code—faulty medicine, or faulty ethics—faulty practice.

One of the latest examples of this trend is seen in the BMA's 1997 revision of the Hippocratic oath, drafted on behalf of the World Medical Association. It contains these words, 'Where abortion is permitted, I agree that it should take place only within an ethical and legal framework'. So, no hope there for protecting unborn human life. It continues, 'I recognise the special value of human life, but I also recognise that the prolongation of human life is not the only aim of health care.' And it goes on, 'I will not provide treatments which are pointless or harmful or which an informed and competent patient refuses.' True, these latter statements are not overtly promoting euthanasia, but there is a sniff of it there, and their tone and content are undoubtedly part of the downgrade, a shift away from that old-style Hippocratic-Christian medicine, and a further move towards the culture of death. It is certainly a huge step away from the high view of human life that prevailed during the preceding centuries. And this downgrade has occurred within just the last fifty years or so.

Of course, the practice of medicine has undergone colossal changes in these last fifty, let alone 2,500, years. It has become vastly more complex, technological, specialized, political and costly. However, we also need to recognize that modern medicine is now practised within a set of frail core values, which include, either by default or by design, this low view of human life. Melanie Phillips and John Dawson drew attention to the 'recentness' of this onset of ethical frailty in *Doctors' Dilemmas* (1985, p. 39), 'It is all very well for doctors and others to uphold with passion the distinction between killing and letting die, justifying the latter but resisting the former; but thirty years ago or less, they would probably have found the idea that doctors would decide not to use standard procedures to save the life of a Down's syndrome baby as outlandish and repugnant ...'

So, modern medicine has gone wrong, first, because it has rejected its earlier codes of ethics, which were powerful, in favour of modern codes, which are feeble. And second, it has gone awry because of the rejection of historic, orthodox, biblical Christianity. This rejection has had a profound bearing upon the collapse of ethical medicine, in addition to advancing the disintegration of almost every aspect of modern life. Biblical absolutes have been thrown out of the window. As a result, personal restraint is now a laughing-stock, the squeaky clean are mocked, traditional family life and values are derided. Instead, financial greed is the new virtue, recreational sex is the new pastime, drugs are the new solution, and so on, and so on. But it is far more than merely an 'old religion' that has been lost. When a society like ours, historically structured upon Christianity, rejects the teaching of the Bible, it undermines its very foundations. So how, without reference to this infinite yet personal God, who, as the Law-giver, has given the biblical system for law, justice and moral values, do we now judge right and wrong, and formulate laws and ethics? The answer is, with immense difficulty. The solid rock has been replaced by shifting sand. Therefore, we now depend not upon given absolutes, but upon debatable, arbitrary values. If fifty-one per cent think, or perhaps more appropriately, 'feel', that euthanasia is right, then that is what will get onto the Statute Book. This is frightening stuff. It illustrates not only the enormity of the downgrade in medical ethics, but also the parlous ethical state of much of our society in which medicine is practised today.

This is the outcome of our society's general ditching of Christianity and its replacement by secular humanism. Secular humanism can be summed up in that ancient phrase, 'Man, the centre of all things', or 'Man, the measure of all things', or the more modern truncated form, 'Me-first'. This has come to dominate our thinking and practice in every part of our lives. It is a philosophy at loggerheads with Christianity. One is theocentric, the other is anthropocentric—one is rooted in the Bible of God, the other in the Enlightenment of man—one is supernatural, the other is naturalistic—one upholds absolutes, the other is relativistic—one is in love with the Triune God, the other is enthralled by modern science. They are poles apart, as different as the proverbial chalk and cheese. But neither is a mere sterile, intellectual exercise, because both determine the actions of their adherents, that is, both produce fruit. Among the fruits of Christianity have been the encouragement of the culture of life, while secular humanism has been responsible for the culture of death.

This is how modern medicine has gone wrong. The cause has been a double rejection—rejection of historic medical ethics and rejection of historic Christianity. It is so simple, yet so disquieting.

3.6 Anti-Christian ethics

The battle lines of medical ethics are thus clearly drawn. They can be variously described as Hippocratic-Christian versus secular humanistic, or the culture of life versus the culture of death, or principled versus arbitrary, or true versus false, or a high view of human life versus a low view. However they are portrayed, the stakes are enormously high. Among other alarm bells that this book wants to ring, is a wake-up call to return to a medicine of principled compassion, a medicine that once produced and maintained that laudable culture of life. Currently, that seems to be a great way off.

While the current position is alarming, it is also a curious state of affairs. By rejecting the Hippocratic-Christian framework, many doctors and ethicists thought that they would automatically become radical freethinkers, finally unrestrained by, as they saw them, ancient dogmas and clapped-out ethics. In reality, such unconditional freedoms are always illusory, they do not exist—these men and women are still in bondage, this time, to new dogmas and new ethics. This time they are called women's rights, or personal autonomy, or freedom of choice. While hating the non-negotiable aspects of Christianity, they have instead absolutized their own measly creeds. They have failed to grasp the fact that genuine ethical freedom does not come about simply by shovelling out 'that old religion'. This entire farrago reinforces the truth that we live in a moral universe—there can be no ethically-neutral thought or action. When one set of values is abandoned, another takes its place. Dumping Christianity just allows secular humanism, or its cousins, post-modernism, situation ethics, moral relativism, or whatever, to invade. It is exactly like it says in 2 Peter 2:19, 'They promise them freedom, while they themselves are slaves of depravity—for a man is a slave to whatever has mastered him.' Good penetrating comment!

This general distain, even hatred, of orthodox Christianity is seen among most modern-day bioethicists and moral philosophers. They are, largely, an atheistic, or at best, an agnostic, lot. Many of them abhor the concept of the sanctity of human life. They especially despise such doctrines as the *imago Dei*, eternal life, and the sovereignty of God.

The British moral philosopher, Mary Warnock is perhaps more mild and perceptive in this matter than many others. In her book, *An Intelligent Person's Guide to Ethics* (1998), she states in the Introduction (p. 7), 'And though ethics ... like the rest of philosophy, has been secularised, it is almost impossible to think about the origins and development of morality itself without thinking about its interconnections with religion.' Nevertheless, she follows this with 118 pages of ethical analysis through the eyes of a secular humanist, or what I have previously called, 'a secular humanist with a Christian memory'.

James Rachels, in his book *The End of Life—Euthanasia and Morality* (1986), presents what seems, at first sight, to be a similarly reasonable approach to ethics. He records (p. 4) that, 'The traditional theory [that, as a tenet of Christian orthodoxy, all human life is sacred] must be taken seriously; not only has its influence been enormous, but from a philosophical point of view it is the only fully worked-out, systematically elaborated theory of the subject we have. Its development has been one of the great intellectual achievements of Western culture, accomplished by thinkers of great ingenuity and high moral purpose. However, I shall be mainly interested in the question of whether this theory is *true*—granted that it has history and tradition on its side, still we may ask whether there is good reason for a rational person to accept it.' This sounds like the approach of the genuine enquirer—'I do not know, therefore I shall interrogate Christianity, and specifically, I shall investigate the Bible to establish if it is true.' But then, a mere four lines later, Rachels comes clean,

'I believe that the traditional view is mistaken at almost every point.' So that is Christianity done and dusted, Rachels-style.

Michael Tooley is a good example of the more strident anti-Christian position. In his influential book, *Abortion and Infanticide*, (1983) he states (p. 312), 'As long as there is good reason for believing that the religion in question is correct, the fact that it is responsible for the sharing of certain moral views raises no problem. But if there are grounds for doubting or rejecting the religion, these will also be grounds for discounting any moral consensus that it has produced, unless that consensus derives from considerations that are independent of its religious claims.' This is, again, a seemingly-sensible statement. You would then expect Tooley to spend at least a few paragraphs presenting reasons for either accepting or rejecting Christianity. Yet nowhere does he do this—he simply rejects it. For him, religions merely '... offered people package deals—part of the package being a set of moral principles.' But, Dr Tooley, are these principles true? Go on, analyse them, explore them, discuss them. No? You're right, it's far easier simply to reject them. So for Tooley, Christianity is definitely false, whereas scientism and secular humanism are definitely true—just don't confuse the issue and ask him why!

An equally disparaging attitude towards Christianity is promulgated by Helga Kuhse and Peter Singer in their pro-infanticide book, *Should the Baby Live?* (1985). They write (p. 125), 'Now we can see why Western thought has ended up with a fundamental ethical principle which is impossible to defend in rational, non-religious terms. The principle of the sanctity of human life is a legacy of the days when religion was the accepted source of all ethical wisdom.' However, even these scathing authors concede that, 'Within the framework of Judaeo-Christian religious belief, it makes some sense. Now that religion is no longer accepted as the source of moral authority in public life, however, the principle has been removed from the framework in which it developed. We are just discovering that without this framework it cannot stand up.' Kuhse and Singer are wrong for at least three reasons. First, they too easily discount the impact of true religion, that is, historic, orthodox Christianity, as the moral basis of Western societies. Second, just because the majority of people, including these two authors, do not accept Christianity to be true, does not automatically make it untrue. Third, the Bible addresses all men—believers and unbelievers. Of course, it makes proper sense only to believers, but the Christian position is that the Maker's instructions are still the best guide to living and dying for all men and women. And this has proved to be so. Think, for example, of the profound benefits we all enjoy because of the Christian ethics of marriage, work, leisure, education, and so on. Moreover, the pro-life movement worldwide is composed of many people who are not Christians—they are the morally sensitive, yet they agree with the Christian position, namely, that it is right to protect and defend all human life. So Kuhse and Singer are also wrong in their conclusion (p. 125), namely, that, 'Here, too, we are unlikely to get an answer that will persuade those who do not already accept the tenets of Judaeo-Christian religion.' They seem to know little about the workings of the real world.

These five authors, men and women, have been cited because they are among those who have been largely responsible for setting the agenda of medical ethics over the last twenty or so years. We should not underestimate their influence, but nor should we overestimate their ethical understanding or intellectual abilities. They are badly informed about the role of truth in ethics. They readily dismiss Christian truth, its presuppositions, and its practical outworkings. Their arguments for rejecting it extend no further than, 'It is old', and 'It is believed by only a minority.' Nevertheless, they are convinced that their modern, widely-believed worldview is better, more certain, more true. But why? On what basis? On the basis that it is humanistic, that they are in control, that it does away with the transcendent God? Of course, biblical Christianity is foolishness and a stumbling block to them (1 Corinthians 1:23). But, dear reader, consider this again. What is the fruit of their worldview? It is easy abortion, secret infanticide, and hovering euthanasia. These men and women want to get rid of the very young and the very old, and woe betide if you are disabled, for then they just want to get rid of you, whatever your age. Do I want to live in a world where their philosophies rule? No thank you!

Many moral philosophers are not nice people. They can be wilful, confused, and blind. They are ignorant of the Bible. Though they have not read it, they are adamant that it is not true. Christians have a very different view of the Word of God. It is primarily, above all, first and foremost, propositional truth. It is candid truth, the whole truth, and nothing but the truth. Indeed, that is the only reason to believe and ever become a Christian—because the Bible is true. That is why the Christian has no problem with setting out the Scriptures as his certain guide to all the edge-of-life issues.

Furthermore, these moral philosophers tend to be in the vanguard of those pressing for the legalization of euthanasia. Yet, while they are eager to talk, they never seem keen to act. So here is the new deal. When doctors are reticent about practising euthanasia, let these moral philosophers be recruited as euthanasiasts. After all, it is a relatively simple needle-and-syringe job and these apparently-intelligent academics could quickly learn the technique. It would certainly solve the problems of those within the medical profession who are averse to euthanasia, those still bound by the Hippocratic oath and the Judaeo-Christian doctrines, those still concerned about doctor-patient relationships, and those who are uneasy about the dual title of healer-killer. These moral philosophers are never dogged by such ethical qualms! But some of these thinkers may object to having this duty forced upon them. Some may feel uncomfortable and ill equipped about undertaking such responsibilities. They may even eventually dream up some moral misgivings and want to duck out. Exactly! This offer of new employment is designed precisely to make them rethink their cloistered position, and to stop them bullying the medical profession into the unnatural role of euthanasiast, and the rest of us into adopting the practice of euthanasia.

So that is the moral philosophers sorted—their bluff is easily called. What about the doctors? After all, they are the ones generally making edge-of-life decisions both for us, and about us. Yet, as we have already noted, their decisions are often made within a set of feeble ethical principles, or sometimes, none at all.

It is time to ask them some searching questions. Can we really trust them? Is the traditional doctor-patient relationship still intact? Will they tell us the truth, and treat us properly, especially when we are dying? There can be little doubt that if euthanasia were to be legalized, then the answer to these questions would often be, 'No'. Even in the absence of legalized euthanasia, we should recognize that in most situations, doctors still have the upper hand—they remain the arbiters of the doctor-patient relationship, the treatment regimen, and the type of care prescribed for their patients.

In 1806, the eminent Berlin doctor, Christoph Hufeland, foresaw these impending predicaments and described them (*Journal der praktischen Ärzneykunde und Wundärzneykunst*, 23:15–16) thus, 'The doctor should and must not do anything other than preserve life. Whether it is happy or not, valuable or not, that is none of his business. If he once permits such a consideration to influence his actions the doctor will become the most dangerous person in the State.' Hufeland's past fears are now present realities. Almost two hundred years later, Fabian Tassano, in his 1995 book, *The Power of Life or Death*, warned (p. 159) that, 'It is dangerously naive to assume that doctors are invariably benevolent and that they operate only on the basis of our best interests, notwithstanding the fact that the profession behaves as if this attitude of submissive veneration were *de rigueur*.'

It is beyond cavil that we are now living in a post-Hippocratic, post-Christian age of medicine. It can be unnerving. Doctors have, by and large, turned their backs on medicine's ethical origins, and now neither they, nor society, have any clear idea of how to formulate or regulate the contemporary ethics of medicine. In effect, every doctor is governed by his own version of medical ethics. And the prospect of legalizing euthanasia is creating an even weirder phenomenon. The emergence of the living will, or the advance directive, (see chapter 20) is allowing each patient to create his or her own version of medical ethics, a sort of do-it-yourself set of moral values. It is like a return to the ancient times when, '… everyone did as he saw fit' (Judges 21:25)—and we know the result of that debacle.

3.7 Christians can be infected too

Christians are never immune to the problems of their society. We must never dismiss these dilemmas of medical ethics as 'a doctor-thing', and therefore nothing to do with us. Our society has already explicitly approved of abortion and has implicitly endorsed the practices of infanticide and euthanasia—our taxes are already paying for these activities, and if we say and do nothing, then our hearts and minds are condoning them. This must be one of the greatest blots on the face of Christianity during the last century. Christians failed to be preservative salt and illuminating lights. Oh yes, we can be pretty adept at justifying our sub-Christian behaviour, our lack of compassion, and our weak leadership. God forbid that we become ensnared by the self-deception of Luke 18:11–14.

Perhaps we should ask, are we really any ethically different from the secular humanists around us? Try a little two-question test. First, would you object less about a case of infanticide if the child were severely handicapped, rather than 'normal'? 'Yes', or 'No'? Second, consider this classic example. A man is a notorious drunkard, and probably syphilitic. His wife is weak and frequently ill and already suffers from tuberculosis. They have previously had one child, but he was sickly and died just six days after his birth. She is now pregnant again. Would you suggest she has an abortion? 'Yes', say those surrounding us, 'Don't let this poor woman suffer any more pain and anguish, and spare her unborn child a future life of sickness and misery.' But this unborn child was none other than Ludwig van Beethoven! Well, did you pass the test? Or did you fall into the secular humanist's snare? Easy to do, isn't it? Without a sure grasp of the biblical framework of ethics, we can be infected so readily by that culture of death, just like those around us.

Who, then, is going to stand up, swim against the tide, and challenge the prevailing ethical consensus? Christians, of course! But are we sure? Too often, we have been uncertain, indistinct, and sadly, even silent. Living by the hapless ethics of this world is far more comfortable. But Christians are under an obligation to live by a new, very different set of ethics, 'Therefore, if anyone is in Christ, he is a new creation; the old has gone, the new has come!' (2 Corinthians 5:17). New person, new thinking, new standards, new ethics, new action. Do you understand the differences between the old and new ethics? Are you discarding the old and developing the new? Excellent! Now you can begin to apply them to the primary edge-of-life issues.

PART 2

The Primary Issues

'Nor love thy life,
Nor hate; but whilst thou livest,
Live well.'

John Milton, (1667) *Paradise Lost*.

True to its sub-title, this book is primary about the issues of dying, death and euthanasia. Therefore, it is quite proper that these three topics occupy the prime position in this Part, as well as the longest chapters of the entire book. Since they are central to all the other edge-of-life matters, that is how it should be. Dying and death are probably the most feared and misconstrued topics (un)known to men and women. Yet, because of their inescapability and nearness they call for our attention. Without some level-headed understanding of dying and death, we will fail to grasp the point of living. And if living has little or no significance for us, then, euthanasia, and all its attendant issues, will seem as nothing.

Two additional primary issues, closely linked to euthanasia, are also presented. These are infanticide, which is neonatal euthanasia, and suicide, which is self-inflicted euthanasia, that is, euthanasia without the help of a third party. The two final primary topics considered are permanent vegetative state (PVS) and eugenics. The scope of modern-day euthanasia cannot be fully comprehended without reference to PVS. It is patients in this state who have become the first regular victims of non-voluntary euthanasia in the UK. Eugenics is the insidious topic that underlies, to varying degrees, all other nasty edge-of-life issues. Many have the wrong idea about eugenics—they think it is old-fashioned, and that it rose, declined and disappeared during the last century. They are unaware that it has re-emerged more recently under new and tragic guises.

Dying and death

'**D**ying is a process—death is an event.' 'Dying has started—death is yet to come.' True maybe, but such neat aphorisms cannot exegete either of these two solemn words sufficiently. Dying is the undoubted precursor of death, and though death is not our eternal end, it is a mightily significant rite of passage. They both therefore demand some serious attention and reflection. For a few of us, death will be instantaneous, perhaps as a result of an accident, or a sudden heart attack. For most of us, death will come after a short, or perhaps a more prolonged, period of dying. Whatever the circumstances and timescale of our death, a Christian should, above all, want it to be a witness to God's mercy and grace. Understanding the nature, meaning and purpose of dying and death is certainly going to help achieve that objective.

4.1 Thinking about dying and death

Our thoughts on dying and death reveal much about our society and, more particularly, about ourselves. A good deal of our uncertainty about the edge-of-life issues is because we are uncertain about dying and death. We can certainly be confused by them. People prattle on about 'a fate worse than death', whatever that might mean. Or, non-Christians parrot, without any understanding of Philippians 1:21, that someone's death came as a 'blessed relief', or 'a merciful end'. Is that what people really think? Because if any of these expressions were true, then death would be nothing but beneficial and the case for euthanasia would be all sewn up. Or, are these off-the-wall sayings, along with the euphemisms for death, like 'kicking the bucket' and 'falling off the perch', proof that people are so bewildered and fearful of dying and death that when confronted by them, they babble stupidly—a sort of whistling in the dark?

It has not always been so. Our forefathers often thought about dying and death and many spent considerable time preparing for them. As a consequence, they were much more assured about them. The quest for immortality, the hope of an afterlife, the reality of a final judgement, were common chitchat among them. These aspirations were expressed, not just in the flamboyance of the pharaoh's pyramids in Egypt, but also in the solemn funeral rites of the ordinary man. Above all, it was Christianity that brought home the intensely personal aspects of death—before long, the dying were going to meet their Maker. Death was not a mere cessation of life—it was a crossroads' experience with eternal consequences. People of a bygone age were certainly more familiar with death—they not only spoke about it, but they saw it, for they lived surrounded by the dying. That did not mean that either were particularly welcome—dying and death were still regarded with considerable trepidation. For many, those fears were ameliorated, albeit falsely, by the increasingly elaborate paraphernalia of dying and death, such as, mourning, cortèges, tombs and cemeteries. The First World War changed all that. Millions of brave men's bodies were buried with little ceremony, in plain graves, or they were simply lost, in foreign fields. Dying and death had been transformed—they had been turned into lonely and remote events. Furthermore, during the ensuing peacetime, both were increasingly taken out of the home and close community, and into the inhospitable hospital. The previously warm social and emotional aspects of dying and death were being replaced by coldness and isolation. They were also becoming taboo topics. Nowadays, they can cause us to be even more irrational and irritable. We are quite likely to demand, 'But why couldn't medicine have done something to halt it, or at least, postpone it?' Or even, 'Well, how much longer have we got to wait?' Such attitudes towards dying and death are absurd and malevolent. They are counterproductive because they confuse, not just our intellectual understanding of these issues, but also our practical caring for those involved.

In view of the absolute certainty of death, it does seem strange that we should be so uneducated and unprepared for it. The combination of human experience and the Word of God tells us that, '... man is destined to die once ...' (Hebrews 9:27). Yet most of us appear to be generally indifferent about it. Most of us have thought so little about dying and death that it is no surprise that our understanding is so hazy and inchoate. By contrast, and unlike most of us, the Bible tackles dying and death, in-depth, and head-on. Death is certainly a central theme of the Bible—one of its recurring phrases is, '... and he died.' Indeed, it has been argued that there are only two topics throughout the whole Book—life and death. These two words occur almost 1,000 times in a ratio of approximately 60:40, and that somehow seems to be exactly the right balance. Most of us operate on a ratio of something more like 99:1—we would undeniably profit from adopting a more biblical ratio in our thinking and living.

4.2 What is death?

The original creation was all about life—death was never part of it. Indeed, creation was judged, by its Creator, to be 'very good' (Genesis 1:31). Death was not there. Death entered our world as a result of sin. It was the disobedience, the so-called Fall of our progenitors, Adam and Eve, which brought about death.

Here is what happened. Creation, as outlined in Genesis 1, was finished. Man and woman stood as the culmination of God's creativity. They were unique and special because they were made in the image of God (Genesis 1:27). Man had a special task, to work and to care for the Garden of Eden (Genesis 2:15), and woman was to be his helper (Genesis 2:18). Here then is unalloyed peace and perfect harmony between the Creator and the created. Man and woman were in perfect union with God. It was a beautiful relationship in which all three parties communicated, and the created lovingly obeyed the Creator. This was the full realization, the complete epitome, of what was later to be recorded as the first and greatest Commandment in both the Old and New Testaments. Moses spoke it in Deuteronomy 6:5, 'Love the LORD your God with all your heart and with all your soul and with all your strength', and the Lord Jesus Christ spoke it in Matthew 22:37, 'Love the Lord your God with all your heart and with all your soul and with all your mind.'

God and man (and, of course, woman too) were not equal—the created were to love and obey the Creator. Yet God had made man significant and free, he was not dust, nor was he a pre-programmed automaton. He was made in God's image. God had given him choice. Without such freedom his life, his dominion of the Garden, and his love towards God would have been meaningless. This freedom was expressed, for example, in Genesis 2:16 as Adam being '... free to eat from any tree in the garden ...' But God had made one tree, '... the tree of the knowledge of good and evil ...' (Genesis 2:17), from which Adam was forbidden to eat. As John Calvin comments, '... the prohibition of one tree was a test of obedience ... that man might know he had a Director and Lord of his life ...' (*Genesis*, Banner of Truth, 1965, pp. 125–126).

Thus, history was ticking, the scene was set. All understood the simple arrangement of Genesis 2:17, '... you must not eat from the tree of the knowledge of good and evil', as well as its dreaded consequence, '... for when you eat of it you will surely die.' The possibility of death was raised, but not realized. So what happened? Eve and Adam were tempted, they disobeyed, and they ate. Sin perforated the cosmos. The Fall occurred, and man and woman immediately became, as promised, subject to death. The whole world was never to be the same again. Who can begin to comprehend the calamity? Man's innocence and obedience disappeared. From then on, 'We all, like sheep, have gone astray, each of us has turned to his own way ...' (Isaiah 53:6). From then on, 'The heart is deceitful above all things and beyond cure. Who can understand it?' (Jeremiah 17:9). From then on, 'You belong to your father, the devil, and you want to carry out your father's desire' (John 8:44).

The Fall is one of the very few truly pivotal events of history—misunderstand it and we misunderstand too much. Its results were, and still are, cataclysmic. The austere promise of Genesis 2:17, '... you will surely die' was fulfilled in at least four ways. First, man became fully corrupted in his body and his spirit, that is, he became totally depraved (Genesis 6:5; Romans 1:29; Romans 7:18; 2 Peter 2:19). Not that he became as wicked as he could be, but rather he became entirely incapable of any good, that is, of pleasing God. Second, man became conscious of his guilt (Romans 2:15; Hebrews 10:2) and aware of his shame (compare Genesis 2:25 with 3:10) before God. Third, man lost communion with his Maker, which began with his hiding from God (Genesis 3:8), and culminated in his spiritual death. Spiritual death means being disconnected from the Triune God, and without such knowing of, and connecting with, the Father, Son and Spirit, man cannot live fully and properly. Therefore, man is spiritually far more than seriously ill, or badly disabled—he is spiritually dead (Ephesians 2:1; 4:18). Fourth, man became subject to physical death—immortal Adam was now mortal Adam and he was going to die, and, sure enough, at the ripe old age of 930, he did just that (Genesis 5:5).

Romans 5:12 is one of the great keys to unlocking the enormity of the global fallout from the Fall, 'Therefore, just as sin entered the world through one man, and death through sin, and in this way death came to all men, because all sinned.' Death is therefore both the consequence *of* sin, and the penalty *for* sin, 'For the wages of sin is death' roars Romans 6:23. Adam and Eve sinned, so they died. We also sin, so we also die. We die because we are human beings, in the lineage of Adam, we are his descendants, and we therefore share Adam's nature, which, at the Fall, became corrupted, disobedient and sinful. We are therefore sinners by nature and by practice—sin, singular, is our nature—sins, plural, are our practice. Now we sin and we cannot help it. And because of this landmark event in the Garden, all human beings, from then on were sinners, and therefore, 'will surely die'. Adam and Eve were the first culprits, but in their place, we would have behaved no differently—the truth of the matter is that even today, we do not behave any differently. Therefore, our guilt before this holy God is entirely deserved. So are our wages, paid in the coinage of death. Likewise, God's wrath towards us is entirely just. Why? Because we have deliberately ignored him, defiantly turned our backs on him, resolutely disobeyed him, and sinned against him regularly and frequently. See what sin has done? The entrance of sin changed this world from what was originally dazzling, to what is today dismal, from what was initially vital, to what is subsequently vile.

Does not all this square with what you observe in the world around you? Does it not have that ring of truth? How else can you explain the wickedness, corruption and evil that are universal to all men and women? Of course, they are present in varying degrees, but nevertheless, they are ubiquitous. A friend of mine who taught sociology at a university used the books of Genesis and Romans as two of the compulsory student texts— what a good choice! How else could his students (and you, and I) understand man, society and the human condition without a firm grasp of these fundamentals?

In summary, Adam's original sin brought about the arrival of death. Its potential was first raised in Genesis 2:17, '... for when you eat of it you will surely die.' Its reality was then confirmed in Genesis 3:19, '... for dust you are and to dust you will return.' The Bible's diagnosis of the intervening state, the condition of all living human beings, is concise and resolute, it says, you are, '... dead in your sins ...' (Colossians 2:13).

4.3 Physical death and spiritual death

Death, as described in the Scriptures, can therefore be two-fold—it can be physical, or spiritual. Physical death is biological, corporeal death, the destruction of the body, or *soma* (Matthew 10:28; Luke 12:4). In other passages, death is the destruction of the spirit, the soul, or *psuche* (Matthew 2:20; Luke 6:9). But because the Bible views men and women as integrated beings, the physical and the spiritual are intimately bound up in the whole person, so in other passages, death is described as the separation of the body from the soul (Ecclesiastes 12:7; John 19:30; James 2:26). However, death is never, according to the Bible, annihilation or extinction. Though our bodies are mortal, and they will die and decay and turn to dust, our souls are immortal, and they will live forever—either in heaven, if we have been reconciled to God and are spiritually alive, or in hell, if we are still strangers to God and are spiritually dead.

This is a good place to scotch the dualist convictions held by some moral philosophers and others. True, the Bible teaches about physical life and death, and spiritual life and death, but these terms are never applied to anything other than a single, integrated human individual. Every human being who has ever lived can be described by a simple permutation of one from each of these pairs. For instance, the apostle Paul is physically dead, but spiritually alive, whereas the current director of the Humanist Society is physically alive, but spiritually dead. Nowhere does the Bible teach that a human life can be divided into separate, distinguishable entities such as, 'personal' life and 'biological' life—every human being is an indivisible human life. True, a human life can be described as, for example, healthy or unhealthy, or conscious or unconscious, but it is always the one life of a human being. In a similar manner, the death of a human being is the death of a human life.

The importance of understanding this fallacy of dualism arises because a living patient can sometimes be described as 'dead as a person', or 'to all intents, dead'. The associated argument is that though the patient is alive, her life has no value, or his 'life is not worthy to be lived'. In other words, some human lives can, so it is said, be deprived, by disability, or illness, or inability, of their value. That philosophical position assumes that to be human requires some evidences of human capacity, some attainment of a pass mark on a checklist of humanness. Furthermore, it supposes that a line can be drawn between those who are human and those who are either 'not yet', in the case of the unborn, or 'no longer', in the case of the incompetent, namely, the senile, comatose, brain-damaged, and so on.

This is secular humanism pitted against the biblical worldview—the latter attributes intrinsic, inalienable value and dignity to every human life because they all bear the *imago Dei*, whereas the former believes that some human lives have these features, but some do not. Incidentally, this biblical view of human value does not imply that all human lives are equal. It is obvious that some are better than others, more full of goodness, and so on. Nor does it advocate that every life must be extended by every possible means, including costly drugs, burdensome treatment, and futile measures—that is a cruel, but popular, caricature of the Christian position. In the final analysis, these two worldviews are contrary and irreconcilable. One leads to a high view of human life, the other a low view. One leads to the culture of life, the other to the culture of death.

4.4 Physical life and spiritual life

All current readers of this book are alive—half-asleep maybe, but definitely alive. We have all participated in this life since we were zygotes, embryos, unborn children, born children, teenagers, and so on. Though now unquestionably physically alive, the effects of the Fall mean that we have also been, or still are, spiritually dead, '... dead in your transgressions and sins ...' (Ephesians 2:1). This is the natural state of man—physically alive, yet spiritually dead. Though we cannot escape our forthcoming physical death, we—and this is the Good News—do not have to remain spiritually dead. We can become spiritually alive. Our spiritual death, which is ours as a consequence of the prehistoric Fall, can be converted, at the beginning of the third millennium, to spiritual life. Our sin, which resulted in our spiritual death, together with our depravity and guilt can be pardoned. Our relationship of estrangement from God can be turned to one of unity.

How can this be? Herein is THE message of the Bible—this is the Gospel.

It is our sin that keeps us spiritually dead—it separates us from this holy God. Sin disconnects us from him. Nothing we do can reconnect us. Yet even as the verdict of death was pronounced for man's disobedience in the Garden of Eden (Genesis 2:17), the cure was also announced, 'And I will put enmity between you and the woman, and between your offspring and hers; he will crush your head, and you will strike his heel' (Genesis 3:15). This is THE scoop of the Book. Enter the God-man, the second person of the Trinity, the Messiah, called Jesus, '… because he will save his people from their sins' (Matthew 1:21). This is the God-inspired, God-accomplished rescue mission—the Lord Jesus Christ would come and 'de-sin' man. His incarnation and its purpose were foreseen throughout the Old Testament, '… and the LORD has laid on him the iniquity of us all' (Isaiah 53:6), and reiterated in the New Testament, '... God so loved the world that he gave his one and only Son, that whoever believes in him shall not perish but have eternal life' (John 3:16). The Cross is where this great de-sinning transaction was accomplished. Here, the Lord Jesus Christ took all of our sins, and standing in our place—he bore the punishment for them. That is, he suffered the wrath of God, which justly should have been our punishment. We deserved it—he took it. And it killed him. His blood became the acceptable sacrifice, which appeased the offended God. Jesus Christ now bridges that gaping chasm that separates sinful man from the sin-hating God. That is why Jesus can say, 'I am the way and the truth and the life. No-one comes to the Father except through me' (John 14:6). That is why he is called the Mediator (1 Timothy 2:5) and the Redeemer (Isaiah 60:16)—he acted as the intermediary between us and God, and he has paid the price of our forgiveness. Because of this, we can now be forgiven and the consequences of the Fall, with its depravity, guilt, disconnection and death penalty, need no longer hang over us. It is a sweet conundrum of Christianity that just as death came in by sin (committed by Adam and Eve, in the Garden of Eden), so sin goes out by death (of the Lord Jesus Christ, on the Cross at Calvary). This is biblical theology at its finest and most profound.

How can you be restored to a pre-Fall condition? By coming to God, repenting of your sins, and trusting in this work of rescue undertaken for you by Christ. A radical change will then occur. The Bible says that you will then become a new creature, born again, 'in Christ Jesus'. As 2 Corinthians

5:17 confirms, 'Therefore, if anyone is in Christ, he is a new creation; the old has gone, the new has come!' As the Lord Jesus Christ said, 'You should not be surprised at my saying, "You must be born again"' (John 3:7). And as Romans 8:1–2 asserts, 'Therefore, there is now no condemnation for those who are in Christ Jesus, because through Christ Jesus the law of the Spirit of life set me free from the law of sin and death.' This is the Gospel—no wonder it is called the Good News!

So the Christian life begins by recovering and restoring what was lost at the Fall. However, this recovery and restoration are neither immediate, nor complete. For example, the Christian is not returned to live in the idyllic Garden of Eden, but instead he continues in this abnormal world, which is still rocked and rolled by sin. Furthermore, the Christian still has to face physical death. But, for the Christian, this physical death is now very different. 'When the perishable has been clothed with the imperishable, and the mortal with immortality, then the saying that is written will come true: "Death has been swallowed up in victory." "Where, O death, is your victory? Where, O death, is your sting?"' (1 Corinthians 15:54–55). Death, for the Christian, is now a conquered and disarmed enemy. That does not mean that our physical death has become of no significance. Death is still uninvited, but it is no longer to be greatly feared—condemnation and hell are no longer the Christian's 'sting'. A proper understanding of our death and the work of Christ teaches us that '... by his death he might ... free those who all their lives were held in slavery by their fear of death' (Hebrews 2:14–15). Now, is that Good News, or what? Can you see what Christ has done for you? Have you begun to experience these benefits of the Gospel? 'For the wages of sin is death, but the gift of God is eternal life in Christ Jesus our Lord' (Romans 6:23). Have you received your gift yet? Hurry—because you never know how soon it will be too late.

'Precious in the sight of the LORD is the death of his saints' (Psalm 116:15). The death of a Christian believer is no longer a tragedy. Nor is it any longer a punishment for Christians—how can it be when Romans 8:1 unambiguously declares that all the penalty for our sin has been paid for by the Lord Jesus Christ? Rather, physical death has become the fruition of the Christian's salvation, the end of wrestling with sin, the final step of sanctification, the release from this abnormal world, and the gateway to heaven.

4.5 Death is awesome

The Christian view of physical death is therefore somewhat ambivalent. On the one hand, it remains an enemy to be faced, though thankfully, it is the last one, and now it is disarmed (1 Corinthians 15:26, 55). On the other hand, it is the access to glory (Philippians 1:21–24) and a whole new beginning for, 'There will be no more death or mourning or crying or pain, for the old order of things has passed away' (Revelation 21:4). Nevertheless, the Bible's overall view of physical death remains negative. Its roots are evil, and even though its power is broken for the Christian believer, it is still a reminder of the influence of sin, and still a daunting prospect. In contrast, of course, for the non-Christian, death should be the most terrifying prospect. To meet one's Maker in an unforgiven state will be to experience the wrath of God. As Hebrews 10:31 affirms, 'It is a dreadful thing to fall into the hands of the living God.'

For both the believer and the unbeliever, death remains awesome for at least three reasons. First, it is awesome because it is the great inevitability. Our days are numbered—death will come to us all, one day. For me, Friday 16 July 2021 has become a date to reckon with. According to http:www.deathclock.com this is the day on which I am going to die. Of course, it is merely a statistical calculation and therefore it is almost certainly wrong. But what is not wrong is that one day I will have that appointment with death, an arrangement from which I cannot absent myself. Oh yes, it will come to me, as surely as it will come to you. Its inevitability is so sobering, is it not?

For completeness and biblical correctness, it should be added that some people, albeit a small minority, will never experience death. For a few, such as, Enoch this has already occurred (Genesis 5:24; Hebrews 11:5) because he, '… was taken from this life, so that he did not experience death …' This also will be the experience of a somewhat greater number at the second advent. When the Lord Jesus Christ returns, that is, comes 'down from heaven', his people, who are still alive on the earth, will be '… caught up … to meet the Lord …' (1 Thessalonians 4:16–17). We should be ready for such an event, though we cannot be sure it will be our experience—it may occur next week, or during the next century. That notwithstanding, most of us will have to face death.

On those rare occasions when we think about the inevitability of death, we imagine it to be years, even decades away. We cling to Psalm 90:10 and expect threescore and ten, or even fourscore, years. And when lives are shorter than this we can feel indignant and cheated—some would say, 'She was cruelly cut short in her prime.' Yet the Bible uses a quite different counting system—'... you have decreed the number of his months ...' (Job 14:5), 'Man born of woman is of few days ...' (Job 14:1), and '... the span of my years is as nothing before you' (Psalm 39:5). Thomas Boston, in his *Human Nature In Its Fourfold State* (Banner of Truth, 1964, p. 328), charmingly regards this span, '... as if our life were but a skip from the womb to the grave.' Whatever our allotted span, it has already had its beginning and one day, soon-ish, it will also have its end.

Second, death is awesome in its pervasiveness. 'Just as man is destined to die once, and after that to face judgement' (Hebrews 9:27). Death is no respecter of persons. It is the Great Leveller. Kings and paupers, men and women, rich and poor, black and white—it makes no difference—we all will die. The death rate has never changed—it is still one per capita. Each year about 54 million people die worldwide. Every year in the UK over 600,000 people die, leaving more than three million close family members bereaved.

Third, death is awesome because of its finality. Of course, earthly life is precious, but it must end. 'All men are like grass, and all their glory is like the flowers of the field. The grass withers and the flowers fall, because the breath of the LORD blows on them. Surely the people are grass' (Isaiah 40:6–7). 'Why, you do not even know what will happen tomorrow. What is your life? You are a mist that appears for a little while and then vanishes' (James 4:14). We can strive to keep death at bay and medical personnel can struggle against death, but eventually it will win. There will be a breath that is your final one, your heart will stop beating, and your life on earth will have come to an end.

4.6 Defining death

This end of breathing and lack of heartbeat have been the time-honoured indicators of death. In practice, they are unfailingly correct, as well as being simple and objective. But, while none doubts the reality of death, actually defining it, as opposed to diagnosing it, can, at times, be far more complex and subjective. In addition, modern science and technology have forced us to redefine the life-death boundaries. For example, in the physiological sense, a body's organs and tissues do not all die simultaneously, and anyway only certain organs are essential for life. Consequently, defining death has become a complicated business. Medical definitions abound. A typical one is that supplied by Gert, Culver and Clouser (*Bioethics: A Return to Fundamentals*, 1997, p. 259), 'Death is the permanent cessation of all clinically observable functioning of the organism as a whole and the permanent absence of consciousness in the organism as a whole and in any part of that organism.' But such definitions border on the incomprehensible, and are of limited utility. For a start, each of their constituent phrases often require mind-numbingly tedious clarification—in the example cited here, this amounts to just over six additional pages from these authors! Forget such academic pedantry. The upshot is that death is now technically defined as, not so much a matter of a lack of heartbeat or respiration, but rather the disintegration between these functions—it is no longer centred on the heart and lungs, but rather on the brain.

4.7 Diagnosing death

If defining death can be tricky and a rather textbookish exercise, grounding it in practicality, that is, diagnosing it, is generally must easier. Diagnosis depends upon definition. In other words, what do we look for to certify that death has arrived? Or, to be more blunt, how do we decide if Mrs Bloggs is really dead?

Reading someone's obituary has generally been regarded as a pretty clear-cut diagnosis of death. Every day I read the obituary columns in *The Times*. No, I am not a melancholic—it can be quite instructive to read how other people mark the death of a loved one. Typically, information about the date and place of death is given, family relationships are recorded, and the details of the funeral are stated. Then there are the usual, 'Donations to such-and-such a charity', and sometimes, the unusual, like, 'Eat a piece of chocolate cake in memory of Peter.' Occasionally, there is the entirely unrealistic assessment of the deceased, like, 'He was loved by all who knew him', or there is a snippet of some pie-in-the-sky philosophy, like, 'Save a place on your cloud for me', or more rarely, a reassuring verse of Scripture, like Philippians 1:21. Reading obituaries can also have a sobering effect because, although we recognize only a tiny minority of the names, they are, as the years tick by, getting to be more and more—our generation is beginning to die, and that means our time is coming nearer too. Nevertheless, although an obituary may be a good and accurate indicator of death, the question remains, how did the doctors diagnose it several days before the notice appeared in the newspaper?

Perhaps surprisingly, after hundreds of years of certifying deaths and issuing death certificates, doctors can still sometimes be unsure about making such pronouncements. The problem is, few entirely decisive criteria exist. Even exceptions to the 'old' criteria can occur. For example, a lack of heartbeat and cessation of breathing, together with the coldness of a body, might indicate only 'somatic', or reversible death. Respiration and cardiac output might have ceased, but resuscitation can sometimes restore them, and circulatory-ventilator technology may maintain them. Likewise, the coldness of the body can also be misleading. Hypothermia can be to blame, especially in the elderly, and, if detected, the patient may be warmed up and resuscitation started. Similarly, careful diagnosis of other conditions like, for example, a drug overdose, or hypoglycaemia, must be made. Special attention must be paid to people who have suffered drowning, electric shock, or airway obstruction.

However, despite the difficulties posed by these exceptional circumstances, the doctor's diagnosis is rarely wrong. The usual diagnosis of death is made by carefully excluding all possible signs of life. A good doctor will first make a rapid assessment to ensure that resuscitation is not needed. The doctor should then look for a deathly pallor, the *pallor mortis*, especially in the face and lips, relaxed facial muscles, a drooping of the lower jaw, and open, staring eyes. A full physical examination is then required to exclude mere 'somatic', or reversible death.

The next step is to diagnose 'molecular', or irreversible death, that is, when the progressive disintegration of the tissues has started. These indisputable signs of death include purpuric death spots, also known as post-mortem staining, which are visible from about thirty minutes after death, muscular stiffness after three hours, and decreasing body temperature from as much as eight hours.

In our world of high-tech healthcare and medical litigation, speedier accuracy is often now demanded in diagnosing death. This requirement has been driven by two main factors. First, there is the need to avoid the ineffectual use of expensive medical equipment. Second, if permission has been given, there is the need to harvest organs for transplantation at the earliest possible time, while they are still in tip-top condition.

These sorts of advances have, over the years, led to the development of four different sets of criteria for diagnosing death. They are, in chronological order, the total and permanent loss of function of, first—heart and lungs, second—brain cortex, third—brainstem, and fourth—whole brain. These criteria reflect improvements in the technology of patient care, such as the use of life-support systems, plus our greater understanding of brain function. Whole brain death is now generally recognized as the only completely satisfactory criterion, especially from a legal standpoint, because it includes both the permanent lack of functioning of the whole organism and the permanent absence of consciousness. Yet, perhaps somewhat ironically, this sophisticated criterion is closely akin to the rudimentary features traditionally looked for by a doctor, such as, the lack of general responsiveness and spontaneous movement, including breathing, and the absence of a pupillary light response. After all, when a person's heart and lungs stop functioning for an extended period of time, then the permanent loss of whole brain function and consciousness will inevitably follow.

For the doctor in a hospital, where about seventy-five per cent of deaths currently occur, the absence of electrical activity in the brain is a relatively easy diagnosis. But the requirement to establish this meticulous criterion of brain death is rarely necessary. In the vast, vast majority of cases, generally estimated to be well in excess of ninety-nine per cent, there is absolute certainty that if the more familiar, long-established criteria of death are met, the person in question has indeed died. This is important to understand because it means that most of us will *never* be faced with doubt at the bedside of a loved one—the doctor's experience in anticipating the proximity of death and then the traditional diagnosis of the cessation of heartbeat and respiration will be true and final.

The precise point at which the process of dying ends and death begins, that is, when somatic death progresses to molecular death, can be of concern for some people. There can be fears that the healthcare team will give up prematurely, or that lurking transplant doctors will be too quick to pounce. Such fears are quite irrational—some people pay too much attention to science fiction. True, it may be difficult to diagnose death with split-second precision. But, we are not unaccustomed to a little vagueness surrounding some of life's crucial occurrences—what is the precise moment of, say, birth, or marriage? Such pinpoint timing is not important for these events. Likewise, death is more than just a technical term. Therefore, we should refrain from getting hung-up on the complexities of the scientific, philosophical and legal definitions and criteria of death. They need not concern us unduly—in ordinary life, there is going to be no disagreement about when someone, Mrs Bloggs, or your dear relative, has died.

4.8 Post-mortem—the aftermath of death

'Dead', and its associated words like 'death' and 'died', have an unequivocal ring of finality about them. They signify a permanence and an irreversibility that are entirely unlike any other event in the human experience—death cannot be repeated, or relived. A death heralds endings, but also beginnings.

For the dead person there is the reality of a new destiny. For the near family, although everyday life will continue, it will never be quite the same again. When a person is declared 'dead', it does not just signify the end of life and medical care, it is also the beginning of numerous other activities. For example, funeral arrangements can be started, a will becomes active, claims on life insurance policies can be initiated, organ donation can get underway, personal loss has begun and grieving can commence. These are the concerns of 'those left behind'.

What happens to the person who has 'gone'? When a Christian dies, the soul goes immediately, with rejoicing, to be with God in heaven (Luke 23:43; 2 Corinthians 5:8; Philippians 1:23). There is no soul sleep, no purgatory, no waiting in limbo. Instead, there is immediate, conscious fellowship with our Maker. In contradistinction, the physical body remains on earth. It may be buried in a coffin, from which it will slowly disintegrate and decay, or it may be cremated, in which case its destruction will be hastened. Whichever method occurs, the body returns to dust, in compliance with Genesis 3:19.

When a non-Christian dies, the outcome is quite different. It is dreadful to even think about it. The Bible gives no indication that the soul of the unbeliever undergoes anything other than an immediate, conscious eternal punishment. Gentle Jesus said so on many occasions, including Matthew 25:41, 46. Read and tremble!

For completion, there is one more doctrine to add here, that of resurrection (John 14:3; 1 Thessalonians 4:16). On that Great Day, all the physical bodies of the dead will be raised from the earth and united with their souls (John 5:28–29; 1 Corinthians 15:50–53). Then we shall all stand before the throne of God to await our final judgement (Revelation 20:11–15). Then all dying and death will come to an end.

4.9 The Christian view of death

If doctors, philosophers, Uncle Tom Cobbley and all can be confused by death and its associated issues, what about the Christian? How should a Christian regard death? As the gateway to life, or the king of terrors? The simple answer is both, but undoubtedly far more of the former than the latter. For most of recorded history, dying and natural death have been an expected and accepted part of human life. This is in stark contrast to the view held by today's typical non-Christian. Nowadays, dying is often regarded as a most distasteful affair, and death has, for many, become offensive. Dying and death tend to be shunned, as if they have no place in the human experience. This detached view is not helpful. Furthermore, it has been compounded by a loss of Christian faith, a decreased personal exposure to death itself, and a misguided belief in the power of modern medicine to render us almost immortal.

On the other hand, the Christian understands the origin of death—it was never intended, but the arrival of sin, and then death, has produced an abnormal, fallen, perishing world. While we live in this world, we are in bondage to its disintegration and decay (Romans 8:21). But it will not last.

Death can therefore be described properly as the *final* enemy (1 Corinthians 15:26). But, here is the uniqueness and brilliance of Christianity. The grace of God comes to liberate us from our fallen state and this fallen world. We are not destined to live forever with our wretched sinful natures, in our decaying bodies. God has a better way. Paradise will be regained. We will know a life of freely living and communicating with God. We are to be transformed back to our original state. And death is the way and the method by which we are released from this earthly life of personal sin and global decay. Now that puts a wholly different perspective on dying and death. Sure, it can be an ugly end, yet, it is also a beautiful beginning. That is the Christian view of death.

So, what can we learn from contemplating dying and death? To summarize this section, I can do no better than to quote the words of the Old Testament teacher, which are as apt and as searching as ever, '… for death is the destiny of every man; the living should take this to heart' (Ecclesiastes 7:2). We must learn to accept our earthly mortality. Our time in this world is limited—we will not be staying much longer. And we must learn that death is not just physical, but also spiritual. The former has already begun—for some of us, manifestly so—but what about the latter? Have we made spiritual progress? Non-Christians, first of all, have much to settle with God. They should seek him as soon as possible (Isaiah 55:6; Matthew 11:28). Christians must then learn to prepare for eternity, to anticipate heaven, and to set their affections above as they finish this earthly race (Hebrews 12:1–3). This biblical perspective of living in the face of dying and death will do us nothing but good. It should alarm the non-Christian, but it should energize and comfort the Christian.

Euthanasia

E uthanasia has developed into one of the hottest bioethical topics of the early part of the twenty-first century. Understand it, or else! The 'else' includes a spectrum of nasty outcomes, from being swept along, like a piece of driftwood, on the tide of secular humanistic thinking, to becoming the actual subject of the euthanasiast's practice. We can, I assume, all agree that it would be preferable to understand the topic, challenge the thinking, and resist the practice.

5.1 True and false euthanasia

When it was first coined as an English word, sometime in the mid-seventeenth century, euthanasia had a marvellous meaning. It was derived from the two Greek words, *eu* and *thanatos*, literally meaning, 'well death'. It represented what everybody wanted eventually, 'a good and happy death'. To die well was therefore euthanasia. Yes, it is true. Throughout history, men and women have aspired to, and made preparations for, a good death. In earlier times, such as during the Middle Ages, the dying were issued with booklets describing the *Ars Moriendi*, 'the art of dying well', to guide them through their last days and hours. Euthanasia was therefore, once upon a time, something people could both hope for and get ready for.

Then came the etymological scam. The Victorians hijacked this nice, smooth-sounding word and twisted its meaning, as first recorded in the Oxford English Dictionary of 1869. From that time, euthanasia took on sinister overtones, associated with the practice of putting people to death before their natural end. Now, in the twenty-first century, euthanasia has undoubtedly become one of our meanest, most menacing words. Modern-day euthanasia is now associated with hovering doctors, doubt, pain, patients' rights, dehumanization, living wills, and bad decisions. It is one of those examples of lexical engineering preceding social engineering—a wretched feature of so much of contemporary bioethics. Another example would be how the realities of mass abortion have been cunningly subsumed under the guise of respectable phrases such as, 'termination of pregnancy', 'removal of the products of conception', or simply, 'a woman's right to choose'. Call it something, anything, that disguises the truth, and hey presto, the majority of the public will begin to accept it, and, in due course, they will even buy it. The public has thereby been lexically confused and socially manipulated. Now a similar verbal cloak is being used to cover up the truth about euthanasia. People insist on dressing it up to try to make it look appealing, or even virtuous—they call it something like, 'the right to die', or 'mercy-killing', or 'self-deliverance'. We should not be so easily fooled. In truth, modern euthanasia is the deliberate administration of death, and it has only two proper names—suicide, or murder.

5.2 A theology of living *and* dying

Our abhorrence at the very word 'euthanasia' should not discourage Christians from seeking to recapture the essence of *true* euthanasia. We have all begun the biological process of dying, now we need to develop the spiritual process. Over the last few decades, Christians have recovered some key biblical doctrines and developed substantially in their thinking and practice with respect to many aspects of living. Examples would be family life, social action, church planting, education, and so forth. Individually, they have become stronger, and their churches have benefited too. That is to say, we have constructed a decent theology of living. Good for us! But, it is my conviction that we need both a theology of living *and* a theology of dying. And I hope that reading this book will prompt many to resolve to do just that—writing it has certainly changed my horizons and done me good. Only such a well-rounded, biblical perspective will enable us to live well *and* to die well. Thinking about and preparing for old-fashioned, true euthanasia will benefit us all.

5.3 Definitions of euthanasia

So, what is this modern-day euthanasia? It is a subject dominated by a secular humanistic, autonomy-driven worldview. We should, at the very least, always be wary of it—it is indeed a fatal practice. Its supporters say that a request for death is a person's right, it is compassionate, it is rational, and it makes good sense. At times, their arguments can seem so reasonable, even convincing. Hence, we need to be on our guard, and ready to meet the challenge of the day. Therefore, think about the issue. Understand what is at stake. Do not be hoodwinked. Be suspicious. Ask probing questions.

For a start, grasp what is meant by modern-day euthanasia. A typical definition would be, 'The intentional putting to death of a person with an incurable or painful disease.' Since this may come about by either an act of commission, or an act of omission by a third party, usually a doctor, a commonly-used alternative definition is, 'The intentional shortening of a patient's life, by act or omission, as part of the patient's medical care.' Can you doubt that this is anything other than either doctor-assisted suicide, or murder? This can all be quite confusing, and for many of us, as bioethical greenhorns, an understanding of the issue will need more definition and explanation.

5.4 Active and passive euthanasia

Euthanasia has been further defined as either 'active', if it is precipitated by a doctor's positive action, such as injecting a lethal dose of drugs, or 'passive', when a doctor acts negatively, such as withholding food, or withdrawing treatment. This distinction is now regarded by many to be false, including even Baroness Warnock, a supporter of euthanasia, whose husband was, in 1995, 'helped to die'. However, some still like to juggle with the concept of active and passive euthanasia because it allows them, so they imagine, to argue that a patient who is starved to death is merely being passively *allowed* to die, rather than being actively *caused* to die. Moreover, they maintain that the former is much nicer than the latter. But these people are muddled. Though there is a *practical* difference between causing death by positive acts, or causing death by negative acts, there can be no *ethical* difference—if the doctor's intention is to shorten and end the patient's life, then it is euthanasia, whatever technique is used. Intention therefore becomes paramount—the means of death, whether by lethal injection (as an example of so-called active or positive euthanasia), or starvation (passive or negative euthanasia), is of minor importance. This division of euthanasia into active and passive categories is a smokescreen. Yet it is easy to be conned by the euthanasia enthusiast's confused thinking and bogus bioethical scruples. For instance, think about this situation. A doctor might inject a barrelful of life-ending drugs into a patient's veins, but would probably never dream of cutting his throat. But why not? Why do people support one action, but abhor the other? What is the difference between the two? The difference is practical, not ethical. After all, a dead patient is a dead patient, regardless of the means used. 'Passive' and 'active', or 'positive' and 'negative' are adjectives that distinguish the methods of committing euthanasia—they do not describe its ethics, nor do they ever justify its practice.

5.5 The importance of intention

So in euthanasia, the 'means' is minor, whereas the 'intention' is major. Moreover, the concept of intention is fundamental. It underlines the premise that our universe is a moral universe—it includes right and wrong—because it was made by a moral Creator, who sanctions what is right, and opposes what is wrong. Man, as one made in the image of God, is a moral and morally-responsible being, who is answerable to this God. Moral intention not only describes *what* we do, but also *why* we do it. Return to Eden. The eating of the apple by Eve and Adam (Genesis 3:6) was the *what*, which was a sufficiently bad action, because it had been forbidden (Genesis 2:16–17). Of course, we could dream up all sorts of mitigating circumstances—perhaps they were hungry, or they thought it was a windfall from another tree, rather than from the forbidden one, and so forth. But *why* they ate is the real key to understanding their original wrongdoing. This was no 'accident'. It was a deliberate defiance, a disobedience with intent. It is what modern law calls *mens rea*, guilty intent. They did it with their brains in gear, and their eyes wide open. Hence, they were responsible. The sin was theirs, it was deliberate, it was their intention—and so their punishment was wholly justified (Genesis 3:14–19). The denouement of this episode is that men and women are indeed moral agents, responsible for their intentions and their actions. This is an essential component of the Christian view of man and woman.

There are some more subtle distinctions here which also need grasping—maybe you will need to read them more than once! Indeed, as an opening example, consider the fact that 'intention' and 'motive' are often confused. The former is concerned with the desired outcome of an action, whereas the latter is concerned about the reason why that outcome is desired. A man's motive may have been to end his mother's suffering, but if his intention was to kill her, then he is guilty of murder. In such a case of deliberate killing, the law takes notice of intention, but ignores motive. Complex? You bet. Thankfully, for those of us who live outside of both the law courts and the ivory towers of academia, this sort of distinction is of negligible importance. For us, what is important is to recognize that euthanasia has been committed if the doctor's intention has been to kill the patient. On the other hand, the administration of a drug in order to, say, alleviate pain, even if, as a foreseen, but unintended side-effect, it hastens death, is *not* regarded as euthanasia. Neither is the withholding or withdrawing of treatment on the grounds that it is futile or too burdensome for the patient, even though such non-treatment may foreseeably hasten death. In both of these cases the doctor's intention is not to hasten death, therefore he is *not* performing euthanasia. The acid test is this, 'What is the doctor's intention in taking, or not taking, a particular course of action?' When the answer is, 'to alleviate the patient's symptoms', then it is *not* euthanasia. When the answer is, 'to shorten the patient's life', then it is euthanasia. These issues are of such importance that they are discussed further, in chapters 18 and 19.

5.6 Voluntary, non-voluntary and involuntary euthanasia

Euthanasia is most often sub-divided into three main groupings. First, there is voluntary euthanasia, that is, killing *with* the patient's request. Its propriety is usually defended with reference to a person's autonomy. That is, a man should have the capacity, the right, and the freedom to choose the circumstances, the time and the means, by which his own life can be deliberately ended. Voluntary euthanasia comes in two categories. In 'straightforward' voluntary euthanasia, the patient makes the decision, although a doctor, friend, or relative performs the actual deed that ends the patient's life. In the other category, known as assisted suicide, the same group of people do no more than help the patient to take his or her own life. In reality, the latter is usually called medically-assisted suicide, or in the USA, physician-assisted suicide, because it is a medical doctor or physician who is generally doing the assisting. Some doctors prefer voluntary euthanasia because, they say, that in assisted suicide the patient is abandoned at the 'supreme moment'. Other doctors prefer assisted suicide because, they say, the actual act of taking the drug puts patients to the test—do they really want to die? Of course, ethically there is no difference between these two forms of killing patients, but some dodgy doctors like to defend their involvement by resorting to such specious moral arguments.

At this point, an important question arises. Why do people seek voluntary euthanasia that is doctor-assisted? Of course, there is the obvious answer, or set of answers, which are associated with issues like, despair, pain, encumbrance, and so on. But is there something else here? After all, it is not difficult nowadays for most people to find, or to buy, the requisite drugs in order to commit suicide on their own. Are these people crying out for something else, something significant in their lives? Is it that their doctor is the most available, trustworthy person they know? Are they seeking a more meaningful relationship with someone, anyone? These are not superficial questions. Christians and the morally sensitive will want to heed them and take them to heart.

Finally, it should be noted that voluntary euthanasia need not be confined to elderly patients with terminal illnesses. For example, the young victim of a motorbike accident, which leaves him paralysed from the neck down, might consider that voluntary euthanasia would end the perceived misery of his disability, and his seemingly-unfulfilled life.

Second, there is non-voluntary euthanasia. This is killing a patient *without* an explicit request. The lack of request is because the patient is incompetent, meaning that she is comatose, or senile, or handicapped, or unable to communicate for other reasons, such as in the case of a newborn baby. The rationale for non-voluntary euthanasia depends upon the proposition that it can be in 'a person's best interests' to be dead. That is, since the patient cannot decide, or cannot communicate her wishes, others will nevertheless decide for her. The fact is that it can now be lawful to kill a so-called incompetent individual by deliberately withholding treatment and, or, withdrawing nutrition and hydration. The landmark adult case in this area is that of Anthony Bland, as discussed in chapter 12. The landmark case with respect to the newborn, otherwise known as infanticide, is that of John Pearson, as discussed in chapter 13.

Third, there is involuntary euthanasia, that is, killing *against* the patient's wishes. It is overriding the express will of a person. It is the strong overruling the weak. The case for involuntary euthanasia depends upon the utter denial of personal dignity, value, autonomy, rights, and so on. It is treating humans as if they were animals—it is the ethics and practice of the abattoir. One of the most appalling examples of involuntary euthanasia is that associated with the Nazi Holocaust, as described in chapter 11.

5.7 The false 'principles' of euthanasia

Being opposed to all categories of euthanasia is a robust, ethical position— it is the Christian position. It can be coherently constructed and stoutly defended. It is compassionate and principled. But euthanasia supporters also want to argue for their own beliefs and values. However, there are some major flaws underlying their alleged 'principles' of euthanasia. We would do well to appreciate them.

Here is the first. It is often claimed by pro-euthanasia campaigners that personal autonomy is the key 'principle' of euthanasia—a person asks to die, therefore a doctor has a duty to comply with that request. However, the interpersonal dynamics of the doctor-patient relationship surrounding a request for euthanasia are most revealing. When a patient asks about dying, what goes on inside the doctor's head? No doctor who practises Hippocratic-Christian medicine would ever kill a patient just because he was asked to. However, if he were a non-Hippocratic-Christian doctor, such an inquiry might trigger his brain to ask himself some big questions, like, 'Does this patient have "a life not worthy to be lived"?', and, if so, 'Should it be terminated?' He might also ask, 'Would death be in this patient's "best interests"?' Hence, all the euthanasia supporter's talk about the primacy, or 'principle', of patient autonomy is a gimmick. The patient may believe it, and expect that it will be taken into account, but the doctor may already be asking himself, rather than the patient, a quite different, and far more sinister, set of questions.

The proposition that a doctor, or anyone else, can judge that a patient has 'a life not worthy to be lived' has two important knock-on effects. First, if such a judgement were true, then there is no reason to restrict euthanasia to the terminally-ill patient, as currently campaigned for by most euthanasia pressure groups. If the patient's life is reckoned to be of no value, then whether dying or not, that life could, even should, be terminated. Second, if the patient is deemed to have 'a life not worthy to be lived', but is incompetent and therefore unable either, to request, or consent to euthanasia, then, is there any reason not to euthanize that patient, especially if the relatives agree to give their consent? If death can be a benefit for the competent, who have 'lives not worthy to be lived', then why should it be denied to those who are sufficiently incompetent that they cannot request such a benefit?

These arguments bring us to the next so-called 'principle'. Pro-euthanasia campaigners maintain that there is a solid and genuine difference between voluntary and non-voluntary euthanasia. Is that true? In his book, *The Value of Life* (1985), the influential British ethicist, John Harris, claims (p. 84) that the case for voluntary euthanasia is open-and-shut. He considers that because it applies to such a relatively small number of people, it is, '... clearly something that society should permit.' On the other hand, Harris considers that the real problem, the ethical hiatus, of euthanasia is with the non-voluntary variety. Harris maintains that, largely unbeknown to, or at least, unrecognized by, the general public, non-voluntary euthanasia is already being practised in three forms. First, as infanticide, against severely-handicapped babies. Second, as the non-offering of resuscitation after medical events, such as cardiac arrest or kidney failure, when the patient has not been consulted. Third, as part of pain control that foreshortens a patient's life. These, according to Harris, are components of every hospital's non-voluntary euthanasia plan, which are currently being widely practised in these healthcare facilities, and controlled by government policies and money. Here then, according to Harris, is the euthanasia iceberg. The tip, which is voluntary euthanasia, is the visible aspect, upon which people concentrate too much, while they tend to disregard the other hidden, non-voluntary four-fifths.

While Harris' remarks may appear to be novel and startling, they are only an amalgam of logic and human disposition. Many advocates of voluntary euthanasia have already openly espoused their wishes for killing in a much wider context—most are already disposed to non-voluntary euthanasia. If the former practice were to be legalized, then the latter would inevitably follow, as surely as night follows day. This is because the boundary between voluntary and non-voluntary euthanasia is so very thin and fragile, in fact, it hardly exists. Logically, once we have accepted that a judgement for euthanasia can be made by a competent patient, then there is no reason why it cannot be made, by equally competent people, even highly-skilled, knowledgeable medical experts, on behalf of an incompetent patient. If death can a benefit for the competent patient, how can it not be a benefit for the incompetent? What is good for the conscious, 'normal' patient must surely also be good for the unconscious, or mentally handicapped, or senile, or newborn patient.

Harris' comments serve to highlight a third flaw in the 'principles' of voluntary and non-voluntary euthanasia. The former falsely assumes that a competent person can possess total freedom or personal autonomy, and therefore it is that person's right to be able to choose his own death. The false assumption of the latter depends upon knowing the unknowable, namely, the 'best interests' of an incompetent person. There is a contradiction between these two arguments. How can an appeal be made for the autonomy of an individual to choose the time and means of his death, as in voluntary euthanasia, while simultaneously insisting that, on some occasions, that choice can legitimately be made by others, without any contribution from the individual concerned, as in non-voluntary euthanasia? Is personal autonomy the principal foundation for euthanasia, or is it not? We should be told.

The fourth false 'principle' considers that euthanasia is based on compassion. 'If it is compassionate to kill the suffering dog or cat, then why not human beings?', it asserts. This argument is flawed, first, because it disregards the specialness of human life—we alone bear the *imago Dei*. Even the bioethicist Peter Singer, who vehemently denies this truth with his own weird theory of 'speciesism', ensures that his severely-disabled mother is cared for, rather than killed. Second, it confuses compassion with convenience. Proper, principled compassion demands that we love one another (1 John 3:11–18) and that we 'Carry each other's burdens ...' (Galatians 6:2), not ditch them, asap. The truly compassionate person seeks to heal and restore, and bring hope and justice to the situation. The falsely compassionate euthanasiast just wants to end it all, and move on. True compassion and euthanasia simply do not mix.

These so-called 'principles' of euthanasia are incoherent and unsound. Hence, the practice of euthanasia is flawed not only medically, but also philosophically, not to mention biblically. There are no principles of euthanasia—there are only twisted arguments and human wish-lists. The supposedly impregnable case for euthanasia, its superstructure and its foundations, have collapsed. But what else would you expect with such an unprincipled, utilitarian practice?

5.8 A brief history of euthanasia

Euthanasia has long had its advocates. In the classical era, Seneca and the younger Pliny were among its early supporters. And in later times, like the seventeenth century, men such as the English philosopher, Francis Bacon, thought that euthanasia was a good idea. Then in 1873, Lionel Tollemache broached the topic by writing about it in the *Fortnightly Review*, a Victorian periodical noted for its radical secular and scientific outlook.

However, the modern euthanasia movement could be said to have begun in 1931, when Dr C Killick Millard used his presidential address to the British Society of Medical Officers of Health to propose that voluntary euthanasia should be legalized. In 1935, under the leadership of Lord Ponsonby, and with the support of some other medical doctors, lawyers and even a few notable Church of England clergymen, the Voluntary Euthanasia Legalization Society (VELS) was founded—the first of its kind in the world. The issue began to be debated in the columns of the medical press, and while the overall tone was one of indifference, there was a growing consensus that euthanasia could be a sensible option for the mentally handicapped. In the same year, 1935, a private member's Bill was presented by Lord Ponsonby to the House of Lords seeking to legalize the practice. It was hedged about with numerous stipulations to prevent accusations of murder, fraud and undue haste. It was defeated at its second reading. During the 1930s, the subject of euthanasia was being debated and campaigning organizations were being set up throughout Europe and elsewhere. For example, in the USA in 1938, the Euthanasia Society of America was formed. Its express aim was to promote euthanasia as, 'The termination of human life by painless means for the purpose of ending severe physical suffering.'

The intervention of the War and the subsequent uncovering of the practices of euthanasia that had occurred in Germany served to curb political discussion and public interest. However, in 1950, Lord Chorley introduced a House of Lords' debate on voluntary euthanasia, but it was withdrawn without a vote. In 1961, the Suicide Act decriminalized suicide, but the 'aiding, abetting, counselling or procuring' of the suicide of another person remained as criminal offences. A 1969 Bill in favour of voluntary euthanasia was proposed in Parliament, this time by Lord Raglan—it was rejected at its second reading. In the same year, VELS changed its name to the Voluntary Euthanasia Society (VES). During 1970, the subject again appeared in the House of Commons in the form of a ten-minute rule Bill, sponsored by Hugh Gray MP, but no vote was taken. Then in 1976, the Incurable Patients Bill, which would have legalized so-called passive euthanasia, was presented to the House of Lords by Baroness Wootton of Abinger. It was defeated, by 85 to 23 votes. In 1979, the VES became Exit. In 1982, Exit reverted to the VES. Lord Jenkins, in 1985, proposed amendments to the Suicide Act, but the attempt foundered after its second reading. Another ten-minute rule Bill promoting euthanasia was introduced in 1990 by Roland Boyes MP, but it was voted out, 101 versus 35. In 1994, the House of Lords' Select Committee on Medical Ethics published its Report on some issues surrounding euthanasia, including its legalization, which it steadfastly opposed. This document is further discussed in chapter 10. In December 1997, Joe Ashton MP, proposed his ten-minute rule measure, the Doctor Assisted Dying Bill—it was trounced in the House of Commons, 234 votes against, 89 votes for.

This brief overview demonstrates that calls for national policies of euthanasia have certainly not been restricted to those in Germany during the 1920s and 1930s. These UK attempts might seem piffling, like so much political tub-thumping, but such efforts have ensured exposure to the issue, for the last seventy years, within the corridors of Parliamentary power.

However, in the UK, and generally elsewhere, the political push for euthanasia has met with little tangible success, so far. Legal success has been greater. This has been achieved by individual 'hard cases' coming before the law courts. The outcomes have produced a chipping away at what were previously regarded as inalienable decrees. In the UK, although there is no law that deals directly with euthanasia *per se*, it remains illegal. Notionally, it is illegal throughout most of the world, but it is obviously practised, often covertly, and probably to a greater extent than many of us would wish to imagine. Indeed, the current law prohibiting it in the UK, as in most other countries, is now regarded as profoundly ambiguous. The 1957 Homicide Act carries a life sentence for murder, and the 1961 Suicide Act carries a sentence of up to fourteen years imprisonment for assisting suicide. For those who kill for 'compassionate reasons', a charge of murder is often reduced to manslaughter on the grounds of 'diminished responsibility'. However, as detailed in section 5.12, sentences for such crimes of euthanasia are usually light, and often carry no terms of imprisonment.

5.9 Doctors and euthanasia

Just as euthanasia has been a subject for debate within the corridors of Westminster and the law courts, it is also an occasional topic of conversation within the corridors of hospitals and health centres. If asked, some doctors would be in favour of the legalization of euthanasia, some would be opposed, and many would be unsure. However, there is an interesting state of affairs occurring here that no such vox pops would highlight. Polls of healthcare professionals have consistently shown that nurses are less in favour of euthanasia than the public, but more so than doctors. The figures are generally of the order of seventy, eighty and fifty per cent, respectively. However, approval is one thing, participation is another. Such polls also reveal that while about thirty per cent of medical personnel would be willing to assist, only fifteen per cent would be willing to administer the lethal dose. In other words, most are saying, 'Yes, euthanasia is good idea, but let others sully themselves.'

However, numbers and percentages, whether for, or against, are almost irrelevant to this issue. What is far more relevant to the practice of edge-of-life medicine are the almost imperceptible changes that are slowly altering it. These subtle changes, which are eroding the ethical component of medical thinking and practice, are rehearsed throughout this book. Despite the extent of this lamentable decline in medical ethics, there are still some doctors practising Hippocratic-Christian medicine, who still continue to offer respect for all human life, who still practise principled care, and who still maintain genuine professional integrity. But it must seem incongruous to them, as successors of Hippocrates, some 2,500 years later on, that the idea of euthanasia appears to be increasingly popular. The paradox is that such a resurgence of interest has arisen at a time when our medical resources are the best ever, especially when compared with times when euthanasia was either forbidden, or largely unheard of.

Furthermore, the medical profession's general ethical weakness is seen in its lack of ability to resist the threat of euthanasia. Where are the doctors willing to stand up against the supporters of euthanasia, who, for example, happily continue to propagate two well-worn misconceptions concerning edge-of-life issues? One, is that death is commonly associated with uncontrollable pain, and the other, is that modern technology will prolong the dying process interminably, and cruelly. Neither should be true, and certainly need not be, if doctors were practising principled, compassionate medicine. And even if either were true, they would be forceful arguments, not for legalizing euthanasia, but rather for promoting good, better, and best medicine.

Not only have doctors been confused by increasingly contentless medical ethics, they have also been faced with an unprecedented increase in medical technologies—better drugs, novel procedures, sophisticated equipment, and so on. These too have caused subtle changes within medicine. They have created a more depersonalized approach to it. This trend has been termed the 'medicalization of medicine', and it has deprived medicine of much of its former glory. This movement has shifted a primary aim of medical personnel away from caring towards curing. For many, medicine has now become little more than a technological battle against illness and death—cure at all costs. Yet doctors with this mindset will always be failures—they will fail themselves, and they will fail every single one of their patients. Such a view of medicine and death is seriously deficient. The medicalization of medicine has led to this 'tyranny of cure', which has become the demanded expectation of patient and doctor alike.

Perhaps, therefore, it is not surprising that modern medicine and its practitioners often handle dying and death poorly. Where there is a prospect of life, they often do brilliantly, but where there is dying, they generally do poorly. Dying is seen as a failure—another bed needlessly occupied. Death is an embarrassment—another patient failed, a doctor's career aspirations again quashed.

If this emphasis on 'curing' represents a lop-sided medicine, then what constitutes 'caring' medicine? 'That's simple. It's erm …' Exactly! Doctors, like the rest of us, have become bewildered. Are you surprised that we are confused? Mull over, for example, the bamboozling message of the medical ethicist, John Harris. He, and others, believe that 'killing can be caring'. Indeed, the fourth chapter in his book, *The Value of Life* (1985), is entitled, *Killing: A Caring Thing to Do?* It is caring, he and they say, if it saves lives, or reduces suffering. So why, they ask, should not killing be part of a doctor's duty? Two examples, classically used to support, or 'prove', this line of thinking are, first, a soldier kills the enemy to defend his country, as in the just war, and second, a homeowner kills the mad, murderous intruder as an act of protecting his family. Therefore, Harris and others conclude, it is obvious, 'killing can be caring'. Then, why not, so their argument goes, kill the newborn handicapped, or the elderly senile? However, this extension of their argument collapses because neither the enemy, nor the intruder, were innocent people—their intentions were to kill, and probably to kill many. In contradistinction, the newborn baby and the senile patient are innocent—to whom are they a threat, what have they done to deserve death? Doctors who kill them are not in the least caring—they are cold, callous and cruel. How can it ever be that 'killing can be caring'? It is a preposterous phrase. Neither doctors, nor we, should be deceived by it.

The euthanasia debate has not only subtly changed the thinking, but also the role, of doctors. They have become more than just expert witnesses, standing on the sidelines, or at the bedside. They have, whether they like it or not, been pushed to the forefront. Despite all the talk of patient autonomy, it is the doctors who are the generals, and the patients who are the foot soldiers, if not mere cannon fodder. And now that mainstream opinion among healthcare professionals is that a human life can be regarded as worthless, the wishes of the patient, as to whether euthanasia should, or should not, be prescribed, have become increasingly irrelevant. The determinant in euthanasia is no longer the patient's wishes, but rather the worldview of the doctor, egged on by the attitudes of many within an increasingly unprincipled profession, and backed up by an ethically-detached society.

This sad state of affairs has already evolved and moved on, especially in regard to the practice of non-voluntary euthanasia, where it is said that it can be in the patient's 'best interests' to die. This topic is further discussed in chapter 17. And the assessment of the 'best interests' is considered to be the prerogative, certainly not of the patient, but of the doctor. We may well ask, how long will it be before the right of the patient to ask her doctor to end her life becomes the right of the doctor to end his patients' lives?

5.10 Two awful doctors

Not all doctors are the same. Some are excellent, high-principled, caring professionals. Many are not so good, and as well as being over-worked and stressed, they are ethically confused. A few are utterly dreadful—they should be struck off the medical register, pronto. From that latter group, here are two examples of blatant euthanasiasts.

On 22 September 1996, Bob Dent, a sixty-six-year-old carpenter with prostate cancer, became the first person in the world to die under euthanasia law. This occurred in the Northern Territory of Australia under its Right of the Terminally Ill Act. Mr Dent had used a computer-operated machine developed and supplied by a doctor called, Philip Nitschke. He had designed his 'death machine' to give his patients control over the time of their death. And because a doctor does not need to be directly involved, it cannot technically be called medically-assisted suicide—except, of course, that the doctor invents, makes and loans the machine, supplies the drugs, and instructs the patient—that sounds like assistance, does it not? That notwithstanding, the patient's consent is indicated by the answers he gives to three questions on a laptop computer. If he answers 'Yes', 'Yes' and 'Yes' and then hits the spacebar, the machine delivers a lethal cocktail of drugs, thiopentone, pentobarbitone and atracurium, into his arm. Commenting on Mr Dent's death, Dr Nitschke is reported to have said that, 'It [voluntary euthanasia] is the greatest thing you can do for a person. I felt at the end of it enhanced by the experience.' Well, he is one real non-Hippocratic-Christian doctor.

These events caused an ethical storm across Australia and this euthanasia law was overturned the following March by its federal Parliament. At first, Mr Dent's action was enthusiastically supported by his son, Rob. But, less than three months after the event, he (Rob, certainly not Bob) changed his mind. After due consideration he came to the conclusion that the right solution to his father's dilemma was that, 'He needed access to proper palliative care.' Somewhat bizarrely, both sides of the ethical divide, those for and those against euthanasia, then joined forces in calling for increased funding for palliative care. Ah, what the application of a little common sense can do! Loving your neighbour is always a better response than killing him.

The second awful doctor is Dr Jack Kevorkian. For years, he has been overly keen to tell the world about his hobby of assisting people, now in excess of 120, to commit suicide. Much of his retirement has been spent building better and better assisted-suicide machines. For years, this unpleasant man has baited the USA authorities to prosecute him. And in April 1999, he was given what he was asking for—a ten to twenty-five-year prison sentence for the second degree murder of Mr Thomas Youk, who suffered from Lou Gehrig's disease. Kevorkian has previously been acquitted three times on charges of physician-assisted suicides. But this time, in 1998, instead of merely assisting, he went the whole hog and delivered the lethal injection himself into Mr Youk's arm. This self-proclaimed Dr Death even prepared a video of the whole event, including the moment of death, and the CBS network in the USA subsequently showed it on the television programme, *60 Minutes*.

Now as the star of prime time television, Jack Kevorkian displayed his bedside manner. 'I am going to inject in your right arm,' he said as he reached for the potassium chloride, watched by twenty-two million Americans. 'OK? Okey-doke.' And with those words, the last he heard in this world, the fifty-two-year-old Thomas Youk went to meet his Maker, just in time for a television commercial break.

5.11 The general public and euthanasia

Apparently, most of the general public, eighty-two per cent, according to a 1996 survey, say that they are in favour of voluntary euthanasia. At least, they are if asked while they are healthy. A similar poll has shown that such support is highest among young, well-educated men, but lowest among elderly women. Not surprisingly, it demonstrates that the most vulnerable are also the most bothered about the issue. On the other hand, euthanasia is appealing to the young and healthy because it reflects their desire for a hedonistic lifestyle, unencumbered by relatives and the demands of the elderly and the ill. However, this enthusiasm for euthanasia of eighty-two per cent plummets to less than four per cent among hospice patients, once their pain and other symptoms are under control. Attitudes towards euthanasia have also hardened with time. When asked in 1986, if doctors should be permitted to end a life when someone requested it, seventy-five per cent said, 'Yes', and twenty-four per cent said, 'No'. Ten years later, in 1996, the results were eighty-two and fifteen per cent, respectively. Other determining factors include religion, ethnic background and regional variations—the Scots are less accepting of euthanasia than either the Welsh or the English. Overall, there can be little doubt that people, in the UK, the Western hemisphere, even the whole world, are beginning to view euthanasia more favourably, particularly when it is prescribed for others!

Additional factors are also at work encouraging this pro-euthanasia ethos. Many of these reflect the loss of a Christian consensus. For example, traditional family structures and relationships are breaking down, if not collapsing. Perhaps nowhere is this more tragically obvious than in our responses to dying and death within the family. Compassion is not always evident in attitudes towards the elderly. Increasing living standards, divorce and family break-up, greater mobility and the cult of youth have all contributed to the way in which the elderly are viewed and treated. As a rule, parents no longer live with their grown-up children, nor are they living just around the corner. Instead, for some, there is the prospect of third-rate nursing homes, where the bills for accommodation and treatment pile up rapidly as the increasingly senile, lonely relative sits in front of the television. In such an unhappy and dysfunctional social climate, support for euthanasia is bound to grow.

5.12 Four recent UK cases

Few can doubt that euthanasia is coming. The first fruits are already here—

it is unlikely that you could now read a national newspaper for a month and not come across a case or two. Just four cases, randomly selected from dozens reported within the last ten years, are sufficient to give a sense of what is happening. These are ordinary cases, with two young and two old victims. None of them has any particular legal significance or ethical merit, except that all four convey a deep sense of sadness and wrongness.

In July 1995, Con and Fiona Creedon from Humberside, applied to the High Court so that their two-year-old son, Thomas, could be allowed to die by stopping him from being tube-fed. Thomas had suffered severe brain damage in the womb and was blind, deaf and unable to control his limbs. The main reason given by his parents for their request was that Thomas was in continual pain. This theme was picked up by much of the media, which portrayed Thomas as 'a child in agony'. However, one key aspect of the case, not reported by either the BBC, or most newspapers, was the judgement by Sir Stephen Brown, president of the High Court's Family Division, that Thomas, '... does not suffer significant pain or distress.' Indeed, doctors caring for Thomas opposed the High Court application. Much of his apparent distress was caused by his age and his frustration at not being able to communicate effectively. Since then, there have been reports of other children, with medical conditions like those of Thomas, who have reached adulthood and who have led contented lives. On 31 July 1995, Thomas Creedon was made a ward of court in order to alleviate the heavy burden he placed upon his parents. The ensuing legal action was expected to take months, even years, to complete. However, before it was resolved, Thomas died of natural causes on Friday 23 February 1996.

The second case is that of Naomi Nelson, from Bournemouth. In November 1995, her forty-two-year-old father, Nigel Nelson, walked into a police station and confessed to the 'mercy-killing' of his 6-week-old handicapped daughter, three years earlier. Naomi had been born prematurely, and she was deaf, blind and had a bowel defect. While she was in hospital in 1992, her father had deliberately raised the prescribed amount of painkillers given to his daughter—the excessive dosage killed her. He was released on police bail. Eventually, the Crown Prosecution Service decided not to bring charges against him.

The third case concerns an eighty-year-old cancer patient, Alice Rowbottom. She died in April 1996, the day after her son, Derek, had tinkered with her hospital intravenous drip in order to give her a massive overdose of diamorphine, '... to ease her agony.' Her son said, 'I knew my Mum would not leave me like that if I was in agony.' He said that he, '... just wanted my Mum to be out of her pain.' If her death was caused by the overdose then Mr Rowbottom could have been charged with murder, which carries an automatic life sentence. However, in many of these 'mercy-killing' cases, it is claimed the patient is so ill that it cannot be said with certainty whether death was caused by the illness, or by the act intended to end the patient's life. In such cases, where the charge is of attempted murder, the judge has complete discretion over the sentence. In fact, the Crown Prosecution Service decided not to charge Derek Rowbottom.

The fourth case occurred in October 1997, when Peter Pitman, a farm worker, was tried for helping his seventy-five-year-old mother, Janet, to commit suicide. She had suffered from crippling rheumatoid arthritis for many years and had previously threatened to kill herself. In May 1997, in a field near their Somerset home, they had hugged farewell before Peter Pitman had held a shotgun to his mother's head while she pulled the trigger. Mr Pitman had then called the police and he was originally charged with murder, though this was subsequently reduced to aiding and abetting suicide. In his summing up, Judge John Foley said that Mr Pitman had suffered enough by having to face a murder investigation and he gave him a nine-month sentence, suspended for two years.

These are undeniably heart-rending tragedies, and so are the scores of other similar cases. They illustrate the fact that our society has already begun to sanction euthanasia for both young children and the elderly. Moreover, if the potential victims are disabled and experience pain then the arguments in favour of them being euthanized, voluntarily or non-voluntarily, are judged to be even more compelling. We have been conned by the twisted logic that says, 'killing can be caring'. In addition, there is a growing sympathy for those who kill such innocent human beings—both the public and the judiciary are increasingly saying, 'Let them go', or even, 'Thank you, case dismissed.'

Chapter 5

5.13 The UK situation, present and future

What of the future? Most Parliamentary watchers agree that legalisation in favour of euthanasia will not come about in the UK as the result of a comprehensive change of law, passed by the Houses of Commons and Lords. There will be no radical law reform that permits the widespread administration of lethal injections, at least not yet. Instead, euthanasia will creep up on us, in dribs and drabs. First, there will be non-voluntary euthanasia for the incompetent, particularly those in a permanent vegetative state. This, of course, has already begun. Second, there will probably be the legal recognition of living wills, or advance directives. This is already being officially discussed. Third, legalized voluntary euthanasia, or medically-assisted suicide, will be brought in, for just a few, with alleged safeguards to prevent abuse of the many. When these three steps have been taken, and found to be increasingly acceptable to the public, then the fourth stage, a comprehensive, permissive Act will be introduced. It will allow direct, wholesale and widespread euthanasia by lethal injection, of both the voluntary and non-voluntary varieties, that is, for those who ask, and for those who do not, because they cannot.

Each of these stages is being introduced, little by little, via difficult and hard cases. An example of this is the tragic situation of Mrs Diane Pretty. She is the forty-two-year-old mother from Luton, who suffers from motor neurone disease. She wants to end her life at the time of her choosing, but she is physically unable to do so because of her disability. Her condition, diagnosed in 1999, deteriorated rapidly so that she became paralysed from the neck down. In August 2001, Mrs Pretty sought immunity from prosecution, under the 1961 Suicide Act, for her husband, Brian, who would assist her to commit suicide. The Director of Public Prosecutions refused to give such an undertaking. In October 2001, she won the right to challenge that decision before the High Court. In November, she lost her case, but was given permission to petition the Law Lords. In December 2001, they too refused her. She then planned to take her case to the European Court of Human Rights in Strasbourg. Perhaps the saddest aspect of this sad case is that Mrs Pretty spent the last months of her life entangled in legal battles, paperwork and court appearances—instead, she should have been receiving palliative care and preparing to die well. In truth, she had become the puppet of pro-euthanasia campaigners—her case was supported and conducted by the Voluntary Euthanasia Society.

Whatever the outcome, there will be other, similar legal challenges. It will be euthanasia by knee-jerk decree. It will be euthanasia by the backdoor. It will come about without extensive discussion and without the establishment of any all-embracing ethical principles, until it is too late, and then the 2008 Euthanasia Act (the date is a sheer guess on my part, but interestingly, while writing this book I have already revised it downwards, twice) will be passed, granted Royal assent, and then enacted. The events, patterns and progress of euthanasia legalization will be similar to those which culminated in the 1967 Abortion Act—if you wish to spot the glaring parallels, then read chapter 6 in *Responding to the Culture of Death*. The two basic questions we need to answer are, when will we wake up to what is already happening? And, what are we going to do about it?

5.14 The global situation, present and future

This thrust in favour of legalizing euthanasia is a global affair. For example, cases of euthanasia are currently passing through the courts of many other countries, including those of the USA. Several states have voted on the issue, but only Oregon, via its Death with Dignity Act, approved on 8 November 1994, has legalized the practice of physician-assisted suicide. Following challenge and counter-challenge, it was not until March 1998 that an eighty-five-year-old woman with breast cancer became the first publicly-reported US casualty of this state law. In 2000, twenty-seven terminally-ill adults were killed under its provisions. Now, perhaps too late, a national debate has emerged on the medical, legal and theological implications surrounding euthanasia. The question there is, 'Do the dying have a constitutional right to ask a doctor for assistance in ending their lives?' The American Medical Association is currently implacably insisting that assisted suicide is incompatible with the doctor's role as healer, but this is seen by some as blind adherence to 'medieval values', presumably referring to those derived from good, old Hippocratic-Christian medicine.

As previously noted, Australia's Northern Territory implemented its Rights of the Terminally Ill Act in February 1996 as the world's first euthanasia bill, though it was revoked the following year. Even so, there is a string of countries, like Belgium, Columbia and Switzerland, which have informally tolerated euthanasia for many years and will probably legally formalize their arrangements soon. Finally, there is Holland, home of euthanasia, which in 2001 became the first country in the world to legalize the practice. The disastrous Dutch situation is further discussed in chapter 10.

What can this introduction to euthanasia teach us? First, euthanasia is wrong. Second, it is always a shabby affair. Third, doctors, you and I are inescapably caught up in the issue. Fourth, every 'case' of euthanasia is more than just a cold statistic—each involves a real, live, human being, as the patient, but also several others, including relatives and carers. Fifth, there are much better ways of treating the sick and dying—a palliative 'cup of cold water', some practical support and comfort are a good start, and far, far better than killing them. Sixth, the legalization of euthanasia is beginning to look inevitable, yet, thankfully, many doctors and ordinary people are still uncomfortable with the idea. Seventh, you and I had better understand the issues clearly because the day of challenge is fast coming—the heat is already on.

Infanticide

Infanticide is that go-between issue, that second of the three dominoes from the culture of death. If ranking these nasty edge-of-life issues were not such an absurd idea, then infanticide would perhaps be the most pitiless and heartless of them all.

6.1 What is infanticide?

Deliberately ending the life of a newborn child, or soon after birth, is known as infanticide, though it is sometimes referred to as neonaticide, or filicide, or more officially, neonatal euthanasia. Like all acts of euthanasia it may be accomplished by commission, as a result of the direct action of someone, perhaps one of the parents smothering the child with a pillow, or a doctor poisoning the child with a huge overdose of sedatives. Or, it may be accomplished by omission, such as simple neglect, or the refusal to provide food or water, so the child starves, or dehydrates, to death. The actual means make little difference—either way, a defenceless, newborn child is killed.

Throughout this chapter, the term infanticide will be used in its general and broad sense, namely, killing by either the parents, or another person with the parents' consent, rather than the restricted English legal definition of only the mother killing her own newborn child.

6.2 What is not infanticide?

The targets of infanticide are often, but not always, severely-disabled newborns. To begin with, the distinction must be drawn between non-fatal and fatal disabilities. Children born with non-fatal conditions, like Down's syndrome or spina bifida, will, with normal care, food, perhaps some routine surgery and other treatments, survive. On the other hand, a fatal disability means that the child's condition is so grievous that there is no possibility of survival, and she will die naturally within a short time, perhaps just a few hours after birth. An example would be anencephaly, which is incompatible with life, and untreatable. Such cases are without hope. That does not imply that her life is useless, or without meaning—

such a life, though short, can have a disproportionately enduring impact for good. The dying child must be treated with respect, made comfortable, fed and given treatment, if required—this is proper palliative care. No drug must be given which will hasten her death, but there may come a time to withhold treatment. After all, the child is fast dying and it would not be sound medicine either to 'strive officiously', or to employ extraordinary measures, to prolong her life. And when she has died, her body is to be treated with reverence. A very young child has died, but this is *not* infanticide. This child's death was no one's intention.

Whether suffering from non-fatal or fatal disabilities, or neither, the life of every newborn is protected by law. Therefore, the killing of disabled newborns will constitute a crime of either murder, or manslaughter.

6.3 Why not infanticide?

Perhaps most people would find the practice of infanticide morally repugnant, on a par with killing an adult, if a so-called 'normal' child were killed. However, the reaction can be quite different when the child is mentally or physically disabled, especially when severely so. In one sense, this attitude is a bioethically-consistent response. Consider abortion—the preborn child who is disabled has long been an especial target of abortionists. We already use prenatal screening, namely, sophisticated sampling and analytical procedures, in the form of amniocentesis, or chorion villus sampling, to detect handicapped children in utero, and when detected they are typically aborted. Furthermore, whereas the 1967 Abortion Act permitted an unborn child to be aborted under ground 4, namely, where there is, 'substantial risk of the child being born seriously handicapped', the 1990 Human Fertilisation and Embryology Act amended this ground (now referred to as ground E) to contain 'no time limit'. So now, if handicap is suspected—note, not necessarily proved—the abortion can be performed right up to the time of birth. If this is the law of the land *before* birth, then why not extend it by a few minutes or hours *after* birth? If we already destroy children in utero, then why not neonatally? What morally-significant arguments can be raised against infanticide in a society that already kills its unborn children of forty-weeks' gestation?

Genetic testing has created a group of children who are now deemed to be undesirable. We have turned the handicapped child into a problem rather than a challenge. We now want children made in our own image, and we ask, even tell, doctors to achieve this. This speaks loudly of our substandard attitudes towards human life in general, and disability in particular. As more and more functions of the human genome are unravelled, so more disabilities will be tested for, and more parents encouraged to abort those who are reckoned to be disabled, whether apparent or real, and if the latter, whether trivially or severely. Society's attitude towards those who escape this ever-widening 'search and destroy' net may change subtly from tolerance to something far less acceptable.

Such societal attitudes have also spawned another criterion to justify infanticide, namely, rejection by parents. This too is fallacious. Sure, parents are entitled to decide whether their child should wear red or blue shoes, but not to elect the very life or death of their child. Under most circumstances, the latter course of action would lead to criminal prosecution of the parents and the removal of the child, if still alive, into care. Yet this brings up an important associated issue. Parents of the disabled are offered little help by society. Yes, there is some financial provision by the State, but there is often only limited care, inadequate advice and poor practical support on offer. If parents feel that they cannot cope with a disabled child, what then? Is the child likely to be confined to a somewhat gloomy institution for a lifetime? None should underestimate the difficulties—the extent and intensity—of caring for the disabled baby, child, or adult. On the other hand, if we are to confront and solve these problems, killing the baby can never be the answer. Going down that route will cause nothing to change in law, ethics, medical decision-making, or professional and voluntary care facilities. Principled compassion is the way forward. Instead, we are currently enamoured with 'solving the problem' by practising defeatist infanticide.

So, when newborns slip through the eugenic net of prenatal screening plus abortion, they can be, and indeed, are, destroyed neonatally, by infanticide. Newborn, disabled babies can be left to gasp and tremble, and eventually die on hospital sluices in Western hospitals. This too can be the destiny for those babies who result from late abortions that 'go wrong', meaning those who survive the abortionist's onslaught and who are then born alive, to the utter embarrassment of all concerned. They too are regularly abandoned, in accordance with the euphemistic policy of 'benign neglect'. In other countries, particularly those of the East, disabled babies, as well as the unwanted, non-disabled, especially if they are girls, are frequently abandoned, often simply left outside, to die. The doctor's weasel words in defence of these practices are, 'Allowing such babies to die is in their "best interests".' This insidious statement obviously takes no account of the patient's preferences, and treatment is certainly prescribed and delivered without the patient's consent. This is twenty-first century, global infanticide. Can you believe it happens? Oh, yes, it happens alright.

6.4 A brief history of infanticide

Infanticide, in common with many of the other edge-of-life issues, has a long and miserable history. It has been practised widely, in many societies, over thousands of years, especially for reasons of disability, but also as a means of sex selection, limitation of family size, and the concealment of illicit pregnancies.

For example, it was regularly practised, mainly by means of exposure, by the Greeks, and then by the Romans. In both Plato's *The Republic* and Aristotle's *Politics*, the practice was supported by arguments that defective and deformed infants should be 'quietly got rid of'. Recent studies have shown that the Roman occupiers of Britain used infanticide to limit the native population. The victims were often girls, which explains the unexpected adult male:female ratio of about 100:65 in Romano-British burial grounds.

However, in spite of the widespread practice of infanticide, it was definitely not the custom of the ancient Jews. They lived under the creational obligations of Genesis 1:28, 'God blessed them and said to them, "Be fruitful and increase in number; fill the earth and subdue it ..."' God repeated this command to Noah and his sons after the flood (Genesis 9:1), and again to Jacob (Genesis 35:11). Indeed, it became a theme of Old Testament life as fathers reminded their sons of it (Genesis 48:4), and as God fulfilled his promise (Psalm 105:24). But this was not a call to mere fecundity. The Old Testament saints were required to live family lives that were blameless, honouring parents, while also cherishing and protecting their God-given offspring. The people of the Old Testament had a proper understanding of children. From Eve onwards (Genesis 4:1), their conception was regarded as evidence of God's continuing goodness to those who deserved no such thing. And the resulting children were regarded as signs of Jehovah's grace and favour, '... children are a reward from him, like arrows ...' and 'Blessed is the man whose quiver is full of them' (Psalm 127:3–5).

Furthermore, the Jews were firmly and repeatedly barred from participating in the infanticidal practices of their pagan neighbours, 'Do not give any of your children to be sacrificed to Molech, for you must not profane the name of your God. I am the LORD' (Leviticus 18:21; 20:1–5). Again, during the times of Isaiah, the prophet spoke against those who, '... sacrifice your children in the ravines and under the overhanging crags' (Isaiah 57:5). The only biblical incident that ever comes close to infanticide was the almost-sacrifice of Isaac by Abraham (Genesis 22). But infanticide has never been God's intention—on that occasion, he was testing Abraham's obedience. Thus, for centuries, the people of God behaved quite differently from their neighbours—they were holy and separate, and for them, infanticide was regarded as an abomination. Much later, the Roman historian, Tacitus, wrote (*Histories*, 5.5) that the Jews, '... provide for the increase of their numbers. It is a crime among them to kill any newly-born infant.'

The coming of New Testament Christianity continued these Hebrew prohibitions of infanticide. Nothing was rescinded. Indeed, the ethical imperatives of the Old Testament were not just maintained in the New Testament, they were considerably strengthened. The early Christians made no distinction between 'normal' and 'abnormal' babies. For them, all human life was made in the image of God and was therefore special. Human life was God-given and God-taken—those who disposed of newborns and infants broke God's law and usurped God's authority.

As already described, it was these Judaeo-Christian doctrines, in tandem with the Hippocratic oath, that fashioned the foundations of the noble ethics and practice of early medicine. The Hippocratic oath expressed a strong respect for all human life and a specific disapproval of abortion, suicide and euthanasia. But it was the coming of New Testament

Christianity that purged the Graeco-Roman world of infanticide. In AD 318, Constantine, the first Christian emperor, issued a decree declaring that the slaying of a child by the father was a crime. By the end of the fourth century, infanticide had become a crime punishable by death.

6.5 More recent infanticide

For the next fifteen hundred years or so, infanticide was regarded as a serious crime by most societies, particularly among those whose ethical thinking was shaped by Christianity. There have been some notable exceptions. For instance, Charles Darwin regarded infanticide, particularly of female infants, along with abortion, as important means of maintaining a check upon human population growth. In addition, whole societies have unequivocally practised infanticide. These include the eighteenth-century Japanese, as well as the twentieth-century !Kung bushmen of the Kalahari desert, the Tikopia of Polynesia, and the Netsilik Eskimo of Canada's North-Western Territories. The latter, for example, have been reported to kill as many as eighty per cent of their newborn baby girls. It is not insignificant that these societies have been largely untouched by the Judaeo-Christian tradition.

In England and Wales, but not Scotland, infanticide has existed as a separate statutory crime since the 1922 Infanticide Act. It took sixty years of campaigning before the Act got onto the Statute Book. It created a non-capital offence, distinct from murder, though the punishment was to be the same as for manslaughter. However, the Act did not define the time limit of 'newborn'. In 1927, less than six weeks was judged to be the limit, whereas in 1936, it was three weeks. Nevertheless, that Act was replaced by the 1938 Infanticide Act, which maintained the unlawfulness of infanticide, but specified twelve months as the limit, and it still is today.

It is a strange eccentricity of English law that infanticide is a crime that can only be committed by a woman, in fact only the mother, upon her own child. Fathers, though they can commit the same deed, will be guilty, not of infanticide, but of murder, or manslaughter. The Infanticide Acts were designed to show a certain compassion towards the mother who kills her child under the age of twelve months where, '... the balance of her mind was disturbed by reason of her not having fully recovered from the effect of giving birth to the child or by reason of the effect of lactation ...', for she would be guilty of manslaughter rather than murder. Furthermore, puerperal psychosis, or post-puerperal depression, has been a defence against the charge of child murder since the middle of the nineteenth century.

6.6 Justifying infanticide

How can infanticide ever be justified, let alone recommended? It is significant that the Bible makes no distinction between the unborn and the born child. This continuity of prenatal and postnatal life, and its attendant preciousness, is endorsed by the use of the same Greek word, *brephos*, for both, as, for example in Luke 1:14 and 2:12. The abortionist may be able to salve his conscience by kidding himself that the unborn child is not 'one of us', after all, she is unseen, untouched and unheard. But what about the born child? What arguments can he now muster to continue fooling himself and excuse his infanticidal activity while in the presence of a visible, tangible, bawling or whimpering baby?

Some argue that the newborn child is not really 'one of us' until as much as one year after birth, until speech, or at least, some form of rudimentary communication, has been established. Astonishingly, the two Nobel prizewinners, who discovered the structure of DNA, support this view. One is James Watson, who has said, 'If a child were not declared alive until three days after birth, then all parents could be allowed the choice only a few are given under the present system' (*Prism*, May 1973, 1:13). Similarly, his Nobel prize collaborator, Francis Crick has stated that, '... no newborn infant should be declared human until it has passed certain tests regarding its genetic endowment and that if it fails these tests, it forfeits the right to live' (quoted by the *Pacific News Service*, January 1978). This is alarming stuff from the elite of the biological sciences. But moral philosophers can be just as unpredictably creepy. Jonathan Glover, a prominent voice in bioethics, justifies infanticide in his book, *Causing Death and Saving Lives* (1977) by arguing (p. 156) that, '... new-born babies have no conception of death and so cannot have any preference for life over death.' Well, have you ever heard so much pseudo-intellectual, yet dangerous, twaddle as that?

Two other modern-day advocates of infanticide are Helga Kuhse and

Peter Singer. In their notoriously shocking book, *Should the Baby Live?* (1985), they present the case for a twenty-eight-day period after a child's birth during which treatment could be legally withheld. Throughout this period, the child could be clinically assessed by some sort of independent review panel, eerily reminiscent of the Nazi child euthanasia committees, before the verdict of life or death is pronounced. These authors recommend (p. 196) the latter course when the patient's '... life will ... be one of unredeemed misery.' This is a remarkably poignant phrase, yet it could readily be applied to millions and millions of this world's people in a general sense, as well as in a specifically Christian theological context. Are Kuhse and Singer seriously suggesting that deprivation and unhappiness should now be used as criteria to justify the killing of such victims, both young and old?

But infanticide is not simply the whim of a few urbane moral philosophers, or the practice of some faraway primitive tribes—it actually occurs on our doorsteps, in our local sophisticated hospitals and clinics. Advances in medical technology have enabled newborn babies, who would formerly have died, to be kept alive and given the necessary preliminary help to live long lives. But in some such cases, parents and doctors have quietly decided not to treat these neonates. These conversations are carried on behind closed hospital doors and few had ever been privy to such infanticidal decision-making activities. That is, until 1973, when two doctors went public in an article published in the *New England Journal of Medicine* (289:885–894). Drs Raymond S Duff and A G M Campbell described how, while working over a two-year period at the Newborn Special Care Unit of Yale University School of Medicine, a total of two hundred and ninety-nine babies had died there. Of these, forty-three had been deliberately 'allowed to die' after negotiations between doctors and parents. These babies often had Down's syndrome with duodenal atresia, or intestinal obstructions, but rather than operated upon to relieve such difficulties, they were starved to death. Duff and Campbell argued that non-treatment was justified for these neonates because their, '... prognosis for meaningful life was extremely poor or hopeless.' The authors clouded the cruel reality of their non-actions by calling them a '... growing tendency to seek early death as a management option.' Whatever sort of

Newspeak is that? And how will such 'management options' ever lead to the development of new and genuine treatments, plus better caring strategies, plus improved symptom control, and so on? Financial constraints and psychological stress for the families were cited as additional reasons for practising infanticide. Such barbarism in the medical profession can never be right. If we cannot cure, then we must care, not abandon the newborn baby to the sluice room to die. However much one may sympathize with the difficulties, present and future, facing the doctors and the parents, there is no escaping the fact that their intentions were to kill these newborn children—and that can never be acceptable behaviour.

6.7 Modern-day infanticide

How much has changed since 1973? Apparently, very little. Consider present-day Holland, for instance, where Down's syndrome infants are routinely starved to death. The official current estimate is that about fifteen cases of hospital-based infanticide of handicapped newborns occur each year, though the real figure is, without a doubt, higher. How many cases occur in the UK? Some estimate twenty, others say it must be three times that. Nobody knows. No parents or doctors are going to volunteer infanticide as the cause of neonatal death. The late John Emery, distinguished paediatric pathologist at the University of Sheffield and the UK's pioneering expert on sudden infant death syndrome (SIDS), considered (*Archives of Disease in Childhood*, 1985, 60:505–517) that one in ten 'cot deaths' was due to infanticide, which doctors had either failed to recognize, or had misdiagnosed. Professor Sir Roy Meadow, professor of paediatrics at the University of Leeds, examined (*Archives of Disease in Childhood*, 1999, 80:7–14), over an eighteen-year period, the cases of eighty-one children, who were thought initially to have died of natural causes, but who had eventually been judged by criminal or family courts to have been killed by their parents, usually by their mothers smothering them. Forty-two of these infants had originally been certified as dying from SIDS and twenty-nine had been given another cause of natural death. This is by no means a challenge to the tragedy of genuine 'cot deaths', but rather it is an indicator of the incidence of infanticide.

What happens in the West, also often happens in the East. The one-child policy of China, started in the early 1970s, is well known. Officials insist on abortions for those who break the rules. But when a pregnancy is detected too late, then infanticide is the Chinese solution. One such horrifying example, reported in the Western media during August 2000, involved Chinese officials in Hubei province drowning a healthy baby in a paddy field in front of the 'offending' parents. It was one example among a total of how many hundreds, or thousands? Who knows? In India, female infanticide remains widespread, especially in rural areas. The practice is rampant among, for example, the Kallar caste in Southern India—in one survey of 640 families, fifty-one per cent admitted to killing a baby daughter within a week of birth. According to some mid-1990s estimates, the numbers of India's so-called 'missing girls and women' range from twenty-five to fifty million. Male:female population ratios are typically about 100:105 for most countries, but in India they are 100:93, and in China only 100:88, reflecting the incidence of female infanticide as well as, of course, the spate of sex-selective abortions, directed against unborn girls.

Where are the voices raised against infanticide? Has a generation of unbridled abortion rendered us numb and dumb towards infanticide? Why, in the new, caring Britain, are the disabled so readily rejected and discarded by parents, doctors and society? Why is there not a worldwide outcry at such practices? Why is the Department for International Development not calling for censure, boycott and embargo of the offending Third World countries? Why are we sending food aid to those who deliberately kill fifty per cent of the intended child recipients? How come the world's feminists are not up in arms at the mass slaughter of the next generation of the sisterhood? What have you and I done to recognize and to help halt this horror?

Suicide

Suicide is defined as the intentional killing of oneself. If the victim carries out an act of either commission or omission, knowing that it will result in his or her death, then it is suicide. In other words, it is self-murder. Suicide and euthanasia are different, yet similar, edge-of-life issues. They are different because suicide is achieved by the victim alone, whereas euthanasia requires another person, typically a doctor, to bring about the death, to help with the dirty work. Furthermore, suicide usually occurs in the midst of life, whereas euthanasia usually occurs towards life's later stages. Suicide and euthanasia are similar because both end a human life, prematurely. And they are also similar because orthodox Christianity has, from its earliest times, together with the Hippocratic oath, condemned them both.

7.1 Suicide and assisted suicide

The linkage, both intellectual and practical, between suicide and euthanasia needs to be forged clearly, especially within the context of this book. This is because the question arises, if suicide is nowadays not generally disapproved of, or, at least, not outlawed, then why is it wrong for that suicidal person to recruit the help of another to assist in bringing it about? If suicide is tolerated, then surely voluntary euthanasia, in the form of medically-assisted suicide, should be too?

Or again, why do we have such pesky misgivings about the different means of committing suicide and assisted suicide? The physical and mechanical means of suicide, like a length of rope, a kitchen knife, a tall building, or a car exhaust, have always been rather abhorrent. On the other hand, the alternative chemical means, a lethal dose, or an overdose, of drugs, and the relatively pain-free way of dying, seem to be more appealing for both practices. Are we in the peculiar business of categorizing these different means of killing, and assessing some methods of achieving them as more acceptable because they offend our sensibilities less?

Furthermore, we display a strange ambivalence when the subject of autonomy is raised in association with procuring death—there is a reluctance on our part to enable people to do it themselves. To that end, the public is normally denied legal access to the sorts of drugs that would terminate life in a rapid and painless way. We disapprove of chemicals being available over-the-counter for people to commit suicide. As a consequence, assisted euthanasia is resorted to. Bring in the doctor-turned-euthanasiast. It is the doctor who can assist in supplying, and even administering, the required drugs. Curiously, the presence of a figure from the medical establishment seems, somehow, to make it all much more acceptable. Yet the role of medical assistant to the suicidal will always be an odd, as well as an unnatural, one for the doctor.

Even if we were to give legislative approval to medically-assisted suicide, it would still be a very ill-defined and poorly-monitored area, and one that would be wide open to abuse. For example, a question that would frequently crop up is, what could the doctor do? To what extent could he 'assist'? Could he prescribe the drugs, purchase the drugs, deliver the drugs, place them on a bedside table, open the bottle, hand them over, put them in the patient's mouth? Where does 'passive' assistance stop, and his 'active' assistance begin? Where does medically-assisted euthanasia begin and suicide end?

Whenever euthanasia is the topic of discussion on television, at work, or in Parliament, it is invariably under the guise of medically-assisted suicide and the benefits thereof. But there is never the analogous promotion of a public policy of straightforward, solitary suicide. Can you explain why that is, because the two acts are so very, very similar? Is it really to do with medical degrees, professionalism and a sense of tidiness?

7.2 Suicide and the Bible

But to return to straightforward suicide. Defined as self-murder, the Sixth Commandment, 'You shall not murder' (Exodus 20:13), forbids us from taking the life of anyone who bears the *imago Dei*, including our own. Suicide is a personal assault against the sovereignty of God in all the affairs of human life. The suicide declares that she has a sovereign rule over her life, and a sovereign reign over her death—neither of which are true. Our lives belong to God. He oversaw our conception, he gave us our first breath, he has sustained us, and he alone has the entitlement to take it. The suicide makes herself the judge in a matter not entrusted to her—God alone is the judge, it is his prerogative both to announce life and to pronounce death. 'There is no god besides me. I put to death and I bring to life ...' (Deuteronomy 32:39), and 'The LORD gave and the LORD has taken away; may the name of the LORD be praised' (Job 1:21). As a result of both creation and redemption, we are to live and die according to the perfect will of God.

For a very, very few, this will mean sacrificing their lives for others, as in rescuing a child from a burning building, or for the defence of freedom, as in war, or as a result of Christian witness in a Muslim country. These three examples are *not* suicides, they are heroic acts in which it was not the intention of the individuals to kill themselves. God never asks men or women to kill themselves intentionally. And that is the point, the heart of the matter—*a priori*, suicide is wrong because it is against the will and purposes of God.

It is true that some believers in the Bible, such as Paul (2 Corinthians 5:6, 8; Philippians 1:21, 23), expressed their desire for death in order that they might be free from sin, and in heaven with Christ. But they never considered it their choice, or right, to take their lives themselves. Suicide for them was never an option. Life was to be lived, service was to be rendered, death was to be awaited. Others were more petulant and less honourable. Although they recognized the sovereign hand of God over human life, they prayed like Jonah did, 'Now, O LORD, take away my life, for it is better for me to die than to live' (Jonah 4:3), or Elijah, '"I have had enough, LORD," he said. "Take my life; I am no better than my ancestors"' (1 Kings 19:4). But their requests were wrong because their intentions were selfish—these men were ingrates, or discontents, in pain, or trouble. Nevertheless, despite their genuine predicaments and their profane yearnings, even they did not resort to committing suicide.

The actual word, suicide, does not appear in the Bible, and while there is little written about it, the Bible is not silent on the subject. It contains at least six examples—all by men. The first was Samson, who pulled the temple upon himself (Judges 16:30). Then the unfaithful Saul and his armour-bearer fell on their swords (1 Samuel 31:4–5), despite the version told by the lying Amalekite (2 Samuel 1:10), although 1 Chronicles 10:14

comments that it was the Lord who actually '… put him to death …' The other three were Ahithophel, the conspirator, who hanged himself (2 Samuel 17:23), king Zimri, the sinful plotter, who set fire to himself (1 Kings 16:18–19), and the only New Testament example, Judas Iscariot, the betrayer, who hanged himself (Matthew 27:5). Their ends were tragic and none of them, with the exception of Samson, was approved of by God.

In fact, the death of Samson was quite different. Hebrews 11:32 and 11:39 include him as a hero of the faith, and Judges 16:31 records that he was honourably buried by his family in the tomb of Manoah, his father. Samson's death should therefore be seen, not as a suicide, but as an example of heroic self-sacrifice, exemplifying John 15:13, 'Greater love has no-one than this, that he lay down his life for his friends.' Samson ended his days opposing the Philistine enemies of God. His intention was not to escape the difficulties of this life by suicide, but rather his death was a courageous giving of his life that others might live. His death was in a different league compared with the other five corrupt and cowardly men who took their own lives—their sad ends are recorded in the Bible as a warning to us.

7.3 A brief history of suicide

Historically, most societies have regarded suicide with a sense of revulsion, though a few have tolerated it. The Greeks had mixed feelings about it, though their prevailing view was that suicide was a crime against their gods and the State. Pythagoras, Plato and Aristotle rejected it as a cowardly way of avoiding life's hardships and evading one's duty to self and the State. By contrast, the more liberal attitude of the Romans was founded on the grounds of personal freedom and compassion, albeit, of the bogus varieties, towards the elderly, the ill and the dishonoured.

The noted eighteenth-century British lawyer, William Blackstone, declared that suicide was an offence against God and king. In his *Commentaries on the Laws of England* (1769) he stated (vol. 4, p. 189) that, '… the law of England wisely and religiously considers, that no man hath a power to destroy life, but by commission from God, the author of it: and, as the suicide is guilty of a double offence; one spiritual, in invading the prerogative of the Almighty, and rushing into his immediate presence uncalled for; and the other temporal, against the king, who hath an interest in the preservation of all his subjects; the law has therefore ranked this among the highest crimes, making it a peculiar species of felony, a felony committed on one's self.' Thus, by and large, it was considered that, besides God, only the State, as the God-given agent of justice, could lawfully take a person's life. Suicide was therefore regarded as wrong and offensive.

However, the contrary view was also beginning to emerge. The publication, in 1774, of Goethe's *The Sorrows of Young Werther* was one potent expression of such thinking. While the author intended that Werther's suicide should be a warning, he actually became an icon. The book seized the imagination of Europe during the 1770s and suicide was put forward as a fashionable way to resolve moral dilemmas such as, adulterous, or unrequited, love. Even so, the literature of emotionalism was one thing—the law of the land was quite another.

And the law of England continued to criminalize suicide. Up until 1823, the estate of the dead suicide went to the Crown, and the victim could be buried at a crossroads with a stake through the heart. This barbarous practice was abolished in 1834, and church burials were later allowed. Eventually, the 1961 Suicide Act decriminalized suicide, but it still included penalties for anyone who assisted the victim. The Act represented a new public tolerance towards suicide, especially for those with apparently-impossible personal problems, for it was designed to show sympathy to the victim, rather than approval or ennoblement of the deed. And that is how suicide is nowadays commonly perceived by the general public—neither unacceptable, nor welcome.

In some other modern cultures, especially those where Christianity has had only a minor influence, suicide has remained an acceptable custom in the wake of either social disgrace, or as a way to atone for misconduct. For example, among some sections of modern-day Japanese society, where the two main religions, Shintoism and Buddhism, hold no such prohibitions, suicide is still supportively practised. From time to time, a failed Japanese banker, or an adulterer will be reported to have jumped from an office window, or to have committed hara-kiri. But such acts are not the Christian way.

7.4 Understanding suicide

Suicide and parasuicide, that is, attempted suicide that is deliberately unsuccessful, are on the increase, worldwide. Why so? More, and better, education, prosperity and health have obviously not provided the life of longed-for personal peace and fulfilment for all people. The common triggers of suicide and parasuicide are associated with stress, divorce, alcoholism, drug abuse, unemployment, financial worries and mental illness—they read like a catalogue of many ordinary people's symptoms over the last fifty years. We now live in a world where work and the family are under pressure and where, despite quantum leaps in communication systems, people are experiencing growing alienation, as well as mounting uncertainties about faith, purpose and the other serious issues of life. In many ways, the rising numbers of suicides and parasuicides reflect these changing values and the subsequent disintegration of much of the moral and social fabric of our world.

These triggers may represent the impetus behind the majority of suicides, but there are other causes too. For example, there is the copycat suicide, which can occur when a teenager's role model commits suicide. And there is a religious motive behind some suicides, especially of the mass suicides of various cults, such as those of recent years in Jonestown and Waco. Finally, there are the previously-mentioned 'suicide gestures', or parasuicides, intentional self-harming that does not result in death, but which are commonly recognized as 'cries for help'. Nevertheless, parasuicides should be taken seriously because there is evidence that approximately ten per cent of them will eventually succeed.

In the past, we have been unduly harsh regarding suicide. Yes, the victim has acted contrary to truth, hated his own flesh (Ephesians 5:29), lacked courage to endure suffering, not established deep personal relationships, failed to fulfil his societal duties as a citizen, and sinned against God. But suicide is now generally surrounded with more compassion and understanding. Yet despite all our knowledge and insight about the practice, as well as our sympathy towards the victim, there is still no psychological or social theory that is sufficient to explain it. However, we do now understand that the majority of those who commit suicide are mentally or physically ill. Most display a lack of integration within society.

They are typically weak, depressed and psychologically-disturbed people, albeit, often temporarily.

Despite all of these tragic surrounding circumstances, suicide can never be endorsed. Apart from the biblical prohibitions, suicide still shows a selfish disregard for those in the aftermath. Suicide can be devastating for the immediate family and friends. It can be seen as an irreversible declaration that they were inadequate in times of need, and not worth living for. For them, the inevitable unanswered questions can lead to long-term, or even life-long, guilt. Besides, such sudden deaths can produce denial, anger, depression and grief among those left behind. There can also be the issues of disgrace and loneliness to be overcome, as well as sometimes, economic problems. In summary, suicide is not good for individuals, families, or societies.

7.5 Suicide statistically

Figures relating to suicides should generally be regarded as underestimates, primarily because of a reluctance on the part of many to admit to suicide as the cause of death.

The total number of suicides worldwide, as estimated by the World Health Organization, is approximately 400,000 per year. There are about 6,500 suicides each year in the UK, which represent roughly one per cent of all deaths. That means that suicide claims one life every eighty minutes, and it has now become the second most common cause of death among young people. Furthermore, a suicide attempt is made in the UK every five minutes, which is one of the highest rates in Europe. Between 1982 and 1996, suicide rates across the UK generally fell. The rate among women declined by forty per cent. During the same period, the rate among all men declined by four per cent, but rose by twenty-four per cent among those aged between fifteen and twenty-four. This increased rate among young men must be of special concern. The 'new lad' image does not recognize the options of having, or exploring, personal feelings, or of finding ethical ways out of depression, or major difficulties—our young men have begun to lose another attribute of what it means to bear the *imago Dei*, namely, true mannishness. That loss is serious.

Overall, several other groups of people are also at high risk. For example, doctors and nurses are more likely to commit suicide than are other professionals. During the 1990s, the suicide rate for doctors was twice the national average, and it was one and a half times among nurses. Students are also prone. A report, published in 2000, by the National Union of Students found that twelve per cent of all first-year undergraduates were depressed to such an extent that they had entertained suicidal thoughts. While suicides among the young, and particularly young men, are growing worldwide at an alarming rate, it is old men, over the age of seventy-five, who have the highest suicide rate within any demographic grouping.

In national terms, perhaps unexpectedly, Hungary has the world's highest suicide rate at 35.3 per 100,000 people, followed by Japan with a corresponding rate of 17.2, which, in 1999, amounted to a record total of 33,048 suicides. And Japanese men are especially vulnerable—they represent seventy-one per cent of the total suicides in that country.

Suicides have always used various methods. Self-poisoning among older men, and for young men, hanging or gassing by domestic supplies, or by car exhausts, have customarily been the chosen methods. The introduction of catalytic exhaust systems on cars has led to a considerable decrease in carbon monoxide poisoning by this latter method. Women have traditionally preferred drug overdoses, but recent advances in producing less lethal forms of some drugs, especially tranquillizers, have resulted in a decrease in the numbers of female suicides.

7.6 The real causes of suicide

When a man or a woman gives up on Christianity, they give up more than they can imagine. Their subsequent view of life has become not just jaundiced, it has become seriously distorted. Listen to the statements of two of the last century's prominent thinkers. First, Albert Camus, the French nihilistic philosopher, who wrote as the opening lines of his 1942 essay, *The Myth of Sisyphus*, 'There is but one truly serious philosophical problem, and that is suicide. Judging whether life is or is not worth living amounts to answering the fundamental question of philosophy.' This is depressing stuff, and though Camus ultimately rejected suicide as a means of escape, the book is not to be recommended as bedtime reading. Second, there is the noted American psychiatrist, Thomas S. Szasz writing in *The*

Antioch Review (1971, p. 10), 'A man's life belongs to himself. Hence, he has a right to take his own life, that is, to commit suicide.' Here is secular humanism, bold as brass. Szasz's position may appear to be reasonable, even valid, but it is based on faulty presuppositions. Quite simply, it is the very antithesis of the Christian perspective. With the likes of Camus' despair and Szasz's errors shaping the mindset of the day, is it any wonder that modern men and women commit suicide?

The truth is that the would-be suicide is alienated—from God, family, friends and society. He believes that there is no point to life. Living has become meaningless. Of course it has! He has discarded the foundation, the only bedrock of human worth and dignity that can ascribe meaning and value to human life. He has rejected Genesis 1:27. Without a grasp of that truth, men and women are inevitably alienated—they cannot live before God, they cannot live with others, and they cannot live with themselves. Perhaps we should be surprised that more people do not resort to suicide.

7.7 Suicide pastorally

I am only too conscious that suicide can be a sensitive and awkward topic. Several readers will have had a loved one, family or friend, who has committed suicide—I have known some myself—and their memories may still be fresh, and their consciences tender. For them, the above introduction, with its facts and figures about suicide, may appear to be unduly stark and unhelpful. If so, I regret it. Nevertheless, I am duty-bound to explain such issues as clearly as I am able—the truth cannot be served without telling it. And that is why this current section has been included—there are important pastoral aspects to suicide. Would the Lamb of God, the gentle Jesus, have nothing to say to his people suffering from suicidal feelings, or the repercussions of suicide, in order to bring them hope and consolation?

How then does the Christian face suicide and its aftermath? First, we should recognize the hugely negative effects that secular humanism has on people. We are not dealing here with some harmless, obscure philosophy that impinges on only a few oddballs. Secular humanism has become the destructive opiate of the twenty-first century masses. Not only does it, for example, encourage the act of suicide, it also demands that we should not intervene. After all, is not suicide a person's right to self-determination, the true expression of personal autonomy? Today, the heart of the injunction of Matthew 5:39, to 'turn the other cheek', has been corrupted to 'turn the blind eye'. It says that we ought not to interfere in the free acts of a person, as long as nobody else is harmed. Therefore, let the would-be suicide do his thing. This, of course, is the spurious logic of the twenty-first century pornographer, paedophile and euthanasiast, as well as the downright, disinterested passer-by—do not look, do not get involved, turn that blind eye. Of course, Christians have a different set of marching orders—they have an obligation to come to the aid of a brother, or a sister, or a neighbour, or a stranger (Luke 10:29–37).

Second, we should understand that would-be suicides have not only negative feelings, but also real despair, about themselves and their 'world'. These, together with a sense of helplessness and hopelessness, encourage them to think that suicide is the only option. The wish to die, to escape, to be released, is common among the suicidal, particularly among the ill and the elderly. Isolation, such as experienced by the divorcee, the widowed and the bereaved can also be a suicide trigger in the older victim. But many would-be suicides do not actually wish to die, or to be killed. Instead, these parasuicides want to 'interrupt' their lives in order to interrupt their intense despair. It is as if they have two personalities—one that wants to live, and one that wants to die. They are confused and therefore they are often indecisive, insecure and impulsive. Some are so bewildered that they are known as 'smiling depressives'—though miserable and suicidal, they hide their emotions behind a cheery grin.

This despair, which precipitates suicide, is a sin—the grace of God insists that no human life need be intolerable. This is not to deny that life can, at times, be difficult, and almost overwhelmingly so. There are often huge, seemingly-insoluble troubles and problems in this life. For Christians there is even an additional problem, 'the trial of faith' (James 1:12; 1 Peter 1:6–7). But despite all these dilemmas, we are not to despair. Tempted, we may be, but sin, we must not. God has promised that, 'No temptation has seized you except what is common to man. And God is faithful; he will not let you be tempted beyond what you can bear. But when you are tempted, he will also provide a way out so that you can stand up under it' (1 Corinthians 10:13). God will never let us go under.

Third, we need to be convinced that ultimately, there can be no approval of suicide—it cannot be regarded as a way of solving life's problems, or even as a legitimate example of self-determination. For the would-be suicide, the Gospel must be applied. There is none who is so desperate, depressed, or downtrodden who cannot be helped by God. In him, there is hope and there is peace. 'He is my loving God and my fortress, my stronghold and my deliverer, my shield in whom I take refuge ...' (Psalm 144:2). The Lord Jesus Christ said, 'I am the way and the truth and the life' (John 14:6)—an encounter and a developing relationship with him leaves the suicidal with no excuses—none is needed. They are loved, beyond measure, by an infinite, yet personal God.

Fourth, to those left in the aftermath, the Christian response must be gentle. It should seek to support in terms of 'being there', and providing practical help. It should not seek to encourage an incessant search for explanations, or to provide a string of tiresome platitudes and facile answers. A reliance on the goodness and the sovereignty of God are the ultimate comforts for everyone in such difficult circumstances.

Fifth, it can sometimes come as a surprise to discover that there can be such little support for parasuicides, or for the family of the suicide, from within the medical profession. Its members can be strongly anti-suicide. Why is this? It is because for some doctors, suicide represents the antithesis of their calling. They are trained to preserve life. The suicide wants to throw it away and this can offend the doctor. However, this observation is not intended to dissuade any from seeking medical advice and care at these tough times. If one doctor is unsympathetic, ask to see another.

And sixth, there is a final, and perhaps most important, pastoral lesson here. Life can be a right rollercoaster. Everything can be going swimmingly, and then suddenly some disaster, real or apparent, can storm into our lives. We need to be prepared. Consider the soldier. He will survive in the frontline only because he has trained beforehand. Those months of manoeuvres and classroom studies are now about to pay off. He is a fool if he paid little attention during these tranquil training sessions, when the enemy was absent. So it is for the Christian. In times of relative ease, we should be arming ourselves—listening to the best preachers, reading good books, rehearsing the doctrines, practising self-discipline, talking with others, attending the means of grace, and so on. The biblical metaphors of soldier (2 Timothy 2:3) and athlete (Hebrews 12) are entirely apposite. Training before the battle or the big race is the essential prerequisite of the 'victor'. A Christian who disregards the means of grace—teaching, fellowship and prayer—will inevitably be a weak Christian, who will almost certainly fall in the heat of the battle, or the struggle of the race. So it behoves us all, pastors and congregation, leaders and led, to be well equipped and prepared.

These are among the pastoral approaches that will allow us not only to avoid suicide ourselves, but also to help others cope with it. In the final analysis, the biblical direction for both the would-be suicide and the bereaved can be summed up in three words—go to God (Matthew 11:28).

We tend to think about and regard suicide and euthanasia quite differently. We consider that suicide is delicate—euthanasia is callous. Suicide is inexpressible—euthanasia is debatable. Yet the linkage between the two is real, though subtle. Suicide is primarily a matter for the individual, 'I want to die, so I'm going to kill myself.' On the other hand, medically-assisted euthanasia can become primarily a matter for the State, 'One of our trained and approved medical practitioners will help you die.' Any endorsement of suicide for the individual can therefore, in terms of both ethics and practice, pave the way for euthanasia of the masses. Therefore, the inevitable flow, in both thought and deed, is from suicide to medically-assisted voluntary euthanasia to non-voluntary to involuntary euthanasia, with the State in control of the latter three. Alarmed? So am I.

Permanent vegetative state (PVS)

Perhaps the first thing to say about PVS is the inappropriateness of its name. A human being cannot ever have been, be, or become another species. A human being can never possess mere vegetative life—a child was not once a potato, a man cannot be a carrot, nor will a woman ever become a runner bean. Furthermore, because the language that people use expresses certain values and conveys their presuppositions, this term immediately devalues the victims of this condition. It can therefore cloud subsequent discussion about them and their treatments. It can cause medical staff and relatives to abandon hope. Our society rightly struggles to rid itself of cruel prejudices and discrimination on the basis of, for example, gender, race and age. Should not PVS now be added to this list?

8.1 What is PVS?

The term 'persistent vegetative state' was invented some thirty years ago by Professors Bryan Jennett and Fred Plum of the Institute of Neurological Sciences in Glasgow (*Lancet*, 1972, 1:734–737). It is used to describe patients who survive severe brain damage, usually as a result of acute injuries brought about by accidents, anoxia, drug overdoses, and so on, though there can be other causes, such as, congenital, or degenerative, conditions. Sufferers are awake, they breathe spontaneously, have a stable circulation, exhibit sleep-wake patterns and reflex responses, but they seem to show no evidence of awareness of either self, or their environment.

PVS is distinct from coma in which patients have their eyes closed and they lack the sleep-wake cycles. A simple vegetative state usually develops from a short period of coma. It can be partially, or totally, reversible, or it may progress to become a persistent, or eventually, a permanent vegetative state. Persistent is usually defined as continuing for more than one month, but implies neither permanency, nor irreversibility. Permanent is the term typically used after at least six, but more likely twelve, months. It is this condition of *permanent* vegetative state that generates major bioethical dilemmas.

8.2 Diagnosis of PVS

All of us live somewhere on a spectrum of human consciousness that ranges from PVS to full awareness, with a state of low awareness somewhere in between. But the borders of these three states are ill defined and not susceptible to precise demarcation.

However, in suspected cases of PVS, a presumed diagnosis can have a sting in its tail, because once that verdict has been reached, active medical treatment may be halted. As explained more fully in chapter 12, in the wake of the Anthony Bland case, 'artificial nutrition and hydration' can now be defined as 'treatment', and this may be lawfully withdrawn or withheld. The outcome is that PVS patients can be refused food and water, which inevitably causes them to die. Yet, perhaps surprisingly, in view of these life-or-death consequences, there is precious little agreement about the criteria of PVS diagnosis, let alone patients' prognosis. Diagnosis is complicated primarily because there are no definitive tests available. As in many aspects of medical practice, the diagnostic judgement of PVS experts is based on probabilities, not certainties. Therefore, uncertainties and errors are to be expected—and that is exactly what has happened in some disturbing cases.

Other aspects of PVS medicine are equally foggy. The 1992 British Medical Association (BMA) guidelines suggested that withdrawal of nutrition and hydration should not be considered until at least twelve months of PVS and that two doctors, plus the patient's doctor, should agree that there is no reasonable hope of the patient's improvement. Additional guidelines, issued in March 1996 by the Working Group of the Royal College of Physicians, recommended that 'permanent' rather than 'persistent' should be applied where irreversibility can be diagnosed with a high level of certainty. Also no diagnosis of PVS should be made until twelve months after a head injury, or six months after brain damage by other causes. Furthermore, the diagnosis should be made by two doctors who are experienced in evaluating disturbances of consciousness. Their main task should be to assess if the patient is sentient. They should also take into account comments from the family and other carers, who spend a good deal of time with the patient.

But determining the awareness of patients with brain injury can be a pig in a poke. It takes time, patience and is, to a large degree, subjective, depending upon the worldview of the assessors. Do they, for example, consider that a human being can have a 'life not worthy to be lived'? Within the last few years, some of this subjectivity has been removed and the diagnostic accuracy improved by the use of the sensory modality assessment and rehabilitation technique (SMART), developed by the staff of the Brain Injury Unit at the Royal Hospital for Neurodisability in Putney, London. Dr Keith Andrews, its medical director, commented, 'The slow-to-recover patient is often incorrectly labelled as being in a vegetative state. Although aware of their surroundings, they are unable to communicate their needs whatsoever. The frustration of understanding what is being said and done around them, but being unable to express their needs and thoughts or indeed respond in any way has been described by patients whose potential to communicate was unlocked by SMART.' This technique records patients' responses to sensory and environmental stimulation over a two-week period. If they respond, it will be detected. Means of communicating with the patient can then be established. This type of assessment and rehabilitation programme has an additional advantage because it encourages participation by the patient's family and carers at a time when they often feel hopeless and helpless.

8.3 Misdiagnosis of PVS

As previously noted, 'presumed diagnosis can have a sting in its tail'. This is borne out by a 1997 survey, published by the Centre of Medical Law and Ethics, King's College, London, of nearly two thousand consultants in neurology and allied fields. It showed that some seventy-five per cent said it was sometimes appropriate to withdraw artificial nutrition and hydration from PVS sufferers. Here is the two-edged ethical sword. If I am suspected of being a PVS patient, I want to be correctly diagnosed, so that I can then be given the proper treatment to aid my recovery. On the other hand, if I am diagnosed as a PVS patient, they will probably want to starve and dehydrate me. Misdiagnosis could therefore actually spare my life. Whatever sort of absurd medicine is this?

Not only would these doctors want to starve and dehydrate me, but also many of them would want to do it in a hurry. Although the 1992 BMA guidelines recommended that 'treatment' withdrawal be considered only after twelve months, a third of these surveyed doctors said they would do it before six months has elapsed. A significant proportion, forty per cent, of them were either 'quite confident' or 'very confident' that they could predict the outcome of PVS patients after only four to six months.

But such diagnostic confidence, even arrogance, seems to be misplaced. Keith Andrews, using SMART, examined forty patients, who had been previously diagnosed as PVS sufferers. He concluded (*British Medical Journal*, 1996, 313:13–16) that seventeen, or forty-three per cent, of them had been misdiagnosed. Up to three-quarters showed some improvement after therapy. The misdiagnosed patients had functioning minds imprisoned in severely-disabled bodies and their efforts to communicate had simply not been recognized. All of these patients had been in 'PVS' for at least six months, and three had suffered for more than four years. All seventeen patients were blind, but, astonishingly, their doctors had often failed to realize this when assessing their ability to track a moving object with their eyes—a standard diagnostic test for PVS. In the same issue of the *British Medical Journal*, Dr Ronald Cranford, a US expert, played down these findings, and anyway, he considered that the quality of life of these misdiagnosed patients was questionable. Dr Andrews rejected this, 'Quality of life is something I have, not something you tell me I have. We have got to give patients an opportunity to live before we give them an opportunity to die. If you are paralysed and cannot speak it is difficult to detect any communication. Assessment needs to be over a long period of time and is a team effort.' The Andrews' team further discovered that many of these patients were capable of communicating. But by this time, the High Court had authorized the deaths of at least eight alleged PVS victims in Britain.

8.4 Proper treatment of PVS patients

Keith Andrews maintains that doctors have been too negative about what could be done for PVS patients because few have had sufficient experience of rehabilitation opportunities. Aggressive treatment is called for at the possible onset of PVS because of the uncertain prognosis. Once stabilized the patient should be given stimulation and rehabilitation exercises.

The view of the Medical Ethics Committee of the BMA (1992, p. 16) is much more forlorn. It says that, '… nutrition and hydration are medical treatments and are warranted only when they make possible a decent life in which the patient can reasonably be thought to have a continued interest.' The latest position of the BMA is to be found in its publication, *Withholding and Withdrawing Life-prolonging Medical Treatment* (2001). It represents one more step down the slippery slope, for there (p. 63), 'The BMA hopes that in future the Courts will decide that PVS cases no longer inevitably require Court review, where consensus exists, as long are such withdrawal is in accordance with agreed guidance.' This negative, lifeless type of medicine sounds just like a prescription for uncaring, non-treatment, which is another name for mistreatment.

8.5 Non-treatment of PVS patients

Good medicine defines a doctor's duty as providing both care and treatment for the patient. Where it is certain that no possible benefit can be conferred upon a patient, a doctor is said to have no duty to provide treatment, otherwise it simply degenerates into 'meddlesome medicine', which is futile and a burden to the patient. This is principled compassion operating as part of proper medicine. However, the case of Anthony Bland redefined all this. The Law Lords decided that, since Anthony Bland was a PVS patient, he would never recover consciousness, and therefore it was lawful to withdraw treatment, because it no longer benefited him. But, in this momentous decision in 1993, 'treatment' was redefined to include nutrition and hydration—food and water. Therefore, withholding or withdrawing these essentials of life was no longer unlawful.

Of course, such a decision must be preceded by a chain of enquiry. This would include independent diagnosis and prognosis, an assessment of the likely benefits and burdens of treatment, the patient's views, if known, and the views of family and carers. Nevertheless, someone, usually the patient's doctor, has to make the first move—unanimity among all those involved is most unlikely. After the Anthony Bland decision, each case for withdrawal of 'treatment' has had to go to the High Court to obtain permission—these are now in double figures, around twenty-five patients, and none has so far been refused. Furthermore, since there is no definitive diagnosis for PVS, and misdiagnosis is commonplace, it seems inevitable that people on the ill-defined margins of PVS will also be coming before the Courts.

The Anthony Bland decision also raised the question of what to do with the other 1,500 or so PVS patients currently lying in hospital beds in Britain. After all, it cost £2,100 a week to keep Anthony Bland in hospital, so altogether they are costing the country almost £200m each year. Some consider that the Anthony Bland decision will eventually pave the way for the 'medical cleansing' of the long-stay wards of our hospitals. Many are worried that this will be just one more example of the law and ethics abdicating to economic and social pressures. Such people are on the ethical ball. We have already witnessed this spectre, with eyes wide open, in abortion, and with blind eyes turned, in infanticide. The medical profession in many of its practices has already succumbed to these pressures.

If lawyers and doctors have already caved in, the philosopher's view is no more reassuring. A typical opinion has been given by Gert, Culver and Closer in their 1997 book, *Bioethics: A Return to Fundamentals*. They maintain (p. 263) that, 'A patient in a persistent vegetative state is usually regarded as living in only the most basic biological sense ... The death of an organism which was a person must not be confused with an organism ceasing to be a person. The loss of personhood in persistent vegetative patients makes it inappropriate to continue treating them as if they were persons. Consciousness and cognition are essential human attributes. If they are lost, life has lost its meaning. Unless there are religious reasons to the contrary, we recommend that nothing be done to keep such patients alive.' Here again is that shocking theme of modern medicine—if patients are encumbrances, if they are very ill, or disabled in some way, if they cost a lot to keep, then they have 'lives not worthy to be lived'—therefore it is in their 'best interests' to die, and that should happen as soon as possible.

You think that I am over-egging my case? Then consider the opinion of the world's foremost medical expert on PVS, Professor Bryan Jennett. He has said that nobody who stays in this state for three months recovers, though he has had to revise this figure upwards more recently. Or again, that most famous of PVS doctors, Dr Jim Howe, has said, 'I would not see it [injecting a lethal dose] as something that would disturb me for patients with PVS, and if it was legal and families wanted it to be done I think I could do it.' Or there is the view, held by many within the medical profession, that any improved consciousness associated with PVS 'recovery' would cause patients to be aware of their condition and that would be a plight worse than the 'oblivion' of the vegetative state.

The lawyer's perspective on PVS is given by Dame Elizabeth Butler-Sloss, president of the High Court's family division. She has stated that the principles established in 1993 by the House of Lords in the Anthony Bland case will not be affected by the 2000 Human Rights Act. In other words, the European Convention will not alter a doctor's right to withdraw artificial nutrition and hydration from PVS patients. PVS patients will therefore receive no protection from the Act, and in particular from Article 2, namely, 'Everyone's right to life shall be protected by law. No one shall be deprived of his life intentionally ...' In the original document of the Act, a list of exceptions was added, but PVS patients were apparently not 'exceptions' because nothing on that list was based on the 'quality of life', or a person's 'best interests'. So what does Article 2 actually mean? Surely, it provides protection for 'Everyone ...', including PVS patients. Not so, says Butler-Sloss, who apparently regards the Bland judgment as infallible.

Finally, the future state of medical practice and ethics with respect to the PVS patient is perhaps best summed up by the recent statement from Derick T. Wade, professor of neurodisability at Oxford. He has gone one step further. Commenting, in the *British Medical Journal* (2001, 322:352–354), on the suffering of PVS patients when food and water are withdrawn, he gruesomely points out that this slow mode of death also renders their organs unsuitable for transplantation. However, undaunted by any sense of callousness, he concludes, 'It would be possible to kill the patient more directly.' Can you believe it? In one of the world's premier medical journals? Wholesome medical ethics, the Hippocratic oath, the Judaeo-Christian doctrines are all heaved out of the window. And you thought that I was indulging in hyperbole! I ask you, if it is PVS patients today, which group of patients is for the chop, or the syringe, tomorrow?

8.6 Non-recovery from PVS

The Anthony Bland case has become the most famous example of non-recovery from PVS. But there are others. Just three are outlined here to give a flavour of what is happening in our hospitals.

Janet Johnston, a fifty-three-year-old grandmother, had been in PVS for four years after taking an overdose of drugs. Mrs Johnston could breathe for herself and could open and shut her eyes, but she did not appear to respond to any stimuli. In April 1996, the Scottish judge, Lord Cameron of Lochbroom, said that Law Hospital in Strathclyde could stop artificially supplying her with food and water. She died of dehydration within fourteen days. This, the first 'right-to-die' case in Scotland, took eight months to pass through the Courts and had been heard by five of Scotland's most senior judges. The Scottish lawyer, or Curator, looking after Mrs Johnston's interests, pleaded that, 'In a world where the frontiers of medical science are never closed, the Curator suggests the Court should prefer that life continues to the certainty of death if treatment is removed. There are people who had been in a coma for months who had recovered.' But the Court ignored the Curator's petition and instead ruled that it was no longer in Janet Johnston's 'best interests' to keep her alive. However, despite being committed to carrying out Mrs Johnston's 'death sentence', the Hospital did pledge that she would be nursed intensively up to the time of her death! That is called an ethical *non sequitur*, or is it an ethical oxymoron, or could it even be both?

In 1997, Sir Stephen Brown, a High Court judge, ruled that a twenty-nine-year-old severely brain-damaged, former university student, known as Miss D, could be 'allowed to die' after being in PVS for eighteen months following a car accident. Her feeding tube had accidentally slipped out and the judge ruled against it being reinserted. Thus, she was starved to death. This case has an added significance because the patient's condition fell short of the generally-accepted clinical criteria that provide a diagnosis of presumed PVS. For instance, she showed visual fixation, she could track moving objects with her eyes, she flinched in response to gestures, and she reacted to the sensation of ice on her body. Nevertheless, the judge insisted that, 'The time for merciful relief has arrived.'

Alan Tombs has been a PVS patient since 1989. He was awarded damages of £1.65m after an anaesthetist's error caused him serious brain damage. His wife, Dena, made visits to the hospital in south-west London, spending six hours each day by Alan's side, 'sharing the trivia of the day with him.' However, unlike the Bland family, she does not want her ordeal to end. She fears that after the Anthony Bland ruling other families will be 'leaned on' to follow suit. She voiced her fears, 'You cannot start killing off people because they are economically unsound.' More recently, she has taken her husband home to care for him there, but she still sees no apparent signs of recovery—Alan recognizes neither his surroundings, nor her.

8.7 Recovery from PVS

Now for something more heartening. The medical literature is thinly scattered with reports of people who have begun to come out of PVS. But let us maintain a true perspective here—it is only a very small minority of PVS patients who have so far been reported to show signs of recovery. This, of course, begs several questions. Have the other PVS patients been enabled, or encouraged, to recover? Have they simply been abandoned? Or, have they been too readily subjected to the so-called 'treatment of withdrawal'? Furthermore, we should appreciate that 'recovery' from PVS is neither instantaneous, nor complete—it is invariably associated with continuing and severe disability. Even so, the fact that a few PVS recoveries have been reported should give some hope to loved ones, as well as motivation to medical personnel. What follows is a selection of five fascinating cases from both sides of the Atlantic.

In 1988, Gary Dockery, a Tennessee policeman was shot in the head while on duty answering a bogus call. He went into a coma and then a vegetative state. In February 1996, at the age of forty-two, he contracted pneumonia and was operated on to remove fluid from his lungs. Upon recovery from the anaesthetic, after seven and a half years of silence, he began to speak to his family and doctors almost non-stop for eighteen hours. He then lapsed back into silence, though later he regained some limited powers of speech. He died in April 1997.

In 1994, a North of England health authority was considering asking the High Court for permission to withdraw nutrition and hydration from one of its patients, a late middle-aged businessman who had been in PVS for seven years. His wife opposed the idea steadfastly and the request was dropped. His condition had originally been diagnosed by Bryan Jennett, though Keith Andrews considered that the man was mentally competent—at least, he could communicate sufficiently to withdraw from a newspaper interview! Professor Jennett's subsequent comment was, 'It's very alarming if he's waking up. I saw him and didn't think there was any doubt it was PVS.'

Also in 1994, Geoffrey Wildsmith, a nineteen-year-old musician in his rock band, *Rich and Famous*, suffered severe head injuries. He spent two years in PVS before being transferred to the Royal Hospital for Neurodisability in Putney. In February 1996, this bass guitarist had begun to move a finger, so technicians rigged up a computer with a buzzer and an alphabet code to enable him to communicate. Police had originally thought that his injuries were the result of a rail accident, but in March 1996, he managed to tap out on his computer a message that someone had actually attacked him and tried to kill him. Of the early days after his injury, he wrote, 'It was pretty awful. I felt so bored to tears.' And to cope with these difficulties, he found inner strength by praying every day.

In 1996, an eighteen-year-old American girl, who suffered severe brain damage as the result of a car accident and had been in PVS for five years, had recovered sufficiently to be discharged from a hospital in Austin, Texas. As already noted, many PVS experts and medical bodies, including the American Academy of Neurology, insist that patients who show no awareness of their surroundings and no response to commands for twelve months can be regarded as irreversibly damaged. Yet, this girl showed no such responses until fifteen months after her accident. After three years she was communicating by blinking and after five years she was communicating using spoken phrases.

Finally, there is the astonishing story of Andrew Devine. He was a postal worker who, along with Anthony Bland, had suffered brain damage as a result of the 1989 Hillsborough football disaster. He too was diagnosed as being in PVS. Five years after this diagnosis, he began to emerge from PVS by looking at people. Then he began using an electric buzzer to communicate more and more with his parents, Stanley and Hilary, who have always looked after their son at home. Then, eight years after the accident, he could count. Andrew Devine is not an example of PVS misdiagnosis, nor has his been a full recovery. Yet his case has certainly prompted serious concern and a general uneasiness among many about the string of cases in which judges have sanctioned the withdrawal of artificial nutrition and hydration from PVS patients.

At the beginning of 2002, I spoke with Andrew's father and he told me how his son's progress had now become much less, 'Others tell me there is still some slight improvement, though I'm the last to see it.' Even so, Andrew appears to be happy most of the time, and although he cannot speak, they manage to communicate as they watch television together and as he takes Andrew out in his wheelchair, '... everyday, except in the very filthiest of weather.' Arguments over Andrew's life expectancy continue. Mr Devine recalled, 'The experts said it would be only two, then three, then five years. But Andrew has proved them all wrong because that was thirteen years ago and now he is thirty-four.' He concluded, 'Yes, it is a strain for us looking after him, but he is our son, he needs us, and so we just get on with it.' My admiration for them welled up.

Joni Eareckson Tada, in her 1992 book, *When Is It Right To Die?*, rightly says (p. 148) that people in PVS, '... aren't dying; they are severely disabled.' She then draws attention (p. 149) to the words of the Lord Jesus Christ in Matthew 16:17, which declare that spiritual insight and knowledge are, '... not revealed to you by man, but by my Father in heaven.' Thus, God can work powerfully in the lives of all men, women and children, even, presumably, when they are mentally incapacitated. After all, the twenty-four-week-old unborn John the Baptist leaped in his mother's womb when he realized that he was in the presence of the Saviour (Luke 1:41–44), and he was filled with the Holy Spirit even as a newborn baby (Luke 1:15). So even a baby's brain can be capable of grasping the most weighty spiritual truths. Evidently, God does not need a fully-formed, wholly-sentient, entirely-functioning, high-IQ brain to work through. Thankfully! And so, when we are confronted with complex edge-of-life issues, and in particular, PVS patients, our motto should perhaps be 2 Corinthians 5:16, 'So from now on we regard no-one from a worldly point of view.'

Eugenics

Eugenics has a bad name and a dreadful history, yet, even today, it is still widely practised. It is the thinking that lies beneath and skulks around many of the edge-of-life issues, especially, euthanasia, infanticide and abortion.

9.1 What is eugenics?

Eugenics can be defined as the genetic improvement of the human race by controlling the reproduction of its people. The eugenic approach has always been two-fold, though one has consistently obscured the other. First, there was the enhancement of what were reckoned to be socially good traits among the supposedly 'desirable' people. Second, there was the elimination of bad traits from among the allegedly 'undesirable' people. That is, there were to be programmes of positive eugenics and negative eugenics. Positive eugenics manifested itself in, for example, the popular and ostensibly harmless 'Fitter Family Contests' in the USA, where healthy, white families competed against each other in sports and intellectual tasks at State Fairs. On the surface, these were about as noxious as a knobbly knees contest at a Butlin's holiday camp. In reality, positive eugenics has achieved practically nothing. This is primarily because human attributes, such as intelligence and personality, are determined by an array of not just genetic, but also environmental, dietary, and other factors. The genetic factors, of, for instance, intelligence will be controlled by dozens, perhaps hundreds, of genes—these have not yet even been partially, let alone fully, identified, so at present we know almost zero about their all-important interactions. Therefore, enhancing good traits by positive eugenics, that is, by selective breeding, has been, and will long remain, pretty much a non-starter scientifically. Nevertheless, in thought, if not in practice, such manipulative schemes have been a consistent part of the eugenicist's portfolio of ideals. As such, they remain a threatening and an ethically-repellent aspect of eugenics.

However, they are nothing like so repugnant as the practices of negative eugenics—these are far more sinister. It was not simply the undesirable genetic traits that the eugenicist wanted to manipulate, but rather it was the very people who displayed such traits. They were to be prevented from reproducing, by sterilization programmes, or, ultimately, by their elimination from the population. Negative eugenics may begin with high ideals, but it inexorably progresses by dominating the weak and vulnerable, and eventually it often ends up with killing such people.

A quick survey of the history of moral ruination, whether personal, familial, or societal, would undoubtedly reveal that two of its major causes have been the abuse of either sex or money. Guess what? Eugenics embraces both of them. Consider, for example, its sterilization programmes. They were developed not just on reproductive, but also on economic, grounds— they were implemented to reduce the costs of institutional care and welfare subsidies for the 'undesirables'. Eugenics always wants to control. Usually its two targets are the curbing of reproduction, and the curbing of financial spending, but it will, if pushed, cut both by cutting down people. These themes are frequently entwined, or, perhaps more appropriately, tangled, components of eugenics.

9.2 A brief history of eugenics

Eugenics became fashionable during the late nineteenth century. It was regarded as a form of social engineering—the application of science in order to better society by assisting the process of natural selection. Darwinism had caught the public's fancy, and eugenics has its roots in social Darwinism. Indeed, it was Francis Galton, one of Charles Darwin's cousins, who first organized the eugenics movement in Britain. In 1883, he invented the word eugenics (from the Greek, *eugenes*, meaning 'well born' or 'good birth') and in 1885, in an article entitled, *Hereditary Talent and Character*, he proposed that society could be engineered 'through better breeding'. Then in 1900, Gregor Mendel's long-forgotten work on the mechanisms of genetic inheritance was rediscovered. This was the catalyst that provoked speculation about, and formulation of, eugenic programmes. Here, at last, was the eugenicists' apparently scientific, but what later emerged to be their mistaken, *raison d'être*, namely that, if the so-called 'inferior individuals' could be prevented from breeding, then mental and physical disabilities could gradually be eliminated from the population.

In 1908, Galton organized the Eugenics Education Society in London to investigate human heredity and to carry out these 'social action programmes'. Altruism may have been the motivation of some members, but for others, the matters of race, class and privilege were clearly on the agenda. There was a widespread fear among both conservatives and liberals that the 'feebleminded' were the cause of growing social problems. Crime, poverty, and the like, were increasing because, it was said, these people, with their 'defective' genes, were being allowed to reproduce at too great a rate. It was argued that natural selection had previously kept the numbers of these 'defectives' in check. Now, with advances in medicine, and with charitable help, these people were being kept alive. Worse still, they were breeding faster than their 'betters' were—an official British report in 1908 showed that 'defectives' had, on average, seven children, whereas the 'normal' had only four.

Eugenics, and particularly negative eugenics, was becoming *de rigueur* almost everywhere. Around the 1900s, the eugenics movement was on the increase in North America, Europe, Latin America and Asia. By the 1930s, twenty-four American states had passed eugenic sterilization laws, under which 60,000 and more Americans were sterilized compulsorily. One enthusiastic US supporter of the movement was John Harvey Kellogg, brother of the cereal tycoon. He once stated, 'We are supporting an idle population of defectives. And we permit these defectives to breed more and worse lunatics, idiots, criminals and paupers.' Think about that as you next crunch on your breakfast cornflakes!

9.3 Eugenics as pseudoscience

Much of the early 'science' of eugenics was based on an amazingly simple error—in truth, it was pseudoscience. These early eugenicists believed that, for example, mental deficiency could be eliminated either by segregating affected individuals from the population, or by sterilizing them—anything to stop them breeding, or as a poster from the London Eugenics Society of the time proclaimed, 'Only Healthy Seeds Must Be Sown!'

Edward Murray East, a champion of eugenics in the USA, argued that the 'problem' of mental deficiency lay in the huge heterozygous reserve affecting about seven per cent of the population. But the now-famous estimate by the Cambridge geneticist, R C Punnett, in 1917, showed that even if all the 'feebleminded' could be prevented from having children it would take more than 8,000 years before their numbers could be reduced to even 1 in 100,000 of the population.

Furthermore, this core of the eugenicist's 'science' was proved to be entirely erroneous by the Hardy-Weinberg principle, first published in 1917. In the 1920s and 1930s, geneticists generally agreed that most mental defects were caused by recessive Mendelian factors, or alleles, as they are now called. But the Hardy-Weinberg equation, $p^2 + 2pq + q^2 = 1$, demonstrated that if such a trait is rare, then most deleterious genes will be hidden in apparently normal carriers. In other words, stopping men and women, who are affected with a particular disability, from reproducing will *not* reduce the incidence of that disability. Thus, the theme song of the early eugenicists, namely, that the 'problem' of the mental defectives could be solved if they were prevented from breeding, was a fallacy, and both their eugenic segregation and sterilization programmes were ineffective public policies, and ultimately, a waste of time and money.

Nevertheless, even after all this was known, eugenics and eugenicists persisted. Indeed, the apparent failure of eugenic 'science' caused many of them to insist that their efforts should be increased and widened, rather than restricted. At that time, eugenicists were enjoying power and prestige within science, government and society. In the USA and elsewhere, they continued to influence many aspects of social policy, including discriminatory immigration laws. These were applied, in particular, to east Europeans, who it was feared were diluting the American gene pool. This forging of eugenics with nationalism has been a common theme of history. Of course, Hitler carried eugenic thinking to its hideous extreme while championing Aryan nationalism and elitism. The Nazi eugenic-based programmes sterilized thousands and thousands of people and they paved the way for both the non-Jewish euthanasia programmes, and eventually, for the Final Solution of the Holocaust, as discussed in chapter 11.

9.4 More recent eugenics

Although eugenic programmes have often been associated with the Nazis, that is not the whole story, not by a long chalk. In Sweden, for example, a law was passed in 1926 that permitted sterilization without the patient's consent. Under it, during the period between the 1930s and 1970s, about 60,000 Swedes, ninety-five per cent of whom were women, were forcibly sterilized on eugenic grounds—racial characteristics, very poor eyesight, mental retardation, and so on. This law was overturned only in 1976. During the last decade, similar practices, again, implemented without the consent of the patients, have been uncovered in Switzerland, Austria and Finland. How could these supposedly democratic countries pursue the social engineering policies similar to those of the Third Reich? How could such seemingly-humane, tolerant countries, often held up as role models of enlightened societies with a caring ethos and advanced welfare provision, descend to eugenics and the physical abuse of their citizens? You can answer those questions yourself.

During the 1940s and 1950s, eugenics waned and it became outmoded primarily because of its links with the Nazis, but also on account of its shoddy scientific basis, and because of its association with class and racial bias. Furthermore, it was becoming evident that many mental diseases were not simply gene-linked, but that other factors had a large part to play in such behaviours.

Eugenics was beginning to get a thoroughly bad name. It became fashionable to propose that the State should be stripped of any claim to control, or to interfere in the lives, especially the reproductive lives, of its citizens. Human rights were in vogue, as evidenced by the Universal Declaration of Human Rights, which in 1948, was adopted by the United Nations. Eugenics and enforced sterilizations were both condemned. In 1949, Lionel Penrose, a noted geneticist and a staunch opponent of eugenics, argued that the proper measure of a society's decency was its willingness to provide adequate care for its most vulnerable and weak members. During the 1950s, this anti-eugenic sentiment became synonymous with a mindset that was anti-State and anti-establishment, and thus it became foundational to modish causes as diverse as patients' rights and the feminist movement. By the 1960s, reproductive autonomy, that is, freedom from any State interference, had become the accepted norm.

9.5 Modern-day eugenics

Accordingly, eugenics appeared to be dead, or at least, mortally wounded. Was it fiddle! Human endeavour and history are rarely that neat and tidy. In fact, the societal base for modern-day eugenics has widened and deepened. Despised and discredited for half a century, eugenics is currently back in fashion. During that fifty-year gap, the appliance of science had occurred in two new areas of medicine, namely, prenatal screening and reproductive technology. And they have both encouraged the revival of the practice of eugenics. Of course, it is not the crude eugenics of an earlier age, this now is sophisticated, high-cost, high-tech stuff. Eugenics is far from finished. Eugenicists abound today, but their science is not so slapdash as their predecessors and they are less naive and more disguised.

Our society has a most uneasy attitude towards genetic disease and abnormality or, at any rate, towards those people with them. It is something unacceptable to many people and some would say that anyone so afflicted is better off dead. This is what some have called, 'the personal tragedy theory of disability', whereby 'disability' cannot be spoken about as anything other than a disaster. Yet, we can be strangely double-minded. We increasingly provide facilities and benefits for the disabled, such as, access ramps and job opportunities, but at the same time, we offer every pregnant woman the opportunity to determine whether her unborn child is likely to be disabled, and if so, the means to destroy him. For more and more genetic diseases, not just Down's syndrome and spina bifida, this is becoming a matter of eugenic prenatal screening. There is now prenatal genetic diagnosis (PGD), used in conjunction with IVF, at three days, or chorion villus sampling (CVS) at nine to twelve weeks, or amniocentesis at sixteen weeks. These are the modern expressions of the search-and-destroy mentality of the old negative eugenicists. The thinking is precisely the same, namely, it is morally right to destroy your child if he is defective. Even *Nature* (1994,368:572) conceded that this policy, '... constitutes eugenics of a mild sort ...' and that it is, '... a eugenic procedure that greatly assists many modern parents.' Once detected, the afflicted, or to be more precise, those who are merely *suspected* of being the afflicted, are squashed in the case of embryos, or aborted in the case of foetuses. This is the new and modern way to 'prevent' the 'undesirables'—to banish them from our population. Such prenatal eugenics is the new apartheid, a blatant discrimination against the weak and vulnerable. And what does this say to the disabled who are already born? 'Oh dear, you slipped through our screening procedures, didn't you?'

The old eugenics was based on poor science, a sort of half-baked Darwinism, plus irrational fears of the handicapped with racial overtones, plus the intervention of the State. The new eugenics is based on the sound science of genetics and assisted reproductive techniques, plus the same illogical fears, plus that very modern State-approved maxim, 'a woman's right to choose'. You see how persistent the fundamentals of eugenics can be?

Perhaps the most recent overtly eugenic law to be passed has been that of China in 1995. Its avowed intent was to decrease the number of disabled children born. Several eminent UK geneticists complained, on behalf of the Clinical Genetics Society, in a letter to *The Times* (5 June 1995), '... this is an undisguised embodiment of eugenic principles the implementation of which has had such a disastrous history in the West.' Under this law, Chinese people with certain genetic diseases have not been allowed to marry unless they agree to be sterilized beforehand. Moreover, any parents with an already handicapped child are forced to abort any subsequent children, whether disabled, or not.

As already noted, wherever there is eugenic thinking, economic considerations will be just around the corner. Sure enough, modern-day eugenics also has a financial side, which is redolent of the American and German situations in the 1930s. One of these modern-day counterparts is found, for example, in the 1991 Report by the Royal Dutch Society of Medicine, which studied the outcome of 2,816 amniocentesis tests. Of the seventy-five abortions performed as a result of these tests, fifty-seven involved 'defective' foetuses. The Report concluded that, 'These analyses cost approximately $1.5m. This is the same order of magnitude as the cost of taking care of one patient with Down's syndrome for 60 years. In the light of a cost-benefit analysis, the conclusion is obvious.' Herein is eugenic economics. It can be used to justify the financial gains to be reaped as a result of that little leap from amniocentesis procedures to the practice of abortion. From there it is but a short jump to infanticide, and then only a small step to euthanasia. In Holland, and in a growing number of other countries, such fiscal calculations are considered by many to be the hallmarks of a modern, responsible society.

9.6 Future eugenics

The future of medicine lies largely with genetic medicine—it will revolutionize treatments and cures, as we currently understand them. Now that the human genome has been sequenced, the prospects of determining which genes are implicated in which diseases have become a reality. Once the genetic basis of diseases, like schizophrenia and Alzheimer's, have been elucidated, many supporters of the mentally ill expect that better diagnoses and treatments will follow, together, they hope, with a more compassionate attitude towards the sufferers and their families. Perhaps, but perhaps not.

If only the science were that simple. So far, the only correlation between identified genes and diseases have been for those caused by a single dominant gene, like cystic fibrosis, or severe combined immunodeficiency (SCID). Most genetically-linked diseases involve a multiplicity of genes acting in concert, plus complicating and virtually-unexplored additional factors, such as environment and diet. Researchers will continue to find a statistical relationship between the presence of certain genes and a behavioural trait. But so what? What does it mean to tell a patient that he has a twenty-five per cent predisposition towards, say, schizophrenia?

But surely eugenics, consisting of prenatal diagnosis and then gene therapy, could be a powerful weapon in the prevention of diseases. The question is, will early detection followed by germ-line gene therapies ever be used to eliminate major genetic diseases? At present, such inheritable treatments are illegal. But will such eugenic medicine be disallowed for ever? And when it is possible to manipulate these germ-line therapies safely, will they be tried? 'Precise, safe and effective', will predictably be their three advertised qualities. After all, prenatal diagnoses plus destruction are already part of our negative eugenic medical services, why not try to extend these by including some real positive eugenic manipulation of humans?

As a matter of fact, we can already practise positive eugenics, albeit in a rather limited form, in the comfort of our own homes. There are already sperm banks offering a wide range of male genetic material by mail order, and female models' eggs are available on the Internet. Now, with a little ingenuity and some serious money, you can, perhaps, produce your own eugenically-designed baby—a child with the looks of a film star and the brains of a Nobel prize-winner. But, *caveat emptor*, it may all go wrong, and you will end up with the reverse!

Eugenics has a bright future within mainstream medicine. Despite the coercive nature of its control of human reproduction, and the subjectivity of what it regards as desirable traits, it is already being increasingly practised in our general hospitals and specialist clinics. It has become the unmentioned motivating force behind so many of the nasty edge-of-life issues, including abortion, infanticide and euthanasia. Eugenics and secular humanism fit together as cosily as glove and hand. Eugenics has percolated into the mindset of healthcare professionals without them knowing it. And although eugenics is finding a new outlet in genetic manipulation, which, let us recognize, has the potential for good by treating genetic diseases, it still retains the potential for future malice by tinkering with such attributes as intelligence and physical appearance, besides its current malevolent role in prenatal screening. Eugenics is also in the minds of some of our politicians and public policy decision-makers— now that is a scary prospect.

Modern eugenics, in its uncharacteristically positive form, could be a benign technology as in the application of somatic, rather than germ-line, gene therapies. On the other hand, in its negative form, it can be an unprecedented evil. It depends who is in control. Eugenics is evil when it is driven by those, in medicine and elsewhere, who believe that some human beings are sub-standard and valueless. Such controllers are social engineers and they believe that the handicapped in the womb, the disabled newborn, the senile, and the terminally ill should be eradicated. That is what so much of eugenic thinking and eugenic practice is all about. You do not have to be a geneticist to be a eugenicist—all you need is the belief that some people have 'lives not worthy to be lived'. Eugenics is a slippery serpent—it wants to do 'a snake in the grass' on you. So, beware of the eugenicist's snake oil!

PART 3
Some Evidences

'There is no manne so deafe as hee that will not heare, nor so blynd as he that will not see, nor dull as he that wyll not understande.'

Thomas Cranmer, (1551) *Answer to Stephen Gardiner, bishop of Winchester.*

None will dispute the gravity of the topics of dying and death as discussed in Part 2, *The Primary Issues*. However, some may doubt the grim analysis of the trends in medical ethics and practice presented there. They might consider that the assessment of the other edge-of-life issues like, euthanasia, infanticide and suicide, was too alarmist, too doom-laden. A few may even believe that it was all just so much rhetoric, devoid of substance.

Part 3 answers these doubters and critics. It seeks to authenticate the arguments of Part 2, to substantiate the allegations and ground them in fact, by examining some specific examples. These examples are a mixture of famous court cases, historical narratives and government reports. They are matched with each of the previously-presented primary issues, but, at times, this sort of correlation defies strict categorization. For instance, the Nazi Holocaust can be coupled with eugenics *and* euthanasia, the Anthony Bland case can be associated with the issues of permanent vegetative state *and* euthanasia. That notwithstanding, and in a sense, entirely because of such multiple connections, the evidences are deemed to be not just additionally alarming, but also overwhelmingly supportive of this book's thesis that much of modern medicine has gone wrong. But, you, the reader, must make up your own mind. So, turn the page!

The Remmelink and the House of Lords' Reports

The United Kingdom and the Netherlands have much in common. We are, after all, near-neighbours in both the historic and geographic sense, and our shared national pastimes consist largely of football and gardening. But, we are also quite different. They speak excellent English, we speak appalling Dutch. They are laid-back, we are uptight. They have legalized euthanasia, we have not. This latter difference was predicated in two important, official Reports published in each country within the last decade or so. The Remmelink Report of 1991 exposed the inevitable road that the Dutch were taking towards legalizing euthanasia, while the House of Lords' Report of the Select Committee on Medical Ethics of 1994 came out strongly against such a legal move. The two Reports give substance to the two countries' differing attitudes and approaches towards euthanasia. They are therefore well worth considering in more detail.

10.1 Euthanasia pre-Remmelink

Although euthanasia has, for many years, officially been a criminal offence in the Netherlands, informally, it has long been tolerated, as in other countries, such as Belgium and Colombia. Nevertheless, it is Holland that has earned the reputation as the 'home of euthanasia'. Indeed, it is the only country in the world where euthanasia has been explicitly practised and, more recently, formally legalized. This medical, legal and public toleration of euthanasia is considered by many to be one of the most disquieting examples of post-Christian thinking and practice among the European nations. Therefore, the Dutch experience has much to teach us.

For a start, the Dutch define euthanasia in an unusual way—it is strangely circumscribed. Typically it would be, 'The purposeful acting to terminate life by someone other than the person concerned upon request of the latter' (Remmelink Report, vol. 2, p. 2). In other words, the Dutch define euthanasia to mean only active or positive voluntary euthanasia and assisted suicide. According to Dutch law, a doctor who intentionally kills either, a competent patient, on request, by means of omission, that is, by withholding food or withdrawing treatment, or an incompetent patient, with no request, by means of either commission or omission, does *not* commit euthanasia. These definitions of euthanasia are oddly Dutch.

In 1984, the Dutch Supreme Court and the Royal Dutch Medical Association (KNMG) issued guidelines concerning euthanasia. These established that prior to being euthanized by a doctor, the patient must have first, experienced intractable suffering from which there are no alternatives, and second, made an explicit, informed, voluntary and durable request. Third, the doctor must have obtained a second opinion, and fourth, each case of death must be reported to the local medical examiner. Whereas the Dutch regarded these guidelines as 'strict' and 'precise', it will be seen that they are 'elastic' and open to numerous interpretations, as well as abuses. Furthermore, it is common knowledge that these recommendations have often been disregarded, and moreover, that rarely have doctors been prosecuted when they have failed to abide by them.

10.2 The Remmelink Report

In January 1990, the Dutch government appointed a commission, consisting of three lawyers and three doctors, to report on 'medical decisions concerning the end of life' that occurred throughout Holland during 1990. Its chairman was the Attorney-General, Professor Remmelink, and the associated quantitative survey was carried out by Professor P J van der Maas. The findings of both the commission and the survey, the Remmelink Report and the van der Maas survey, were published in September 1991.

The Remmelink Report (including the survey) reviewed 26,350 cases in which doctors had acted or not acted either 'partly with the purpose of shortening life', or with the 'explicit purpose of shortening life'. It reported the occurrence of 2,300 cases of voluntary euthanasia, plus 400 cases of assisted suicide, which together amounted to about two per cent of all Dutch deaths that year. But, because of the Dutch narrow definition of euthanasia, these are gross underestimates since only the so-called voluntary and active varieties were counted. These Dutch data have been reanalysed by John Keown, a lawyer at Cambridge University. In a 1995 book, *Euthanasia Examined*, Keown reveals (p. 261–296) that when incidents of non-voluntary and passive killings are included, the Dutch euthanasia figures increase almost fourfold. The real total is 10,558. These are cases in which doctors had acted (that is, performed active, or positive euthanasia, or euthanasia by commission), or refrained from acting (passive, or negative, or by omission), with the 'explicit intention to shorten life'. Furthermore, of this total, 5,450 patients had been killed *without* their explicit request. These latter examples of non-voluntary euthanasia account for fifty-two per cent of the total euthanasia cases. In addition, it was shown that in over seventy per cent of cases, doctors had failed to report instances of euthanasia and assisted suicide to the relevant authorities. During 1990, the total number of people who died, from all causes, in Holland was almost 130,000, therefore 1 in 12, or just over eight per cent, of all Dutch deaths were the result of euthanasia, that is, brought about by doctors whose primary intention was to hasten the death of their patients.

10.3 Euthanasia post-Remmelink

Were the Dutch shaken by these findings? Apparently not. The Remmelink Report did little to change Dutch practices—they continued to take a liberal, even relaxed, attitude towards euthanasia. This contrasts with the British, who, on 15 March 1995, were genuinely shocked by the television documentary, *Death on Request*, which featured Dr Wilfred van Oijen euthanizing one of his Dutch patients, Cees van Wendel de Joode, on the night of his sixty-third birthday. Mr de Joode was severely disabled by a neurological condition, but in no sense was he terminally ill. Serious questions arose. Why were antidepressants not prescribed? Was the diagnosis really correct? Why was no palliative care available? Of course, it was all clever, pro-euthanasia propaganda. Though initially appalled at the spectacle, the fact is that we too could, in the near future, become blasé about such killings on, and off, the box. One way we deal with such emotional overload is to sidestep the truth and absolve ourselves from any personal involvement—it is called denial. It is a most dangerous defence mechanism. Then again, Christians, above all others, should be stirred by the demands of truth and personal responsibility.

Incidentally, in 2001, this same Dutch doctor, Wilfred van Oijen, was found guilty of murdering one of his eighty-four-year-old patients, but he faced no penalty because it was considered that he had acted, '... honourably and according to his conscience.' This judgement was given despite the fact that the patient had made no request for euthanasia—as it happens, she had actually said that she did *not* want to die.

In the years following the Remmelink Report, euthanasia in the Netherlands increased. A 1996 survey, again conducted by Paul van der Maas, showed, for example, that the number of initial requests by patients asking for euthanasia had grown by thirty-seven per cent. The number of explicit requests had risen by nine per cent, and the proportion of these granted had increased from thirty to thirty-seven per cent. The only other changes that had occurred were minor administrative ones, such as the reporting of euthanasia cases, which had improved, from less than thirty, to forty-one per cent, but still represented only a small share of the total, in spite of their professed 'strict' and 'precise' guidelines. It all seems so casual and matter-of-fact. While the Dutch probably considered these to be significant improvements in their supposedly well-regulated system, others have made far less sanguine judgments. One such is Professor Lord McColl, a member of the Lords' Select Committee investigating euthanasia, who, after a fact-finding tour of the Netherlands in October 1993, said, 'Our visit convinced me that euthanasia is impossible to police and will be abused.'

10.4 The Dutch future

Nor will matters improve for the Dutch people because, on 28 November 2000, the Lower House of their Parliament approved a Bill to legalize euthanasia, which was then passed by their Upper House on 10 April 2001. Thus, the Netherlands became the first country in the world to decriminalize this practice. Now the Dutch, including their children as young as sixteen, can legally opt for euthanasia. However, those aged between twelve and sixteen will first have to obtain the consent of one of their parents!

Some commentators considered that this new Dutch legislation merely brought their law into line with their long-running practice of tolerance towards euthanasia and leniency towards those who abused it. For others, it was an occasion for celebration. For example, the US-based Hemlock Society, responding to this historic shift in law and medical ethics, stated, 'We are very excited. We have admired what the people of Holland have been doing for the last twenty years.' But, the Dutch have changed more than just a single law of their penal code—they have sent out other important signals to the world. As the head of the Voluntary Euthanasia Society in Britain commented, 'A psychological barrier has been broken with the legalization of voluntary euthanasia. Once one country has accepted the principle and laid it down in law, the question must be, "Why can't other countries do the same?"' That may not happen swiftly, but already there are fears, within Germany and other countries, that Holland will become a centre for 'death tourism', besieged by foreigners travelling there—with, of course, one-way tickets—to be euthanized.

But let no one run away with the idea that Holland is the place to find 'death with dignity'. A Dutch doctor-assisted suicide will not necessarily be 'a good and happy death'. Research, published in the *New England Journal of Medicine* (2000, 342:551–556), showed that a quarter of such cases were botched. Patients had to endure numerous complications like, coming out of induced coma, prolonged waiting for death, vomiting and fits. Instead of just 'assisting', twenty per cent of doctors had to act decisively to actually kill the patients themselves. And they call that 'death with dignity'?

10.5 Pro-euthanasia activity in the UK

From time to time, the UK public shows some interest in euthanasia. For example, in 1985 a poll reported that seventy-two per cent would support its legalization. Yet, there are few vociferous calls for it from the general public, the majority of the medical profession has exhibited little sustained interest in it, and not many politicians openly advocate it. Furthermore, UK citizens are not exactly queuing up for the privilege of having it administered to them.

Nevertheless, during the last century there has been an increasingly strident minority who wish to see voluntary euthanasia legalized. They include those who subscribe to organizations like, the Hemlock Society and the Voluntary Euthanasia Society, and among them have been some high-profile media names like, the journalist and broadcaster, Ludovic Kennedy, and the embryologist and science commentator, Lewis Wolpert. In addition, as outlined in section 5.8, there have been several Parliamentary attempts to introduce it. However, all such efforts have been defeated, not, it must be said, primarily as a result of moral reasoning, but on pragmatic grounds, because Parliamentarians and others recognize that any such laws would be both unworkable and open to abuse.

10.6 The House of Lords' Report

The last time that euthanasia was a serious subject at Westminster was when the House of Lords' Select Committee on Medical Ethics examined the subject and published its Report in February 1994. It came out opposed to euthanasia—well, mostly. This anti-euthanasia stance was something of a surprise, and a relief, because the members of the Committee were an ethically-diverse lot. On the other hand, when elderly Lords and Ladies examine the subject of euthanasia we might well expect them to oppose it! Nevertheless, the Report was not all good, indeed, in places, it was decidedly shaky—beneath its surface lay some disturbing features.

True, the Report strongly opposed any change in the law to permit euthanasia. And while it rightly endorsed (p. 48), '... the right of the competent patient to refuse consent to any medical treatment ...', it also emphasized that, 'The right to refuse medical treatment is far removed from the right to request assistance in dying.' The Committee heard about twenty oral presentations and read about eighty-five written submissions from various pro- and anti-euthanasia individuals and organizations. After considering all of the pro-euthanasia arguments, the Committee decided (p. 48) that, '... we do not believe that these arguments are sufficient reason to weaken society's prohibition of intentional killing. That prohibition is the cornerstone of law and of social relationships. It protects each one of us impartially, embodying the belief that all are equal ... We believe that the issue of euthanasia is one in which the interest of the individual cannot be separated from the interest of society as a whole.' And furthermore, the Committee considered (p. 49) that, 'It would be next to impossible to ensure that all acts of euthanasia were truly voluntary, and that any liberalisation of the law was not abused.'

The Committee also rejected the creation of a new offence, namely, mercy-killing, for which punishment might be more lenient. It concluded (p. 53), 'To distinguish between murder and "mercy-killing" would be to cross the line which prohibits any intentional killing, a line which we think it essential to preserve.'

Good stuff, so far. Nevertheless, and here is the rub, the Report defined (p. 10) euthanasia as, '… a deliberate intervention undertaken with the express intention of ending a life to relieve intractable suffering.' This is a most inadequate definition, with overtones that are reminiscent of the Dutch quirkiness, because, while it encompasses positive acts, namely, euthanasia by commission, which kill the patient, it excludes negative acts, namely, euthanasia by omission, which kill the patient. This failure of their Lordships to recognize the existence of euthanasia by omission is especially poignant in the wake of the 1993 Law Lords' judgement in the Anthony Bland case, an event that occurred exactly twelve months prior to the publication of this Report. After all, it was a deliberate omission, specifically, the withdrawal of nutrition and hydration, which was sanctioned by the Law Lords, that killed Anthony Bland. This case is rehearsed in chapter 12, but let us be entirely clear at this point—the classification of euthanasia into categories, such as active and passive, or positive and negative acts, may be helpful in distinguishing the means of euthanasia, but ethically, it is meaningless. The big question to ask is this— what was the intention of the doctor? The means he uses, whether they are positive or negative acts, are of little consequence if his intention is to kill the patient. Euthanasia by commission, such as giving an injection of lethal drugs, or by omission, such as the withdrawal of food and water, is still euthanasia. If the doctor's intention is to kill his patient, then the means, poisoning or dehydration, are of no ethical significance.

The Select Committee's Report contained other flaws. While maintaining the right to, '… refuse consent to any medical treatment …' (p. 48), it failed to distinguish such refusals that were suicidally motivated. Furthermore, it commended, '… the development of advance directives' (p. 54), but it did not discuss those made with the intention of suicide. It also considered (p. 56), somewhat naively, and entirely disputably, that, '... no other group of people is better qualified [than doctors and their colleagues] ... to take ethical decisions about life and death ...' Moreover, the Committee members were equivocal, and therefore so was the Report, about the practice of withdrawing or withholding medical treatment, even when that is food and water, from patients, especially PVS patients. It stated (p. 52) that, '... a treatment may be judged inappropriate if it will add nothing to the patient's well-being as a person.' While this might be construed as an example of 'futile and burdensome medicine', and therefore ethically acceptable, it should be noted that it occurs in the Report in a section entitled, *Treatment-limiting decisions*, and not in the context of patients who are competent, but those who are incompetent. Complicity with the Law Lords' decision in the Bland case is all too obvious.

Finally, on the more positive side, the Report concluded (p. 57) that, '... the rejection of euthanasia ... entails a compelling social responsibility to care adequately for those who are elderly, dying or disabled.' To that end, it made some important recommendations (p. 57). Among these were, the need for the development, growth and wider provision of 'high-quality palliative care', more 'research into new and improved methods of pain relief and symptom control', as well as more training for healthcare professionals 'for the weighty ethical responsibilities which they carry.'

10.7 The UK future

So where does the UK now stand with respect to the legalization of euthanasia? Our law, as in most other countries, is quite unclear. Notionally, euthanasia is illegal, but it is practised, perhaps even extensively. Yet, at present, there is not much obvious promotion of euthanasia, certainly not wholesale euthanasia, within either of the Houses of Parliament. But, we cannot believe that the Lords' Select Committee Report (1994) will be the last word on the subject. There is currently plenty of activity within the courts, sanctioning the death by dehydration of PVS patients, and within our hospitals, deciding against the vulnerable, whether they are elderly, or newborn. Furthermore, the state of affairs in the Netherlands can be seen only as a lever creating mounting pressure upon our legal, medical and political authorities to follow suit.

We are close to the Netherlands in so many ways, physically, culturally, socially, and so on. However, the Remmelink and the House of Lords Reports—one condoning euthanasia, the other restraining it—show how far we are apart ethically. But for how long? Five years, perhaps ten? The new Dutch euthanasia law came into operation on 1 January 2002. Before the ink was dry on that document, the Belgian Parliament was busy preparing to become the second country in the world to decriminalize euthanasia. Men and women, it is coming closer!

The Nazi Holocaust

The Nazi Holocaust is a shameful subject. It is probably the biggest blot on the history of twentieth-century medicine—its only rival could be the worldwide legalization and practice of abortion. The relevance of the Nazi Holocaust to twenty-first century euthanasia is two-fold. First, ethically, it marks the formal introduction of the concept that some people can be regarded as having 'lives not worthy to be lived'. Second, practically, it reveals the origins of a national policy of euthanasia, which was both doctor-driven and publicly-approved.

Everybody knows that the Holocaust happened, some know *how* it happened, but few know *why* it happened. Shelffuls of books have been written about it, but few accounts are as moving as Michael Burleigh's 1994 book, *Death and Deliverance: 'Euthanasia' in Germany 1900–1945*. As well as being a masterly piece of historical research, it manages to convey the sheer ordinariness of the people and events—this is what makes the book, and, needless to say, the Nazi reality, so chilling. Borrow the book, read it, and be moved.

11.1 The euthanasia plan developed

So *how* and *why* did the Holocaust develop? History can often be exceedingly complex, but by grasping just a few major threads, it is possible to weave together some of the events and motivating forces that eventually led to the Holocaust.

One of these threads emerged during the nineteenth century. Germany had, at that time, developed into the focal point of much of the world's most exciting medical research and practice, as exemplified by innovative specialisms, like neurology and biochemistry. But new-fangled disciplines can challenge old ethical assumptions, and there is a human tendency to cut loose and explore beyond traditional boundaries. One presupposition to be contested was the old Hippocratic oath's, 'do no patient any harm'. Nor was this challenge simply cerebral, it was also practical—some doctors, under the pretext of medical progress, began to get involved with hastening dying and causing the premature death of their patients, especially among the poor and vulnerable, the incurably ill and the mentally disabled. To be sure, some aspects of medicine were getting out of hand. Euthanasia was beginning to lose its wholesome Greek meaning. One man who foresaw the potential dangers of these activities and who predicted the ensuing slippery slope, was the German doctor, Christoph Hufeland. His far-sighted statement (*Journal der praktischen Ärzneykunde und Wundärzneykunst*, 1806, 23:15–16) has already been quoted (section 3.6), but it bears repetition, plus some extension, here, 'The doctor should and must not do anything other than preserve life. Whether it is happy or not, valuable or not, that is none of his business. If he once permits such a consideration to influence his actions the doctor will become the most dangerous person in the State. Once this line is crossed, and the doctor believes that he is entitled to decide upon the necessity of life, then it is only a matter of logical progression before he applies the criteria of worthy, and unworthy, in other situations.'

During the 1890s, with a blatant disregard of such forewarnings, the German polemicist, Adolf Jost, redefined the concept of euthanasia to include the two additional notions of 'the right to die' and 'human worthlessness'. The former phrase introduced the idea of a voluntary category of euthanasia. The latter phrase, since it was particularly directed at the mentally and incurably ill, launched the idea of an involuntary category of euthanasia. Then came Ernst Haeckel. He was the professor of zoology at the University of Jena, an enthusiastic exponent of Darwin's ideas, and a theologically-confused Monist. Perhaps then, it is not surprising that some of his ideas were crackpot, and they were not helped by his often-unsubstantiated speculations and his carelessness over factual details—there is no doubt that he was a shoddy scientist. Nevertheless, his thoughts and opinions captivated the German intelligentsia throughout the first half of the twentieth century. Haeckel was eager to espouse his approval of infanticide and his opinion that euthanasia was 'an act of mercy', which would, he claimed, be a cost-effective policy against the unproductive. These two men, together with several others, were the forefathers of the German euthanasia programme. They were the ideas' men.

Their ideas were picked up again in 1920, when another two Germans, Karl Binding, a retired expert in jurisprudence, and Alfred Hoche, a professor of psychiatry, published what was to become a most provocative pamphlet entitled, *The Sanctioning of the Destruction of Lives Not Worthy to be Lived (Die Freigabe der Vernichtung lebensunwerten Lebens. Ihr Mass und ihre Form)*. In it, after some considerable beating about the bush, they dared to pose this ominous question, 'Is there human life which has so far forfeited the character of something entitled to enjoy the protection of the law, that its prolongation represents a perpetual loss of value, both for its bearer and for society as a whole?' It was philosophical dynamite.

Binding and Hoche maintained that indeed there were people with 'lives not worthy to be lived' and they were to be found predominantly among three groups of people. First, there were the terminally ill and the mortally wounded, who were familiar sights throughout Germany after the Great War. These might voluntarily express a wish to die, to be euthanized. Second, there were the mentally healthy, who, through battle or accident, were now unconscious and therefore incompetent in terms of consenting to euthanasia. Third, there were the 'incurable idiots', especially those who resided in psychiatric hospitals. To these latter people, Binding and Hoche drew special attention, not only because of the emotional and financial burdens that they were putting on their families and communities, but also because the care of these so-called 'full idiots' was costing the German State huge sums of money each year. Binding and Hoche actually did the economic sums to prove their case. Alongside these ideas was some talk among medical professionals about throwing overboard the 'Ballastexistenzen', or 'dead ballast', from the 'ship of fools'. In reality, what was developing among the medical and academic elite was a deliberate denial that the weak and the vulnerable were real human beings. And if they were not human beings, then why should they not be treated according to the rules of the farmyard and the abattoir?

Thus, in post-Great War, pre-National Socialist Germany, some of the philosophical and ethical threads of the euthanasia movement were being interwoven. The fabric contained social threads too. There was, for example, the harsh aftermath of the First World War. Millions had died in the fighting, and for the survivors in Germany, economic hardship and hunger had begun to set in. These warps and wefts consisted of post-war depression among a defeated people, the realities of deprivation and suffering, a weakened Christian church that had largely forgotten its powerful Reformation roots, the decoupling of Christian doctrine and practice, the eugenic 'solutions' propagated by social Darwinian ideology, and the eagerness of psychiatrists to improve their social status and function. And there were the physically and mentally handicapped people, who had now become stigmatized as being both unproductive and costly. Of all of these factors, two were paramount. First, there was a person's racial fitness. This was a peculiarly German concept that historically had symbolized a person's acceptance by, and usefulness to, the State. Second, there were the prevailing financial privations. Eugenics and economics had met again. These threads were decisive in fabricating the unthinkable—a national policy of euthanasia.

A final thread, probably the last straw, came from the best-selling author, Ernst Mann, also known as Gerhard Hoffman. In one of his books, *Moral der Kraft*, he had previously called upon war veterans to perform one 'last heroic deed' and kill themselves in order to spare the German State the expense of their pensions. Evidently, Mann was not a man to dither, or mince his words. In 1922, he suggested to the Reichstag, that in addition to the advantages of 'mercy-killing' for the terminally ill, those who were mentally ill should also be exterminated, and that even children, who were crippled and incurably ill, should be killed too. He considered that a combined plan of eugenics and euthanasia would bring about a double benefit for Germany—it would be seen as an act of mercy, and it would be financially sound. In 1922, Mann's ideas were considered by the vast majority of the Reichstag's politicians and Germany's general public to be far too extreme, way beyond the pale. But wait—just a decade later, they had become official German policy!

11.2 The euthanasia plan implemented

The euthanasia programme was thus laid and hatched. It began to be implemented in July 1933, six months after Adolf Hitler came to power, when the Law for the Prevention of Hereditarily Diseased Progeny was published. This eugenic plan authorized the compulsory sterilization of those with congenital defects, schizophrenia, manic depression, epilepsy, severe alcoholism, and a variety of other conditions. Between 1934 and

1945, some 400,000 people, or about one per cent of the child-producing German population, were sterilized.

The slippery slope was all too evident. Hufeland was right—the doctor could become 'the most dangerous person in the State'. Six years later, in 1939, it became compulsory to report the births of all physically and mentally disabled children. Many parents agreed to send their special-needs children to asylums for what they thought would be specialized care. Once there, a committee of three would meet secretly and decide, usually without even seeing the child, who should live and who should die. The latter children were sent to special clinics and given overdoses of barbiturates, or, more cost-effectively, they were deliberately starved to death. Parents would then receive a letter explaining the cause, picked randomly from a standard list, of their child's sudden death—sometimes appendicitis was given as the reason, even though the child may have already have had his appendix removed!

So, first, there was compulsory eugenic sterilization of adults, then second, there was non-voluntary euthanasia for children. But there was worse to come. The child euthanasia plan was but the forerunner of the adult euthanasia programme. This systematic plan to exterminate all psychiatric patients throughout Germany was called, Aktion T-4. It began in 1940. Its code name was derived from its administrative head office at Tiergartenstrasse 4 in Berlin. Under its auspices, residents of State institutions could be euthanized if it was considered that they could not be 'rehabilitated for useful work'. Therefore the mentally disabled, psychotics, epileptics, the old and senile, those with infantile paralysis, Parkinson's disease, multiple sclerosis, brain tumours, even bed-wetters, and those with poorly-formed ears, were killed because they were considered to be 'useless' and a 'burden on society'.

This adult euthanasia plan was responsible, first of all, for the destruction of some 275,000 German, non-Jewish, institutionalized patients. They were human 'guinea pigs', killed in experimental gas chambers in the drive to perfect the methods and to train the technicians to be used for the later Jewish exterminations in concentration camps, the so-called Final Solution. That horror of mass involuntary euthanasia accounted for the destruction of some six million Jews.

11.3 After the Holocaust

After the Second World War, the Allies felt compelled to take steps to ensure that the Holocaust would never be repeated. One such measure was the Nuremberg doctors' trial of 1946 and 1947. The twenty-four doctors and public health officials, who were accused of being war criminals, were shown to have been willing collaborators with the Nazi regime. Indeed, half of all German academic biological scientists at that time were members of the Nazi party. These scientific personnel knew exactly what they were doing. Many of their experiments were conducted under the pretext of respectable health initiatives, such as, screening for tuberculosis, free gynaecological examinations, or anti-smoking campaigns. But behind such façades of human decency and medical progress, there lurked something unquestionably more deadly, the execution of this immense euthanasia programme. The Nuremberg trial ended after 149 days of hearings and the submission of 11,500 pages of transcripts. Seven of the accused were hanged, five received life sentences, four were given sentences of between ten and twenty years, and eight were acquitted. Most of those imprisoned were released within ten years. Few of the Holocaust survivors, or the victims' families, have ever been compensated.

11.4 The lessons to be learned

Here then is a bit of history with its own frightening momentum. It began with a little novel science, a few academic treatises, several political mavericks, some seemingly-outrageous ideas, a number of popular articles, various economic hardships and numerous emotional challenges. It ended up as the Nazi Holocaust. Its essential fabric had been woven and largely accepted by a society within a relatively short time-span—perhaps as little as twenty years.

But perhaps the most frightening aspect of this cheerless episode it this—it was not just the crazy Führer and a few of his more madcap henchmen, who devised and carried out these atrocities, but rather it was educated, professional men and women, who planned and implemented the whole thing. There was a clearly discernable pattern of personal involvement. Moral philosophers and politicians first raised some controversial issues. Then the medical and scientific professionals, especially some doctors and others, including psychiatrists, followed. Once medicine, its ethics and practice, had been corrupted, the law and its practitioners formulated the necessary legal provisions. Next, there was acceptance by the general public, and finally, the 'open door'. Can you discern the uncanny progression? We have witnessed similar patterns elsewhere, have we not?

Above all, it was the German medical profession that failed the ethical challenge—they had turned their backs on Hippocratic-Christian medicine. They had assumed that proper medicine and Nazi ideology were compatible. Driven by eugenics and economics, they had compounded such erroneous thinking into a programme of euthanasia. While upholding the apparently unassailable idea of Aryan purity, they considered that the mentally and the physically disabled, together with homosexuals, gypsies, Jews, and others were sub-standard, non-persons with 'lives not worthy to be lived'. Consequently, they considered them to be expendable, and that the implementation of such an enterprise would be for the social and economic good of the State.

So where were the German protesters? Where were those who cherished and protected all human life? There were some opponents, who spoke of Christian truth and charity, who argued against such gross utilitarianism, and who warned of the dangers of embarking down such a slippery slope. But they were relatively few in number, and generally ineffective in their opposition. The vast majority of doctors and nurses were apparently easily persuaded to work within these euthanasia programmes. Scientists became yes-men. Lawyers and judges acquiesced. Perhaps most appallingly, ministers of religion generally turned a blind eye, or even worse, actually colluded in these policies. In fact, about half of those killed in the first phases of the euthanasia programme actually came from asylums funded and administered by the German churches!

And think, all this happened just seventy years ago, about 700 kilometres away from Britain—trifles in time and space. Can you believe that? Here was a society that had forgotten its historic Christian roots—the land of Luther and the emergence of the Reformation, no less. A people, who had forgotten that they, and all others, bore the *imago Dei*. A medical profession, which had forgotten the Hippocratic oath and its basic tenet, 'do no patient any harm', as well as the Christian commandment of Matthew 22:39, 'Love your neighbour as yourself.' It started with a denial of the specialness and inviolability of all human life, and it ended with the acceptance of the slogan that people could have 'lives not worthy to be lived'. Once that Rubicon had been crossed, then all forms of human abuse began to be justified. This was an indisputably authentic slippery slope. Two generations on, nothing much has changed. The parallels are all too obvious. Today's international calls for the implementation of programmes of euthanasia are just as menacing.

Yet, understand this if you can. After all the film clips, newspaper reports, personal testimonies of the survivors and of the victims' families, the records of the liberating armies, the physical evidence of the gas chambers and the camps, some people, moreover, some highly-intelligent people, are still denying that the ghastly events of the Holocaust ever occurred. They are still trying to deny the incontestable horror of it all, they are still suppressing the truth. Despite all the evidence to the contrary, for some, it simply never happened. Matthew 15:14 is as true as ever, 'Leave them; they are blind guides. If a blind man leads a blind man, both will fall into a pit.'

For us, the Holocaust should be the wake-up call. It should shatter any remaining ideas we may have about the innate goodness of man, and the inevitability of human progress, kindness and decency. I shudder every time I read this chapter—few narratives can move me to tears so readily. As has been rightly said of the Holocaust, 'All who live after it must confront it.' The lessons of history are there to be learned. Many of the very same philosophical, ethical and social threads that were present in the 1930s, are still with us in the 2000s, still prowling around.

The case of Anthony Bland

Getting to grips with the issue of euthanasia certainly entails getting to grips with this historic case—in effect, it legalized non-voluntary euthanasia, euthanasia by omission, in Britain. Understand it, and you will begin to see where the debate on euthanasia, and more seriously, the practice of euthanasia, has come from, and where it is heading. The bioethicist, Peter Singer, certainly recognized the pivotal significance of the Bland case. In the Prologue (p. 1) to his *Rethinking Life and Death* (1995), he wrote, 'After ruling our thoughts and our decisions about life and death for nearly two thousand years, the traditional western ethic has collapsed. To mark the precise moment when the old ethic gave way, a future historian might choose 4 February 1993, when Britain's highest court ruled that the doctors attending a young man named Anthony Bland could lawfully act to end the life of their patient.'

12.1 The events

Anthony David Bland was seventeen years old when he became a victim of the disaster that took place during the FA Cup semi-final football match between Liverpool and Nottingham Forest at the Hillsborough stadium, Sheffield on 15 April 1989. In the crowd mayhem, which erupted during the first few minutes of the match, his chest was crushed, his breathing stopped, and his brain was deprived of oxygen.

When his breathing was restored his brain cortex, but not his brainstem, had been severely, and apparently irreversibly, damaged. He was taken to Airedale General Hospital, near Keighley, where he stayed for the rest of his life. His condition remained stable and he was diagnosed as being in a persistent, and later, a permanent, vegetative state (PVS). He was not dying. And, contrary to popular belief, and as erroneously, and repeatedly, reported in the media, he was *not* connected to any high-tech apparatus, such as a life-support machine—he was able to breathe on his own. He could respond to loud noises. But he required constant nursing care—he was turned every two hours—and he was fed through a nasogastric tube.

When infections occurred, and on two occasions they nearly claimed his life, they were treated with antibiotics.

In the summer of 1989, just four months after the accident, his doctor at the hospital, Dr Jim Howe, considered that feeding and antibiotic treatments should be discontinued. However, he was advised that such a course of action might lead to criminal prosecution, so he proceeded no further down that avenue, at least, not for several months.

12.2 The judgements

The next significant event occurred in 1992, when the Airedale NHS Trust applied, with the agreement of Anthony Bland's parents, to the Family Division of the High Court for two so-called 'declarations', in order that they might withdraw all medical and life-sustaining treatment, including nutrition and hydration by artificial means, from the soccer fan. On 19 November 1992, the High Court made these two declarations and ruled that Anthony Bland should be allowed to die. One of the judges, Sir Stephen Brown, president of the High Court's Family Division stated, 'His spirit has left him and all that remains is the shell of his body.'

The Official Solicitor, acting on behalf of Anthony Bland, then went to the Court of Appeal in order to overturn the decision of the High Court. The appeal was dismissed, but leave was given to appeal to the House of Lords. On 4 February 1993, the five Law Lords unanimously upheld the Court of Appeal's ruling and delivered their judgement, namely, 'That despite the inability of the defendant to consent thereto, the plaintiff and the responsible attending physicians may, a) ... lawfully discontinue all life-sustaining treatment and medical support measures designed to keep Anthony Bland alive in his existing persistent vegetative state including the termination of ventilation [even though, as noted above, it was not being used], nutrition and hydration by artificial means, and b) ... lawfully discontinue and thereafter need not furnish medical treatment to Anthony Bland except for the sole purpose of enabling Anthony Bland to end his life and die peacefully with the greatest dignity and the least pain, suffering and distress.'

The Law Lords thus declared that it would not be unlawful to withdraw treatment from Anthony Bland, so enabling him to die. They further stated that Anthony Bland's life could be prematurely ended because 'treatment was futile' and 'invasive', and such a course of action was in 'his best interests' since he was a 'living death' with 'no dignity'. Although their ruling was unanimous, the five Law Lords expressed considerable personal unease and declared that Parliament, rather than the courts, should be dealing with this sort of issue.

So on 22 February 1993, Dr Howe switched off the pump of the twenty-one-year-old's nasogastric tube, and nine days later, on Wednesday 3 March 1993, Anthony Bland became the ninety-sixth victim of the Hillsborough disaster. The investigating pathologist, Jan Lowe, reported that Anthony Bland had died of kidney failure and bronchial pneumonia. The coroner, Mr James Turnbull, recorded a verdict of accidental death as a direct result of injuries sustained as the patient was crushed in a crowd.

12.3 The reactions

For many, this ruling of the Law Lords caused anger and dismay. It was disturbing because it was not a case of rejecting meddlesome medicine, or withholding futile 'treatment' from someone about to die, but of causing premature death on the grounds that it was in 'his best interests'.

There is nothing new about withholding or withdrawing medical treatment. It is frequently exercised when it will be of no benefit to the dying patient. When properly implemented, it rightly counteracts the indignities of futile and meddlesome medicine. For example, it is a common, and ethically-sound, practice not to provide antibiotics for the terminally-ill old man who is in the terminal phase of dying, or for those newborns with fatal conditions that are indubitably incompatible with life, such as anencephaly. There is nothing ethically amiss with providing terminal patients with palliative care rather than burdening them with treatment that may be harmful and will certainly never be curative. But this ruling, in the case of Anthony Bland, was quite, quite different. The Law Lords considered that medical treatment was artificial feeding and hydration. This was their lamentable decision. But food and water do not fulfil the criteria of medical treatment—they are the provisions of basic care to which everybody is entitled, even those at the very outer edge of life. We all know what happens to those who are not given food and water— their outcomes are entirely predictable.

The established test for deciding what is an appropriate medical treatment for a patient is whether the benefits outweigh the burdens. Treatment should be withdrawn only when it is ineffective or disproportionately burdensome. So the decision should hinge on the value of the treatment itself, never the perceived value of the patient's life. Treatment is in a patient's best interests if, and only if, it saves his life, or improves, or prevents deterioration in his health. How then, could it be in 'his best interests' to be starved and dehydrated? Tube feeding, even if it were to be re-defined as a treatment, nourished Anthony Bland, it did not burden him. On the contrary, it undoubtedly benefited him—it had kept him alive for almost the last four years.

The Law Lords' re-defining of food and water as 'treatment' caused, and still causes, ethical uproar whenever the Bland case is discussed. Death by starvation and dehydration is a horrible, slow way to die—it is not being 'allowed to die', and it is certainly not 'death with dignity'. As Melanie Phillips (*The Guardian*, 5 February 1993) perceptively observed, 'If it [nutrition] is treatment, then what precisely is the ailment for which food is the remedy?' The guileless Christian response comes from Romans 12:20, 'If your enemy is hungry, feed him; if he is thirsty, give him something to drink.' Yet Anthony Bland was nobody's enemy. The fact was, the Law Lords were making arbitrary law, that is, unprincipled legal judgements on the hoof. As a consequence, our courts now permit us to starve to death British citizens while, for example, we are simultaneously trying to rescue the starving citizens of Third World countries. Welcome, yet again, to the topsy-turvy world of modern medical ethics.

And another question arises. What is the difference between withdrawing 'treatment' that keeps a patient alive, and taking positive action, such as administering a lethal injection with the intent of ending his life? The latter is still regarded as murder. Why is not the former? What is the difference between a slow, nine-day death and a lethal injection, which would kill the patient swiftly? Baroness Warnock in her book, *An Intelligent Person's Guide to Ethics*, considers this very question and concludes (p. 33), '... morally speaking it would usually be less cruel to give a lethal injection than to allow a patient to die of thirst and starvation ... as a general rule, I can see no ethical difference between deliberately killing and deliberately letting die, though the former may avoid the extra charge of cruelty.'

Dreadful cases of miscarriages of justice, such as Anthony Bland's, affect all of us. Indirectly, they cause us varying degrees of grief, doubt and anguish. They also affect some people much more directly, in particular, the healthcare team and the victim's family. Lord Mustill, one of the Law Lords, recognized this as he expressed profound disquiet and misgivings about almost every aspect of this case. For instance, he drew attention to the stress placed upon the nursing staff, especially during the period leading up to Anthony Bland's death. He knew it would be against all their human instincts and training—it was a betrayal of the Hippocratic and Judaeo-Christian undergirding of good medicine. Perhaps the most directly involved people were Anthony Bland's parents, Allan and Barbara. They had visited him every day, talked to him, held his hand, played his favourite music, tuned into soccer matches on his bedside television, and brought him football mementoes. Yet, they had supported the Airedale NHS Trust's application to stop feeding their son. Allan Bland commented, 'To me, euthanasia is direct injection and killing with a needle unlike our case. When Tony's tube was removed it was very, very dignified and peaceful.'

12.4 The ramifications

For lots of people, the case of Anthony Bland was straightforward. He had been in this PVS for over three years. He seemed to be incapable of seeing, or hearing, or talking, or swallowing. He lay there, day after day, month after month, like a heap of inert flesh. Surely, it could not be right to prolong this mere human existence. Surely, Anthony Bland has lost his dignity and this could best be restored only by allowing him to die. 'Let him go in a dignified way', they said.

But, if Anthony Bland's condition had stripped him of his dignity, how could allowing him to die, by starving him, somehow restore it? Human dignity is a complex matter. Dignity is intrinsic to human beings, regardless of their physical or mental conditions. Dignity and worth are the very attributes of all those who bear the *imago Dei*. It is alien to Scripture, and also to English law, to treat the human body as a mere vehicle for the human person—on the contrary, we are complex, integrated beings. Why then was the manifestly-living Anthony Bland judged no longer to have a human life? The apparent answer is because nothing was going on in his head. But that can be said of many others, none of whom we would seek to kill (yet). The entitlement not to be killed, like other basic entitlements, belongs to all human beings because of their inalienable dignity and immutable worth, not because of some distinctive value associated with activities of which they may, or may not, be capable. Here comes the ethical impasse. For there can be no agreement with the advocates of euthanasia, or with their wicked old contention that one may intentionally kill those judged to have 'lives not worthy to be lived'. The solitary Anthony Bland case may appear to be light years and a million miles away from 1930s Germany, but its mass euthanasia programme casts too long a shadow to allow us to get forget its origins, slogans and outcomes.

And what of the doctors' role in all this? A doctor's duty can be wide-ranging and onerous, but, as Hufeland reminded us way back in 1806, it can never be to decide who of his patients has a worthwhile life, and who is better off dead—if it were so, then euthanasia would already be lawful. A doctor may use the concept of 'quality of life' in assessing whether a given *treatment* is worthwhile, but it is never to be used to decide whether a *patient* is worthwhile. Once the concept of a worthless life has been established, then so too has euthanasia. Every innocent human being, however deprived and debilitated, should be allowed to enjoy the basic entitlement of not being intentionally killed. To make this entitlement dependent upon the enjoyment of a particular quality of life is to abandon justice in the care of patients for arbitrariness and convenience. The Anthony Bland case pushes us nearer to classifying all patients into one of two groups—those who are worthy of minimum care, such as basic nursing and feeding, and those who are not.

It is cases like that of Anthony Bland that are resetting the ethical boundaries at the edge of life. Most of us will never have any firsthand experience of them, but we will all be infected by them, from a distance. Little by little, the limits are being driven back. The British Medical Association was generally satisfied with this 1993 ruling of the Law Lords, though the Royal College of Nursing expressed some reservations. Medical staff can now withdraw treatment, including food and water, even though they know that, as a result, the patient will die prematurely. Each court case, sanctioning the death of another PVS or senile patient, is one more small step down Euthanasia Alley. Much of the legal and medical establishment is apparently already sauntering along it.

The case of Anthony Bland was a victory for the euthanasia lobby. It was a defeat for the practitioners of Hippocratic-Christian medicine. It was a salutary warning for the rest of us.

The case of John Pearson

The case of John Pearson has become the most famous example of infanticide, or neonatal euthanasia, to go through the UK courts in recent times. It was contentious two decades ago, and even today it is still contested in bioethical, medical and legal circles. But you do not have to be a moral philosopher, doctor, or lawyer to understand, and to be appalled, by this poignant story.

13.1 The events

Briefly, the events are these. At 7.55 am, on Saturday 28 June 1980, in Derby City Hospital, Molly Pearson gave birth to a son, John Pearson. He was found to have Down's syndrome and for that reason, he was resolutely rejected by his parents. His mother apparently said to her husband, 'I don't want it, Duck'. Consultant paediatrician, Dr Leonard Arthur, was called and at noon, four hours after the birth, he prescribed treatment for the child by writing on the hospital notes, 'Parents do not wish it to survive. Nursing care only.' This latter was to be a regime that included no food, but regular doses of an analgesic called, DF118, or dihydrocodeine.

Baby Pearson was put in a side ward and died three days later at 5.10 am, in the arms of Margaret Slater, a nurse, and herself the mother of a brain-damaged child. The police were called in to investigate the incident and, on 5 February 1981, Dr Arthur was charged with John Pearson's murder. The trial at Leicester Crown Court began on 13 October 1981, before Mr Justice Farquharson. After two days of legal submissions, in the absence of a jury, the charge was reduced from murder to attempted murder. The eighteen-day trial ended on 5 November 1981, with Dr Arthur being acquitted.

13.2 The judgements

Some aspects of the case are cause for grave concern. During the trial, fears and prejudices leaked out—for example, the late Mr George Carman QC for the defence, declared that Down's syndrome babies are 'a time-bomb' of infection and defects.

Moreover, the Judge's summing-up was particularly flawed, and at times, irrelevant and misleading. Mr Justice Farquharson attempted to distinguish between 'allowing to die' and 'causing to die'. He accepted that there was a 'spectrum of actions' ranging from complete non-treatment, what he called, 'allowing nature to take its course', through to direct killing. So where, the Judge wondered, were Dr Arthur's actions on this 'spectrum'? Were 'nursing care only' plus DF118, merely negative and intended to 'allow the child to die'? Was it a case of negative inaction, or non-treatment? Mr Justice Farquharson explained that some non-treatment, such as refusal to operate, would not constitute murder. This may be true, but it was irrelevant, because the law stated that refusal to feed a patient, that is, starving him to death, was murder.

Although John Pearson was given no food, Mr Justice Farquharson erroneously continued to assume that water and large doses of DF118 were 'feeds'. Furthermore, administration of DF118 was not 'negative inaction', or 'non-treatment', it was positive. The noted pathologist, Professor Usher, who performed the post-mortem examination on John Pearson's body, maintained that DF118 was the cause of death—John Pearson died from broncho-pneumonia and lung stasis due to poisoning by DF118.

Later, during the Court proceedings, it was revealed that John Pearson had had heart, lung and brain defects, and in essence it was these disclosures that caused the charge to be changed from murder to attempted murder. However, these medical conditions made John Pearson even more vulnerable to DF118, because its mode of action is to suppress lung and other functions. Down's children tend to be susceptible to respiratory infections anyway, therefore a drug that suppresses lung function is especially dangerous and inappropriate. In fact, the manufacturers of DF118 say that it is not recommended for children under four years of age, and that it should be taken *with* food. This was not 'allowing to die' or 'allowing nature to take its course', this was positive intervention to stop natural processes—the baby boy wanted to eat and breathe. The healthcare team denied him both.

If there was infection present, what John Pearson needed was antibiotics. Genuine non-treatment would have withheld these too. Instead, John Pearson was given only huge doses of an analgesic, which was finally given by tube at a concentration equal to twice that which would be sufficient to kill an adult.

The defence counsel made much of the medical staff's efforts to ensure that the child was comfortable and to relieve his distress and pain. But there was no evidence that John Pearson suffered any such thing. The child's major cause of discomfort was hunger, which could easily have been remedied—he did not need analgesics. The so-called 'nursing care only' regime was denying the child the very thing he needed, namely, milk.

Nevertheless, Mr Justice Farquharson proposed that this regime was a 'holding operation', that it was a reversible, non-final form of treatment and therefore could not be described even as attempted murder. But was the intention of the medical staff to reassess, and ever reverse, such treatment? No temperature charts, and only a limited medical history, were recorded. After the initial treatment prescription, Dr Arthur apparently did not see his patient again. So, was 'reversibility' ever likely? Had not the hospital, as well as the parents, 'rejected' John Pearson?

The fact that John Pearson's parents had 'rejected' him should have been irrelevant to his subsequent care. Such 'rejection' may have some weight in human emotions, but it can have none in law. It is also worth noting that the severity of Down's syndrome cannot be adequately assessed for several months, maybe up to two years, after birth. Nevertheless, the Judge misrepresented Down's syndrome. He played on the jury's emotions concerning 'the stigmata they bear', 'lolling tongues', and 'oriental appearance'. He concluded that such people were faced with 'the most appalling handicap'. Such descriptions were not only immaterial to the case—they were disgraceful comments, and offensive to sufferers of Down's syndrome, and to disabled people in general.

13.3 The reactions

Dr Leonard Arthur was, perhaps because of much of the medical confusion and legal misdirection, eventually acquitted. Nevertheless, the case did send shockwaves through the neonatal wards of our hospitals, and paediatricians began to practise a more defensive medicine. Charities, such as Mencap and the Down's Children's Association, urged more counselling for parents around the time of birth to help remove the idea that all such children are doomed to a mindless and unrewarding life. And the trial did give a much-needed insight into the normally closed world of neonatal medicine. Medical taboos need demythologizing. Since medicine affects every one of us, its ethics and practices should be open for all to see, and for all to discuss openly.

Above all, the Pearson case said something blunt about our attitude towards the disabled child—it said that some should die. It also confirmed that a doctor can stand by, and allow a child to die, as long as that child is disabled and unwanted by his parents. But alas, the case failed to establish any ethically-sound legal guidelines for the future treatment of severely-disabled children.

The trial also told us a good deal about the interaction of medicine, law and public policy decision-making. The case made new law, albeit it bad law. Criminal proceedings do not usually produce new law, but this one did. There are only two other landmark precedents in this area. One was R. v Bourne in 1939, in which the members of the jury were directed to acquit Dr Aleck Bourne if they found that he had performed an abortion on a fourteen-year-old girl 'in good faith' to save her from becoming 'a physical or mental wreck'. They did, and as a result, the law concerning abortion was significantly liberalized. The other case was R. v Bodkin Adams in 1957. If Dr Bodkin Adams had administered painkillers to a patient with the primary intention of relieving her pain then he should be acquitted of murder, even if the increased dose of medication contributed to her death. Thus, the law relating to euthanasia was altered and the principle of 'double effect' was introduced into English law, as explained in chapter 18.

The new law, as a result of R. v Arthur, was that it became not unlawful to treat a baby by providing sedation, but no food or drink. This was hedged about with two provisos—first, that the child should be 'irreversibly disabled', and second, that the child should be 'rejected by its parents'. The term 'irreversibly disabled' is not helpful. Most blind people are irreversibly so. Furthermore, what is 'irreversible' today, medical science may make 'reversible' tomorrow. Similarly, 'rejected by his parents' is a pejorative phrase. It does not mean that the child has been abandoned, totally, by everyone. A child rejected by his parents can certainly be accepted and loved by others—an 'unwanted child' is a misnomer, a solecism.

13.4 The finale

It seems that Leonard Arthur learned the least of all from the John Pearson case. In February 1981, eight months after John Pearson had died, Peter and Margaret Anderson consulted Dr Arthur about their six-week-old daughter, Elizabeth, who had fluid on the brain, a heart defect and was partially blind. They asked him to operate, but he said, 'No. She has such gross congenital abnormalities it would be better if we didn't operate. Don't you realize that she will be a vegetable? She is uneducable and will break up your marriage.' Her parents persisted, and Elizabeth was eventually treated and cared for elsewhere. Some years later, far from being uneducable, she was doing well at a nursery school, and her parents' marriage had not broken up. Dr Arthur had got it wrong, yet again.

On Christmas Day 1983, after a long illness following the discovery of a brain tumour, Dr Leonard Arthur died. He had endured one of the worst ordeals for any doctor—he had been charged with the murder of one of his patients. He was a slightly built and gentle-looking man. He had devoted much of his professional life to looking after disabled children and much of his private life was spent as a volunteer helping their cause. One of his obituary writers described him as, '... humane, tenacious and principled.' He died, aged fifty-seven, and he left a widow and six children.

Let the then President of the Royal College of Physicians, Sir Douglas Black have, almost, the final word on the John Pearson case. He testified at the trial, 'I say it is ethical that a child suffering from Down's syndrome and with a parental wish that it should not survive, it is ethical to terminate life, provided other considerations are taken into account, such as the status and ability of the parents to cope in a way that the child could otherwise have had a happy life.' Many within the medical profession would share Black's heartless views. Infanticide is, without a doubt, a savage crime. We have no idea how widespread it is—we will always underestimate its numbers. The fact that it occurs at all, and often in our best hospitals, says much about the declining state of medical ethics and practice in our land, and it also discloses something rather unpleasant about us too. John Pearson's death diminishes us all—we are less than satisfactory, less than protective, less than caring towards our most vulnerable children. Infanticide will always mock us.

PART 4
Some Secondary Issues

'When I use a word', Humpty Dumpty said in a rather scornful tone, 'it means just what I choose it to mean—neither more nor less.'

Lewis Carroll, (1872) *Through the Looking-Glass.*

There is a considerable posse of secondary edge-of-life words, concepts and issues that will be encountered whenever you read publications, hear presentations, watch the media, take part in debates, join in discussions and talk with your neighbours. Here, they are called secondary, not because they are necessarily of minor importance—at times, they can actually become the centre of attraction—but rather because they tend to be peripheral to, or appendices of, the primary edge-of-life issues.

More than a dozen of them are discussed in this Part. They range from the uncontroversial, like ageing, to the philosophical, like autonomy. Others are entirely medical, like double effect, or practical, like living wills, or contentious like, the slippery slope. This is far from an exhaustive list, but grasping the meaning of even these, and understanding how they are employed, will enable the reader to comprehend the primary issues more firmly, and to discuss them, and respond to them far more cogently.

Ageing, ageism and medicine

It may be a hackneyed saying, but, we are all getting older. This is a truism, with serious consequences, because as we get older, sure enough, our risk of dying increases inexorably. Benjamin Gompertz expressed this joyless principle mathematically in 1825. Like compound interest, he argued, adult mortality rates increase exponentially with age. What that boils down to is this—our probability of dying doubles for every extra eight years that we live. That little statistic may well confirm your lifelong aversion to mathematics!

14.1 Some problems of ageing

While it is unquestionably true that the elderly are getting even older, they are now becoming record-breakers in the process. A fifth of the UK population, representing about twelve million people, is currently over sixty years old, and by the year 2030, this will rise to nearly a third, or some nineteen million citizens. In fact, those over eighty years old are now the fastest-growing age group in the UK. Compared with their predecessors, these 'oldies' are now better educated, with greater disposable income, and far more vigorous in health. No wonder their potential social and financial clout is often referred to as 'pensioner power'.

All this longevity is a wonderful testimony to several advances in medicine, nutrition and general healthcare, but it also comes with a price tag—it is creating novel problems. Just four examples illustrate the point. First, many of these aged folks will, sooner or later, require long-term, residential care—how are we going to pay for it? Second, there is a huge, volunteer army of, largely female, carers, already looking after the elderly. If they were to receive a realistic wage for the work they do, it could cost the country as much as £8bn a year. Third, many of the support services for the aged are currently inadequate, inequitable and poorly co-ordinated—to improve these will require radical organizational and financial changes, and soon. Fourth, the growing numbers of 'unproductive' pensioners together with the declining numbers of paid workers are creating fresh economic dilemmas. For instance, State pensions for the former have to be paid for by contributions from the latter. Non-index linked State pensions, raising the age of retirement and encouraging private pension schemes are just some of the remedies that have been suggested to ameliorate these new-found predicaments.

Of course, the issue of euthanasia is not irrelevant here. With all these oldsters sucking up scarce financial resources, getting in the way at the garden centre, and filling up our hospital wards, it must have entered the minds of some (typically younger) people that euthanasia could be just the solution we need to overcome these problems of ageing. Now, where have we come across that sort of argument before?

14.2 Ageing statistically

Bear with a few more statistics. The world's population is greater than ever. It is currently growing at a record eighty million people per year—now it is about six billion and by 2050, it is estimated to reach ten billion. Only Europe is bucking this global trend—here the population is actually declining, and by 2050, its population will be the same as it was during the 1980s.

But the more pressing demographic issue, in the context of this book, is not population growth *per se*, but life expectancy. Remarkably, in 1900, this was only 49 years for British men, and just 45 for women. Currently in Europe and North America, the life expectancy figures are about 75 for a man and nearly 80 for a woman. By the year 2050, these will probably have risen to 87 for men and 92 for women. Or look at it from another angle. Of our forefathers born in the 1850s, only about sixteen per cent reached the age of 75, whereas of those people born today, about sixty-five per cent will achieve this grand old age. In 1951, there were only 300 centenarians in the UK, but by 2030, there will be about 34,000 of them (or perhaps us!). No wonder the Queen has given up sending out centenary birthday cards.

Above all, it is these changes in human longevity that have highlighted the issues of ageing, and turned them into pressing topics of medical, demographic and social debate, as well as a thorny challenge for policy-makers. This phenomenon of ageing populations is most pronounced in the developed world, generally meaning, the First World, or Western countries. By contrast, the countries of the developing world, or Third

World, are exhibiting the greatest growth in the numbers of their young people. Even so, in global terms, we are moving towards a situation where the elderly will outnumber children. As birth rates fall, and life expectancy increases, our societies will need to respond to these changes, otherwise children will be competing with the elderly for limited resources, including medical resources. We are not well prepared for this—while most Western countries may boast of adequate paediatric care, most have singularly inadequate geriatric facilities.

14.3 Ageing and medicine

What is ageing? It is the effect of the passage of time upon our bodies—we are all gradually wearing out. We tend to recognize it by silver hair and baldness, by physical weakness and slowness, and by mental impairment, but scientifically, what is it? There is no simple, unified answer to this question, yet it seems to be caused by an accumulation of damage to our DNA, mitochondria and other cellular structures. And, this damage is a function of our genes, environment and lifestyle. Yet, contrary to all the assurances of glossy advertisements, health gurus, and even mothers' gumption, there is nothing significant we can do to halt this damage and the ensuing process of ageing. Sorry, but it is true—all resistance is both vain, and in vain!

Though death is the inescapable end-point of ageing, diseases and disorders need not be a part of old age. Ageing, and the disabilities associated with old age, are not necessarily linked—healthy ageing is possible, indeed, it should be one of our goals. Proper medicine aims not so much to extend life, but rather to reduce the amount of time that people suffer from diseases and disorders. We have a duty to look after this body of ours, to keep it healthy, certainly not to abuse it—'Do you not know that your body is a temple of the Holy Spirit, who is in you ...?' (1 Corinthians 6:19).

The healthiest old people are those who are relatively rich, well-educated, non-smokers, and mentally and physically active—we may not be able to modify the first item on this list, but we can certainly have a serious bash at the latter four. Indeed, evangelical Christians might be expected to be among the healthiest people alive since most of us keep mentally alert, we read, listen to sermons, visit and talk to others, we do not abuse drugs, we know the value of bodily exercise, we lead a simple lifestyle, know contentment, and so on.

Our mental and physical, and of course, spiritual, health is important. Yet, health promotion and geriatric medicine can often be misunderstood subjects. For example, coronary artery disease is often thought to be a disease of middle-aged men, but it is actually more common among elderly women. Surprisingly, a Caucasian, post-menopausal woman is ten-times more likely to die of coronary artery disease than of breast cancer, or hip fracture. Watch it, mother! Anti-smoking campaigns are often aimed at the young, but the number of elderly smokers is increasing in many societies. And smoking remains the leading cause of chronic illness and premature death among the elderly. About half of those who smoke will be killed by the habit. So give it up, granddad! We should also take seriously the three current mainstays of nutritional advice—eat less fat, less salt, and more fibre. Anti-oxidants, such as selenium, flavinoids and vitamin C, may protect against some age-related disorders, therefore eat more fruit and vegetables. The recommended intake is five portions of them each day, so eat more broccoli and tomatoes—yum, yum! Physical exercise is good for us. Most of us do too little—leave that car behind and use those legs and get that heart pumping more each day. Do not buy a dog, take your spouse out, and walk and talk. There is so much we can do to help ourselves by way of sensible, preventative medicine. In effect, many of these measures are seeking to minimize the accumulating biochemical damage of ageing by enhancing our natural repair systems. Of course, eventually most of us will succumb to diseases and disorders, some temporary, some permanent, but, while we are able, we should make earnest efforts to stay fit and healthy and keep away from the doctor's surgery as much as possible—it is a strategy that will do you good.

Of course, the link between ageing and health will be broken at death. Mortality used to be dominated by acute infectious diseases, such as tuberculosis or typhoid, but today these claim less than one per cent of people. Nowadays, chronic degenerative diseases are the major causes of death in the West. These include circulatory diseases, such as heart attacks, which account for forty-four per cent of deaths, and neoplasms, such as cancer and tumours, which make up a further twenty-six per cent. This shift in the pattern of mortality is known as 'epidemiological transition'—smart name for a grim topic.

14.4 Ageism and medicine

Ageism is not the same as ageing. Ageism is that stereotypical view of old people, and sometimes the very young too, which is negative and therefore, in terms of medicine, leads to policies and treatment decisions that disadvantage them. Alas, ageism has become a structural part of our society's thinking and practice. It is even found in various forms within the National Health Service (NHS). For example, it is current NHS policy in the UK to exclude women over sixty-five years of age from breast cancer screening, despite the fact that they have the highest incidence of the disease. Though they can be screened on request, few women are aware of their rising risk of breast cancer with age, so less than two per cent of this segment of the population attend for screening. Likewise, though large numbers of elderly patients admitted to hospital have experienced adverse drug reactions, the elderly are often excluded from clinical trials of new medicines and it is often difficult to extrapolate from young to old patients. Elderly people also often miss out on other medical benefits like, chiropody and influenza vaccinations. Those over sixty-five years of age currently account for about fourteen per cent of the population throughout all the developed countries. Yet, they consume about thirty per cent of all medicinal drugs. In other words, they are already a disproportionately ill and costly sector of the population. There is some evidence that such elderly people may be patronized, neglected, ignored, or badly treated by healthcare personnel. So, if we are going to eradicate the discrimination of ageism, changes in attitude, organization and behaviour are required, by the medical profession, as well as by the general public, meaning, you and me, too. Otherwise, euthanasia will again begin to raise its ugly head and seek to gain yet another toehold.

14.5 Ageing and caring

One in three British households is currently headed by someone aged sixty or over. Sixteen per cent of pensioners live alone. Much of the responsibility for the long-term care of these elderly people falls on the immediate family, and particularly the women—wives, daughters and daughters-in-law. But these women are increasingly joining the workforce, and that, together with the restructuring of families, such as, in the aftermath of divorce, means that the numbers of women available to care in this way are decreasing. In addition, at least in the UK, a large proportion of long-term care, which was previously provided by the NHS, is now being provided by the private sector. This care is expensive and must be paid for by the elderly, their families, or all of us as taxpayers. That notwithstanding, there is currently concern that this private sector care is in economic trouble, and may even be beginning to collapse. Certainly, during the last few years, privately-run care homes have been closing in unprecedented numbers.

In conclusion, a word to the elderly, but healthy—there is another facet to ageing and caring. More and more hale and hearty people are retiring earlier, through either choice, or redundancy. The post-war baby-boomers are starting to give up on paid work. This is creating a massive pool of human resource, the self-styled Third Agers. Charities, agencies and society as a whole, could benefit by using some of these men and women to transfer skills, values and experience to a younger generation in both the workplace and in the community. Such schemes might also help close the generation gap—somewhat like the benefits of the extended family. What a waste of assets if we consign the able and willing elderly to non-participation in our national life. Christians should always be thinking about making a difference, and not necessarily just around the corner, but also perhaps around the world. Agencies for short-term service with overseas churches and missions exist—they would be delighted to hear from you.

Ageing is an old problem. Whatever the successes or failures of past generations, we know that we must face its impending, and significantly increasing, challenges. There are responsibilities to embrace that are both individual and societal. The aged must never be discounted. Ageism must be stamped out. The healthy aged must live life to the full. Overall, we must learn how to provide high-quality opportunities and care for our ageing population in ways that are ethically robust, socially sound and economically acceptable. Euthanasia must never become even a considered option. In short, we must be concerned about upholding and improving the quality of life for all, but especially for those at the edge of life—so read on.

Quality of life

Like so much of the vocabulary of modern bioethics, 'quality of life' has a double meaning. It can be like a poisoned apple. It can look so appealing, so eminently sensible—'My quality of life is important. I want to enjoy my life to the full, and not be a lumber to myself or others'— yet it also can taste of death and be rotten to the very pips. On the one hand, a proper quality of life assessment can, and should, lead to the provision of more appropriate and better healthcare for the patient. On the other hand, the great fear is that a 'pass mark' will be set and those who fail to reach it will be condemned, or at least, prescribed sub-standard treatment. This fear, of course, is not without real substance, or historical precedent, as much of this book demonstrates. Quality of life assessments can have dangerous eugenic overtones, and they have long been the starting point for much of the practice of abortion, infanticide and euthanasia.

15.1 Measuring quality of life

It is now generally recognized that physical factors alone, like, the degree of immobility, or the size of a cancer, cannot be used to assess illnesses adequately. Such disorders also consist of psychosocial factors, like pain, anxiety, family responsibilities, financial burdens, and so on. But how can these be measured, especially at the edge of life, particularly, in say, the disabled and the elderly?

Despite the fact that 'quality of life' need not be a malevolent concept, even its benevolent aspects can be awkward to assess quantitatively. Moreover, they are constantly changing. What measurements can be used to assess them on a scale of say, zero to ten? Despite these huge potential problems, the so-called 'Calman gap' has provided a useful rule of thumb. This evaluates a person's hopes and aspirations against his reality—the gap between the two is the patient's 'quality of life deficit'. Good medicine aims to minimize this gap.

To begin to measure a person's quality of life, two kinds are information are required, namely, functioning and well-being. The first involves an assessment of physical performance, which is primarily an objective measurement, such as, 'Can you climb the stairs in your house?' The answer must be either a clear-cut, 'Yes', or 'No'. The second involves a subjective measurement, such as, 'Do you still enjoy reading novels?' The answer here is going to be much more wide-ranging, perhaps depending on the day, the book, the patient's mood, and so forth. What is more, when the results of such questionnaires are completed they must be compared against some predetermined, predefined standard, or norm. This can also be problematic because these types of subjective appraisals can depend too much upon psychological factors that are often unrelated to general health. Our everyday experience acknowledges the existence of such anomalies. For example, sometimes I like people around me, sometimes I do not. If it is my birthday, come on in—if I am revising a manuscript, stay away! One day, I can appear to be gregarious, the next day, an anti-social loner. Yet, on both days, though my self-assessed quality of life can be equally high, it might appear otherwise to an unfamiliar outside observer. Furthermore, in a society as hedonistic as ours, quality of life is often judged to be peculiarly high for the physically fit and intellectually capable, yet these are sometimes the most miserable of all people. On the other hand, the disabled and the senile can be among the most contented of all.

15.2 Life is more than quality

At the heart of quality of life assessments is the notion that truly objective norms and standards exist. Many of these are set by 'the big, the bright and the beautiful' and thus they commonly reflect the aspirations of an elite, or to put it more bluntly, a group of predominately youngish, secular humanistic men and women. They have forgotten, or tend to blur the truth that all men, women and children are made in the image of God and therefore have their own inherent dignity, identity and purpose. In other words, we are all different. Despite the manifest truth of such a statement, modern-day administrative structures want to pigeon-hole us. Our world has this penchant for dull uniformity, or at least, conformity—if you do not fit the pattern, then there must be something wrong with you, therefore you are a problem. This idea, from the heart of sociological psychobabble, has penetrated medicine too. So much so, that quality of life assessments can now prompt the question among healthcare professionals, 'Do we aim to uphold life, or uphold the quality of life?' Then the next dread question becomes, 'Does this person have a life worthy, or not worthy, to be lived?' Now, where have we heard this before?

Let us go futuristic. Could it be that, in the not-too-distant future, a family will appear before a quality-of-life court with a senile, confused, incontinent old woman, who, not incidentally, is also a mother, wife and grandmother, to argue for her to be 'put out of her misery' because she has been assessed to have a low 'quality of life'? Perhaps a doctor and a nurse will support the family's case. Would it be dismissed? What about in five years time? Ten years time?

'Quality of life' can be a decent and useful concept, but it must never be used to denigrate human life, or justify terminating it. Instead, quality of life assessments are to ensure that the patient is receiving all the required principled compassion. The patient's quality of life can be improved by the correct use of science, by care, by hope, by being a bridge to others and by the adherence to proper ethics. This is not just good medicine, it is good, wholesome living—an enterprise in which we should all want to be full participants.

Autonomy, freedom, rights and choice

This quartet is central to much of the ethical thinking, speaking and action of present-day men and women. Challenge them to justify a bioethical decision, and a modern man will answer gruffly, 'That's my business—I do what I want because I'm autonomous.' Or a woman will stridently assert that, 'I did it because it's my right, my freedom, my choice.' Sound familiar? At times, such talk, spiked with these vexing words, can be enough to scare us into silence and withdrawal. For Christians, this foursome can be nothing other than daunting, in fact, they are a real nuisance.

16.1 Autonomy and freedom

Autonomy (from the Greek, *autos*, self and *nomos*, law) means 'self-government' or 'personal freedom'. However, like several other bioethical words with respectable origins, autonomy has now taken on a more ominous meaning. Autonomy has become a key feature of secular humanism. It came to the fore of bioethics during the 1970s when medicine began to focus on the patient as a person, rather than just a case of illness. Now you cannot escape it. It is, for example, the predominant theme that runs through the 2000 Human Rights Act, as well as all the edge-of-life issues. Autonomy elevates the individual above all others, and it puts self, rather than God, at the centre of everything. Think of all those ugly, unChristian, self-type words like, self-centred, self-righteous and self-sufficient, and you will begin to unpack the meaning of misapplied autonomy.

It is certainly a two-edged word. In one sense, it can be helpful because it denotes the moral responsibility that each of us should exercise. For example, 'patient autonomy' means that I no longer kowtow to my doctor, but rather I question him about the course of treatment that he is proposing for me. I am not merely a set of doctor's notes, or a drug company's test subject—I am a human being with worth and dignity, who ought to be treated as such. Therefore, I ask questions of my doctor, we talk, then I decide. True, he is the doctor, the technical expert, but I am the patient, the sick subject. This sort of exercise of my personal autonomy is proper and beneficial to all concerned—it is reminiscent of that good old Hippocratic doctor-patient relationship, as opposed to that awful paternalism, so characteristic of much of the last century's practice of medicine.

Mull over this theme in the context of euthanasia. It may be that most doctors would consider pursuing a policy of euthanasia only if the patient or relatives gave their consent. But in practice, are there not other subtle pressures at work here? Patients, and their families too, often regard doctors as unchallengeable experts and can find it difficult to question, discuss, or politely argue with them. Edge-of-life circumstances are typically fraught and it can be relatively easy for healthcare professionals to coerce patients and relatives to agree with their point of view. They would be resolute people (including you, I hope), who were sufficiently sure of themselves and the importance of the issues involved, who would question the 'expert' opinion. For that reason, a good dose of personal autonomy—speaking up for yourself, or on behalf of others—would go a long way to minimizing the threat of euthanasia, which could come about simply by unspoken complicity.

In its other sense, autonomy can be wholly unhelpful. Nowadays, it is generally used to express the idea that we have the right to do whatever we want with our own lives, as if there were no limits to our individual freedom. This entails setting our own rules and our own standards for morality and behaviour. No longer is there any absolute, given truth. This is post-modernism and moral relativism, *con brio*. All is now considered to be relative and I am free to 'make' my own 'truth'. For the Christian, this is baloney, for at least three reasons. First, the Christian holds that the Scriptures are propositional truth, given absolutes and unqualified precepts, by which all men and women must live (2 Timothy 3:16). Second, the biblical propositions that you were created 'in the image of God' (Genesis 1:27), and 'You are not your own' (1 Corinthians 6:19) are the very antithesis of modern autonomous thinking. Again, these propositions apply to all human beings, whether they are God's by creation alone, or by creation plus redemption. Third, the Christian knows that all people are not free, but rather that they are in bondage—they are 'slaves to sin' (Romans 6:20). Even '... the glorious freedom of the children of God' (Romans 8:21) is a qualified freedom—it is not absolute because, '... now that you have been set free from sin and [you] have become slaves to God ...' (Romans 6:22).

Therefore, this expression of autonomy, meaning that we are 'free to do whatever we want', makes no sense for the Christian, and is utter nonsense for non-Christians too because none of them is entirely free—absolute freedom is a wild delusion. Besides, we all live within boundaries, as conformists—as members of society we all accept certain confines which limit our freedom—we keep off the grass, we do not 'borrow' food from Safeways, and we do not mug old ladies.

Nevertheless, the notions of unfettered autonomy and freedom have become the philosophical bases of the majority of pro-euthanasia campaigners. Indeed, they have become the principal justifications for their demand for the legalization of euthanasia. They insist that patients must be free to decide autonomously how and when they should die. They major on the erroneous beliefs that total self-government is an unqualified good, that self, and self alone, is all that counts, and that 'being in control' is the ultimate goal. These, they believe, are the trademarks of genuine freedom—they are completely wrong.

Of course, misapplied autonomy and the myth of freedom are the source of self-centred responses like, 'It's my body, it's my life, and it's my decision' and, 'I will choose when and how I die.' The outcomes of such excesses can be disastrous. They allow the individual to take centre stage, to be the attention-seeker, the spoilt brat. So, for example, it excludes others from what would best be family-based, or even society-centred, ethical decisions. It repudiates historic ethical systems, it ignores wise counsel, and it sidelines friends and family from crucial edge-of-life experiences and judgments.

In small doses, autonomy can sometimes be beneficial, but it can be injurious when overdosed. Self-interest, self-delusion and self-indulgence are just some of its ugly fruits. It can also be used to justify intolerable behaviour towards others, 'Because I am free, I am free to exploit you'. Of course, it can also be used to counter such bad behaviour, 'Since I too am free, you must not exploit me.' Ultimately, it brings about a clash of self-interests, a battle of wills. Therefore, claims for personal autonomy and its associated supposed freedoms always need to be very carefully examined.

16.2 Rights and choice

Human rights and choice are also part and parcel of the secular humanistic baggage. There is a modern obsession with 'rights', and a corresponding neglect of 'duties' and 'responsibilities'. The doctrinaire autonomist loves the first, and hates the others. That is why many Christians have real difficulties with rights. Rights talk comes from a Western, liberal, individualistic tradition rather than the orthodox Christian ethical framework. Their origin was an attempt, during the eighteenth-century Enlightenment, to create a secular hybrid of Judaeo-Christian thought and action, yet without the indispensable Christ-centered life as the driving force—it was a concept about as useful as the proverbial chocolate teapot.

Whenever we place self at the centre of our moral universe, we get confused and we begin, for instance, to label our 'desires' as our 'rights'. 'What I might like', readily slides into, 'what I must have'. Therefore talk of rights muddles us and frequently conceals what is actually being claimed, namely, duties *from* others. There are no true rights without responsibilities. If we want to exercise our 'right to die', we immediately lumber someone else with the responsibility of doing it. In addition, even in the case of suicide, our own irresponsibility is further emphasized by our discounting the effects that such actions will have upon the doctors and nurses caring for us, as well as upon our family and friends.

If we are going to formulate arguments and policies on the basis of human rights, then we will have to clarify their origins—do they come from nature, society, or our innate humanness? What are their limits—do we have a right to euthanize all terminally-ill, senile and disabled men and women? Is there a pecking order of rights—does the right to consent supersede the right to treatment? How can conflicts between different rights, such as, the rights of the senile patient and the rights of her relatives, be resolved—do they go to law, medicine, the church, or their horoscopes?

The notion of choice is closely allied to the other three. It comes full-throttle from the abortion issue. It was a stroke of misguided genius, in the 1960s, that plucked this word out of the dictionary and used it to transform the world's thinking about killing off its unborn offspring. 'A woman's right to choose' became the mantra of a medical revolution during the last century. Could 'a man's right to choose' do the same for euthanasia this century?

Good choice, bad choice—men and women really do have choice, genuine choice. This is not an illusion because we are not pre-programmed machines. Think of the authentic choice that Adam and Eve were given in the Garden. Perilously, our choices reveal our characters. Whenever we choose we expose our presuppositions, desires and beliefs. A good choice is made as a result of understanding a particular issue, the options and the consequences. That is part of the motivation behind this book. There could be no better framing of this view than in Deuteronomy 30:19–20, 'This day I call heaven and earth as witnesses against you that I have set before you life and death, blessings and curses. Now *choose* life, so that you and your children may live and that you may love the Lord your God, listen to his voice, and hold fast to him.'

To limit or deny other people their autonomy, freedom, rights and choice, especially over their own destiny and ultimately their death, may appear, at least initially, to treat them as incompetents, as less than human beings, as those without worth and dignity. It might appear that we are seeking to make them subordinate to our purposes, that, somehow, we know what is best for other people. Fascinatingly, we think that way, precisely because we have been brought up, and are caught up, with this quartet's way of thinking. Autonomy, and its three ugly half-sisters, are indeed powerful forces—they have beguiled most of us. The Christian needs to be wary of them and extremely cautious when they are raised as arguments in favour of practices, like suicide, infanticide and euthanasia. The Christian, far from wanting to control or deceive others, seeks to warn, forbear and care for them. Is that somehow wrong?

Herein lies the core problem of those dreadful edge-of-life issues and practices. The secular humanist sees his life primarily as of value to himself, 'It's my life, and I do what I want with it.' The post-modern secular humanist may go even further and say, 'I'm not interested in anyone else, the only reality is me and what is mine.' The Christian worldview is so very, very different—it is poles apart in its foundations and its outcomes. It is our duty and privilege to challenge the non-Christian, to show him the errors of his presuppositions, and to assure him that the acceptance and exercise of the Christian position would be better, far better, for him, and for society too. It is at this point that the Christian must begin to articulate his all-inclusive worldview with its more-than-sufficient answers.

A person's best interests

This has become another of the slogans of the euthanasia movement. Perhaps most famously, it was heard during the case of Anthony Bland. The Law Lords decided that his life could be prematurely ended because death was in 'his best interests'. But how can it be in anyone's best interests to be starved and dehydrated to death? Yet, these four little words are repeatedly being used in our High Courts, and elsewhere, whenever judgements are made to allow the withdrawal of artificial nutrition and hydration from PVS patients, the senile and others.

17.1 The true meaning

This little preamble is becoming repetitive, but necessary. Like much of modern bioethical language, this phrase, 'a person's best interests', has two faces. If we are aware of only one, then we will have a lop-sided view of the world of bioethics. It is, of course, entirely possible and proper to act in a person's best interests. For example, I could supply you with some information, like, 'You have a bald tyre and your car is therefore dangerous to drive', or I could give you a gift of £500. Consequently, you would be better informed, or wealthier—either, or both actions, would be 'in your best interests'. You would, at least, in general terms, be happier.

17.2 The false meaning

But would you be happier to be dead? Now, there's a question! Happiness has become the catch-all criterion for assessing what is in a person's best interests. To answer this question honestly, I would need to know, first, how much happiness you are currently enjoying, and second, what is going to happen to you after death. The first is impossible to know exactly, especially if you are very young, or unconscious, or senile, or in some other way, incompetent. The second is also tricky, if not impossible, to know, especially where there is uncertainty about life after death, as there consistently seems to be among proponents of euthanasia. Combine these two unknowns and it becomes clear that it is entirely out of the question to know if it is in someone's best interest to be put to death. And to claim to know, is to claim to know the unknowable.

Consider it from another direction. You are ill and your doctor advises that this treatment, or that surgical procedure, is in your best interests. That advice is, you trust, based on past experience, which has shown that his patients have benefited from such medical interventions. You could even check out his patients' recovery and survival records. This gathered evidence demonstrates whether such treatment would benefit you, the patient. But there is no corpus of information, no empirical evidence to support the claim that a patient's deliberately-procured, premature death will benefit the patient.

The truth is that these types of argument are not centred on the best interests of the *patient*, but rather the best interests of *others*. What the euthanasia lobby actually wants is permission to kill someone who has become a burden to others—maybe it is to the system, medical facilities, social services, the State, healthcare professionals, family or carers.

The proper response to these bogus pro-euthanasia claims is to seek genuinely to act in a person's best interests. What the patient needs is principled compassion in the form of good medicine, palliative care, financial resources, emotional warmth and spiritual comfort. It will *not* include killing the patient to alleviate *our* psychological, physical or financial burdens, or to fool ourselves that we are acting in the patient's 'best interests'.

Chapter 18

The principle of double effect

Christians, and the morally sensitive, all agree that it is utterly wrong 'to kill intentionally an innocent human being'. This statement is derived from four constructs. First there is the unambiguous meaning of the verb. Second, at least for the Christian, there is the value and worth of the 'human being', as made in the image of God. Third, there is the word 'innocent', which, in this context, means 'without harm', since the victim has committed no crime. The fourth construct is the word 'intentionally'. This distinguishes between deaths caused by accidents, which are unintentional and often impersonal, and those caused by the deliberate intentions and personal actions of others, as is the case in abortion, infanticide and euthanasia.

18.1 The use of double effect

This concept of intention is a formidable one in bioethics, and especially with respect to euthanasia, as discussed in section 5.5. It frames the question, to what extent can we be held responsible for our actions? Or, more precisely, and in the context of this book, what are we and doctors trying to achieve by a particular action, or course of actions? Most of the time, our intentions are only too plain. But there are genuinely difficult cases. The classic illustration is that of the pilot who drops bombs on the enemy's weapons factory. His intention is to wipe it out and shorten the war, but he also knows that several bombs will probably miss their target and kill civilians. Their deaths are not his intention, but he knows that they are a likely side effect of his action. They are a foreseen, but unintended, part of his duty. The knotty question is this, is the pilot responsible for the civilian deaths?

Roman Catholic moral theology, which has a longer history and is generally more developed than anything modern evangelical Christians have so far achieved, has handled this dilemma by introducing a device called, the doctrine, or principle, of double effect. Basically, this is used to justify the occurrence of any bad side effects, which may be foreseen, that may result from what is essentially a good action, with the aim of beneficial effects. Hence, 'double effect' refers to both the intended good effect, plus the unintended bad side effect. Another example, more appropriate to this book, is when a doctor prescribes larger and larger doses of an analgesic in order to control the increasing pain of a terminally-ill patient. The doctor knows that the drug has side effects that may shorten the patient's life, but it is the doctor's intention to control the pain rather than hasten, let alone cause, the patient's death. The latter would be the unintended consequence of the drug's dosage. The doctor, with the painkillers in his hand, can therefore perform the same action, that is, increasing the dosage, with two quite different intentions—one would be to help the patient, the other would be to kill the patient.

There are four generally-recognized criteria for the correct implementation of this principle. First, the action, taking the case cited above, the prescribing of analgesics, must be morally good. The principle does not apply if the action is wrong or forbidden, such as, injecting the patient with a heart-stopping drug. Second, the intention, which in this example is the well-being and comfort of the patient, must not be wrong. So it would not apply if the aim were merely to stop the patient from bothering the nursing staff. Third, the good effect, pain relief, and the bad side effect, possible shortening of life, must be coincident. That is, death must not occur before pain relief. Fourth, the good effect must outweigh the bad side effect, that is, it is forbidden to do harm in the hope that some good may come of it.

Double effect theory was introduced into English law as a result of the case of R v Bodkin Adams in 1957. In his summing-up of this ground-breaking case, Judge Devlin presented it like this, '… the proper medical treatment that is administered and that has an incidental effect on determining the exact moment of death is not the cause of death in any sensible use of the term.'

18.2 The misuse of double effect

The propriety of the principle of double effect has been challenged on two main fronts. First, can there be a distinction between the intended act, the good effect, and the foreseen act, the side effect? That is, can a person who foresees the side effect, not intend that side effect, by committing the act?

When the doctor gives the particular painkiller, he knows that it will reduce the pain and perhaps shorten the life, but can his intentions be separated? Second, can the doctor not be responsible for the side effect, which he foresees, but does not intend?

Mary Warnock in her book, *An Intelligent Person's Guide to Ethics*, includes (p. 27) an example similar to the one above—a doctor increases the dosage of morphine until the patient dies. In the same context, she then quotes a real-life doctor who wrote, 'We doctors are practising euthanasia all the time.' She continues, 'The way such doctors let themselves off the hook when challenged is through the argument from double effect ...' Baroness Warnock says the principle of double effect, '... makes me uneasy ... there seems something artificial and indeed Jesuitical about the argument itself and the distinction on which it hinges.' She goes on (p. 29), '... it seems not only absurdly pedantic but morally reprehensible to attempt to separate the intention from the foreseen consequence of the act.' She regards it (p. 30) as, '... a very dubious and shifty argument ...', but nevertheless she is, '... thankful that it has become more and more generally recognised.' The World Health Organization in its 1990 Report agrees—it has no ethical problems with double effect. Nor have two other very different bodies of authority, the Vatican's Declaration on Euthanasia (1980) and the ethical guidelines of the British Medical Association (1998)—both approve of the principle and its use. By contrast, the Voluntary Euthanasia Society considers it to be full of hypocrisy and calls it, 'society's wink to euthanasia'.

18.3 Some additional thoughts

Consider two counter-arguments to the Baroness Warnock-type doubts. First, some doctors would claim that they cannot foresee the consequences of a particular action, in the sense that they do not know how a particular patient will react to a particular dosage of a particular drug. The practice of medicine can legitimately be regarded as always somewhat experimental. Second, if the side effect is foreseen, then surely it must be intended? This is not necessarily the case. There are many examples from everyday life to illustrate this distinction. When I drive my car, I know that such an action is wearing it out, but that is not my intention, otherwise I would encourage it by adding some grit to the engine oil. Similarly, sitting and working for long hours at a computer gives me eye strain, but that is not my intention in writing this book.

Perhaps this all sounds too much like armchair casuistry. Back in the real world, on the hospital ward, the doctor is devising a course of action with regard to treating one of his patients. For this particular patient, who is terminally ill, in serious pain, and soon to die, the doctor has decided that the priority is that the patient should be made comfortable in dying and made ready to face death. Therefore he, together with the patient, has decided to give pain relief rather than undertake an officious striving to give a possible few more hours or days of life. That is both the doctor's strategy and intention. The doctor's primary intention is to relieve pain, not shorten the life of the patient. The doctor does not intend to cause the side effects. That seems to be consistent with the practice of good medicine. And the principle of double effect concurs.

The principle of double effect has no clear support from the Bible and at times its application can be complex, as indeed can be the situations to which it is applied. On the other hand, it does introduce a moral dimension to what can otherwise be somewhat ethically-sterile discussions about medical decision-making. It underlines the importance, not just of the action, but also of the intention behind the action—and that must be a welcome additional feature to the practice of medicine at the edge of life. In that respect, the principle of double effect certainly stands opposed to the utilitarian idea whereby an action is judged solely by its outcome—that is the alarming pragmatism of the 'means to an end' mentality. That undoubtedly *is* bad medicine.

Ordinary and extraordinary means

When is treatment ordinary? When it sustains life in a beneficial way. When is treatment extraordinary? When it merely postpones or prolongs the act of dying. Herein lie some complicated areas of medical practice. But that does not obviate us from seeking to understand them—occasionally we may even have to confront them in the hospital, or the home.

19.1 Ordinary means

Ordinary means are considered to be those treatments which offer a reasonable hope of benefit to the patient and do not entail great expense, pain, or other inconveniences. It is reasonable to expect a person to consent to these means. All of us have benefited from ordinary means, such as, courses of antibiotics, or analgesics, prescribed by our general practitioner. Many of us have similarly survived and prospered as a result of ordinary means of treatment in hospitals—minor surgical procedures, intravenous drips, broken bone repairs, and so on.

19.2 Extraordinary means

On the other hand, a person may not necessarily be expected to submit himself to extraordinary means, which may be treatments that are too expensive, too painful, or those with uncertain outcomes. An example of the latter would be an eighty-year-old man with terminal lung cancer—he has a sudden heart attack, but he refuses to submit to a heart by-pass operation. That is right and proper—for this patient, such extraordinary means of treatment would be correctly classed as futile, burdensome, or meddlesome medicine. Extraordinary means are typically treatments, which, when used properly, enable the patient to be carried through a temporary crisis.

19.3 Additional real life problems

But real life is sometimes even more complex than that. There may be at least three complications in this area. First, the patient may not be able to communicate his wishes—he may be incompetent. For example, decisions often have to be made on behalf of the very young, the comatose, or the mentally incapacitated. Second, the distinction between ordinary and extraordinary means is somewhat arbitrary and the latter tends to develop into the former with medical advances and with time. For example, the brief, but rapidly-changing history of anaesthetics, or kidney dialysis, were both at one time regarded as extraordinary means—now they are generally held to be ordinary. Third, the distinction is subject to the nearness of death. The onset of pneumonia would generally be countered by the ordinary treatment of antibiotics, yet, for those who are very near to death, such treatment may be considered as extraordinary and the pneumonia, the 'old man's friend', allowed to take its course. Thus the diagnosis of the last stages of dying, heralding the arrival of that irreversible state and the proximity of death itself, is all-important. When death is imminent then that ethical crossover in medicine is reached and there is a change in direction of thinking and practice, namely, changing from life-saving medicine to providing palliative care.

19.4 Recognizing death

This switch is *not* sinister. *And we MUST recognize this.* I fear that some readers will misconstrue, or object to, this assertion. There are those who would want to continue to seek to defy death. They are wrong. They have misunderstood the role of medicine. Their attitude is as fruitless as 'chasing after the wind'. Of course, medical treatment, in the form of ordinary or extraordinary means, should be provided when they will be beneficial, but when death is near, aggressive treatment, the use of extraordinary means, is not the practice of good medicine. The patient is dying and the inevitability of that must be clearly recognized. Medical interventions will one day fail all of us. We must die. And good medicine will recognize that and prepare us for that great day.

Any consideration of ordinary and extraordinary means, like so many other aspects of these edge-of-life issues, brings us back to one of the great lessons of this book. Time and time again, the truth has been impressed that our death is at hand, and inescapably coming. Hopefully, by now, well over halfway through this book, we have all learned that lesson and begun to think about, and prepare for, it.

Living wills, advance directives and proxy decision-makers

These devices are largely the inventions of pro-euthanasia advocates. They are the consequence of a combination of the decrease of the practice of Hippocratic-Christian medicine, and an increase in the overdosing on personal autonomy, freedom, rights and choice. They signify that not all healthcare professionals can be trusted to 'do the right thing' and furthermore, they indicate that we want it 'done our way'.

Living wills and advance directives may have different names, but fundamentally, they are the same thing, a bit like a philatelist and a stamp collector. They are both documents drawn up by patients at a time when they are competent. They specify the patients' preferences about the types and extent of medical treatments that they would want for themselves in the event that they become incompetent, that is physically or mentally incapable of consenting to, or of refusing, such interventions. A proxy decision-maker is a person, who is appointed, either by the competent patient, or, as often happens in the US, by the courts, to make medical decisions on behalf of the patient, should he or she become incompetent.

20.1 Their negative effect

The effect of making a living will that would be legally binding upon doctors is unhelpful and undesirable. In many instances, doctors would be obliged to substitute bad medical practice for good. They would be compelled by law to follow the prescription, signed by the patient, perhaps years earlier, who is now incapacitated, rather than follow what is now clinically best for that person. In addition, of course, it would overlook the benefits of any recently-discovered treatments. That cannot be called good medicine.

Proper medicine insists that a patient is given full information about her state of health and the best treatment options. However, she can still refuse to accept this best treatment. But by doing so, any subsequent treatment she accepts is bound to be less than best. That cannot be called good medicine.

Another drawback of a living will is that it sends out a strong signal. It 'says' that the patient does not want much, or even anything, done. What, of course, the patient actually said, perhaps years before, is that she does not want certain types of treatment. But this could be so easily misinterpreted by the healthcare team. Even when the specifics of a living will are clear, they can still lead to sub-standard medicine. Consider, for example, the case of a woman who has specified that she never wants to be tube fed. She suffers a mild stroke and develops problems with swallowing, a common complication. The healthcare team read her living will, understand her proscription against having a nasogastric tube fitted, so, instead, they give her a meal normally. But because of her swallowing difficulties, she inhales the food and develops pneumonia. Can you understand how the team is going to feel stymied and unprofessional, knowing what to do for the best, but not being allowed to do it? That cannot be called good medicine.

The passage of time causes additional problems. A woman enthusiastically produces an advance directive, while she is young and fit, but she has no idea if, when, or how it will be used. Now, in old age, she may have even forgotten about its existence. Now, she is unsure about its effectiveness and suitability, let alone how to amend, or reverse it. This latter aspect is especially important because one of the crucial factors about edge-of-life illnesses is that they often change a patient's perspective on life and death. What seemed good and sensible while in full health, can look quite different from the perspective of sickness and dying. By definition, the deathbed is a novel experience for the patient and it can concentrate the mind like no other previous experience. To ignore that possibility cannot be called good medicine.

As time moves on, so does medicine. Medical practices, technologies and capabilities change and improve. By contrast, a living will is static and can become dated and out of touch with medical advances rather quickly. Of course, living wills can be updated, but herein lies yet another problem.

Such a revision may well be suggested when a serious illness is first diagnosed. Imagine—a frail old lady, who has just been told that she has mild dementia. She is then asked, would she now like to sign on the dotted line so that no treatment need be given, and that food and water can be withdrawn when she deteriorates? Would she be in any fit state, psychologically or medically, to make such a declaration? Might she not fall under some pressure, from doctors and family, to consent? Consent has become a central component of modern medical practice. A patient must give consent, oral or written, prior to any medical intervention. But it is not just consent that must be provided, it is *informed* consent. Yet how can anyone give informed consent five, ten, or twenty years before receiving some unidentified treatment for an unidentified condition? 'Every case will be judged on its merits', is a phrase popular with politicians and others. In some ways, it describes proper medicine—every patient is different with different needs requiring different treatment, especially with reference to edge-of-life medicine. Yet proponents of living wills are arguing for the introduction of just the opposite—a blanket directive, regardless of individual circumstances. That also cannot be called good medicine.

It is sometimes argued that such advance statements can be very helpful to medical personnel. For instance, it is said that the healthcare team can mention them during discussion in a non-threatening way in order to determine if a patient has made such a declaration. The sort of question used could be, 'Are you the type of person who has clear wishes about treatment and non-treatment?' But, of course, this is ethically legitimate only if the caring team is prepared to practise both euthanasiastic and non-euthanasiastic medicine. And what a wimpish lot they would be, if governed by the whims of the patient, rather than the ethical obligations of good medical practice. Such directives would turn doctors and nurses into mere technicians.

The perceived advantage of the proxy decision-maker is that the appointee looks from within the situation, giving a subjective dimension, in determining what is in the patient's best interests. This contrasts, so it is said, with the objective and outsider-type decisions of the healthcare team. Such a distinction is unconvincing, and certainly no guarantee that the patient will receive good medicine. Perhaps the patient and the proxy have not discussed treatment options recently—the patient may, during the course of the illness, have changed her mind without informing anyone, including the proxy. And anyway, patients and doctors, with or without proxies, can all still make the wrong, or even the worst, medical decisions.

20.2 Are they legally binding?

Currently, living wills and their like are not binding under UK law. Only the contemporaneous consent or refusal of a patient is binding, and a living will is, by definition, not contemporaneous. However, there is evident confusion about this matter, some of which has been deliberately stirred up by pro-euthanasia organizations. Much has been made of a case that came before the courts in 1993. It involved a schizophrenic man with a gangrenous leg—his doctors advised him to have it amputated, but the patient refused. The doctors went to the High Court. However, Mr Justice Thorpe granted the man an injunction banning amputation, not only for the immediate future, but also for the distant future, even if the man became incompetent. Advocates of euthanasia have seized upon this case, claiming that it has made all living wills legally binding. This is not so because that judgement was specific, for one condition, for one man. Nevertheless, the trend is towards the legalization of such devices. The British Medical Association and the Law Society of Great Britain are generally in favour of them, and other countries, such as, the USA, Canada and Australia, have long been wrestling with implementing their legality.

20.3 Their positive effect

Modern medicine has become perverse. All the above arguments have been against living wills. Now for one, perhaps in their favour. During 2000, it was revealed that doctors were commonly writing, 'Do not resuscitate' (DNR) on the medical notes of old people in hospital, without first seeking their consent and without informing their families. This illicit practice was reported to be endemic in the NHS. In response, patients' organizations called for the introduction of living wills in order to specify a patient's wish *not* to receive such non-treatment. Are we about to descend into a battle of the living wills? Could there be those that state, 'Do nothing', and those that state, 'Do not do nothing'? As yet, I am not a card-carrying member of the anti-euthanasia club. If only we could return to practising Hippocratic-Christian medicine, I would not even have to think about such an outlandish possibility.

20.4 Prior preparations

What is the way forward for Christians and the morally sensitive? All this negative talk is very well, but let's cut to the chase—who is going to ensure that I am treated properly if I become incompetent when I am dying? The answer must be rooted in edge-of-life education and communication. Just think, if this had been done during the last two generations, Hippocratic-Christian medicine would not now be such a rarity and this question would be largely irrelevant. But back to reality. Have you resolved these issues yourself? Have you discussed them with your spouse, your family, your pastor and your doctor? Do they understand your wishes—indeed, they should share them. If, and when, you have done all this, then relax, because only a minority of us will ever need any such intervention on our behalf. Of course, some will then raise their fears that they might get caught dying away from home and cut off from such safeguards. Unlikely, but possible. Then why not carry a card stipulating contact with these people if you were to be found under those circumstances? 'But', you say, 'I might forget it, or it would get lost.' Yes, there are any number of other similar situations and dilemmas we could concoct, for which there are no cast-iron answers or 100 per cent guarantees. In the final analysis, when we have exhausted every such argument and fear, and taken all sensible precautions, we will have to exercise faith, and counter our worries with truths contained in passages like those of Matthew 6:25–34, John 14:1–4 and Romans 8:28–39. Take a break, when you have finished this chapter, and read them. The issue then becomes, do you trust your heavenly Father to look after you? Has he, or has he not, promised to care for you, prepare a place for you, and never leave you? This is Christian consolation. Trust him.

To choose death, either in advance, or instantaneously, whether one's own, or that of another, is not an option for the Christian. Such actions deny that the God of life is sufficiently sovereign and trustworthy in death. By contrast, living wills and their like are marks of human autonomy, asserting that human life is best lived and ended independently of God. Could there be any clearer signals that secular humanism is rampant, and that modern medicine has gone astray? Stay away from living wills, stay close to God.

Of slippery slopes, wedges and dominoes

Various bioethical commentators have borrowed these three somewhat mundane images from the world around us, and then used them to vivid effect. They have applied them to practices, both ancient and modern, to illustrate a bioethical trend, which, to most of us, seems to be nothing other than downright obvious—the flow of traffic on a slippery slope is forever downwards, doors, once wedged, are easier to open, wider and wider, and up-ended dominoes sequentially knock one another over.

21.1 The 'law' of bioethical entropy

Everything, not just bioethical issues, is on a slippery slope. Physics expresses this phenomenon in its universal law of entropy—in all systems, chaos reigns. That is to say, disorder will always increase. Or, in the vernacular of the tabloid newspaper, 'Things can only get worse.' Take, for example, biology. Here, entropy is a recognized fact of life—everything that now lives, be they fish, bacteria, grass, or people, will go down the slippery slope of death and decay. In the realm of bioethics, previously-unthinkable practices, once commenced, will descend from good, to bad, to worse, to worst. It is like an incontrovertible law.

This 'law' of bioethical entropy has four discernable stages. First, a previously unthinkable practice begins to be tolerated (stage 1), on behalf of just a very few people, the so-called 'hard cases'. With the passage of time, that practice becomes permitted by law, but with seemingly-tight boundaries (stage 2). Next, and before long, it becomes accepted, and even expected by, and for, the majority of people (stage 3). The final phase (stage 4) is when that practice is considered to be required, indeed essential, and even laudable. Put another way, the downward trend is:

❶   **❷**   **❸**   **❹**

unthinkable $\Rightarrow$ tolerated $\Rightarrow$ permitted $\Rightarrow$ expected $\Rightarrow$ required

Come what may, the first stage leads to the second, and so on. And, if the first step is unethical, then so too are all the subsequent steps.

21.2 Do examples exist?

I can almost hear the protests, 'What rubbish! If examples exist, tell us about them!' Well, it depends to whom you wish to listen, because there are three general answers—some say, 'Yes', some say, 'No', and some say, 'Perhaps'.

First, the affirmative. Consider, that keystone of bioethical issues, abortion. From the earliest times of organized medicine the practice of abortion was shunned. The Hippocratic oath and the Judaeo-Christian doctrines forbade it—it was an 'unthinkable' of medicine. Even less than a hundred years ago, the unborn child was regarded as 'one of us', to be protected and cherished. Then during the first half of the last century that view began to be eroded. Some abortions were tolerated for 'hard cases', or for hard cash (stage 1). Then, in 1967, came legal permission (stage 2). The 1967 Abortion Act permitted, under limited circumstances, abortion for the few, like the overstressed, sick mother, with several children already, living in poor housing, and with little financial support. In retrospect, it was a rather modest, restrictive piece of legislation. But, within a short time, coaches and horses had been driven through its boundaries. Then came the growing acceptance (stage 3), so that for the last thirty years, wholesale abortion, 'abortion-on-demand', or 'the free supply of abortion', has been the expected—indeed, it has now been practised in the UK on at least six million unborn children. Nowadays, abortion is regarded as the required norm (stage 4). Any pregnant woman presenting at a hospital or a health clinic can require, even demand, to be given an abortion. This practice, once unthinkable, has now been proclaimed as a liberating force within society, and as a magnificent victory for women, giving them control over their bodies and their reproductive lives. See the slippery bioethical trend, from the unthinkable to the required? Yet perversely, this is regarded by many as exactly the reverse—for them it is considered to be an ascending triumph, from the outlawed to the lauded.

Second, some say, 'No'. They say these trends do not exist, they are nothing to lose sleep about. Consider, this time, an example of wedgery, from the practice of infanticide. As previously discussed in chapter 13, Dr Leonard Arthur, an eminent paediatrician, was, in 1981, charged with the murder of John Pearson, a Down's syndrome baby, who, under Arthur's regime of prescribed analgesic and 'nursing care only', died four days later. Dr Arthur was acquitted. This was the unthinkable stage 1. A few months later, Ian Kennedy, who was, at that time, one of the leading experts on medico-legal matters, rejected the wedge argument. He wrote in *New Society* (1982, 59:13–15) an article entitled, *Reflection on the Arthur Case.* In it, he stated, 'I am not persuaded of the inevitability of the wedge argument—that one step down the road towards removing one class of the disabled, the very severely disabled child, from our midst—means that we must inevitably take the next step.' But John Pearson's death did nothing other than add grease to the slippery slope. It wedged open the door that leads to stage 2, though, it is true, we have yet to go through it in a formal, legalized way. However, as discussed in section 13.3, there can be no doubt that the John Pearson case has become a case law precedent for the practice of killing newborn children, who are 'irreversibly disabled', and who are 'rejected by their parents'.

Third, there is the 'Perhaps' view. It comes, in this instance, from Mary Warnock, regarded by many as Britain's foremost moral philosopher. She has written about slippery slopes in her own inimitably confused and confusing way. In her book, *An Intelligent Person's Guide to Ethics* (1998), she expresses her contempt for the concept of the slippery slope. She maintains (p. 37) that it is, '… not strictly a logical argument at all.' Indeed, in her view it is, '… essentially an argument to be used by people who do not trust doctors or hospital ethics committees.' Well, she has a point there!

Earlier in her career, she chaired the Committee of Inquiry into Human Fertilisation and Embryology and co-authored its subsequent document, known as the Warnock Report (1984). She has thereby become intimately identified with the Report's infamous 14-day rule. This allows human embryos to be experimented upon until this upper time limit, but insists that they are then destroyed. This 14-day rule is supposedly based upon the appearance of the primitive streak. But this is a developmental step of little consequence and no moral significance, which means that the 14-day rule is entirely arbitrary. Nevertheless, in her book (p. 48), Baroness Warnock insists that this block, this 14-day rule, is based on, '… a genuinely morally significant distinction.' Then, on the same page, but switching to the issue of euthanasia, she continues, 'It is largely because it is so difficult to think of an equally simple block on the slippery slope in the case of euthanasia that I am opposed to any attempt to change the law, to render some kinds of euthanasia legitimate.' So, to summarize. Slippery slopes are illogical and used by contemptible people, but somehow, eleven pages later, good people recognize them with regard to euthanasia, and they need stopping, by some arbitrary block, the nature of which, however, cannot even be imagined. That's clear, isn't it? No, I don't understand her either!

So, do ethical slippery slopes and wedged doors really exist? Is there a 'law' of bioethical entropy? If one of our leading medical lawyers is asked, the answer is, 'No'. If one of our leading moral philosophers is asked, the answer is, 'Yes' and 'No'. Personally, I would rather resort to asking the proverbial 'man on the Clapham omnibus'. And I am inclined to think that he would unequivocally answer, 'Yes, of course they do!'

21.3 Slippery slopes and euthanasia

If the vast majority of us consider that slippery slopes and wedged doors exist in the practices of abortion and infanticide, will they not also exist in euthanasia? Of course, they will. This is the reality of the domino theory applied to bioethics and medical practice. Knock over the abortion and infanticide dominos and they will without doubt topple the third, euthanasia.

The euthanasia issue is also subject to the 'law' of bioethical entropy, whereby the unthinkable practice eventually becomes the required and laudable procedure. As the practices of abortion and infanticide have already shown, the eugenic principle, namely, that there are 'lives not worthy to be lived', is firmly rooted among many of those in medicine, as well as among the general public. This principle is fundamental to all bad edge-of-life practices. It is therefore fundamental to euthanasia. The view that some human beings, including the very young as well as the old, do not qualify even for basic care, or routine medical treatment is now becoming more widely ingrained. Some neonates and some of those in a permanent vegetative state (PVS), plus some elderly people have already suffered the unthinkable. Thus, they, and we, have already completed stage 1. Indeed, it can be argued, and convincingly so, that we are already at stage 2 because the case law created by, for example, the Anthony Bland case, means that the legal, albeit limited, killing has already started. Yes, non-voluntary euthanasia is not just tolerated, but is currently permitted in the UK.

The full legalization of stage 2–type euthanasia, encompassing non-voluntary and voluntary, will be, to change the analogy, a can of worms. It will be virtually impossible to produce legislation that is sufficiently watertight to hold back the floodgates. Just where is that ethical line which separates voluntary from non-voluntary euthanasia? Are the authorities absolutely positive that all those PVS patients they have already dehydrated to death were diagnosed as indisputably hopeless cases? How will they prove that the person asking to be voluntarily euthanized is making a genuinely unfettered request? Can you see how stage 2 will irresistibly proceed and merge into stage 3? What will stop it doing so? Strict and precise guidelines? Oh, you mean like the Dutch have had for the last two decades? Get out of here! Voluntary euthanasia is now legally and widely practised throughout Holland, so too is non-voluntary euthanasia and it is being increasingly condoned. The Dutch may resent comparisons of their euthanasia practices with those of the Nazis, but they are using the same basic concept, namely, that patients have 'lives not worthy to be lived'— *lebensunwertes Leben*, the very maxim of the Nazi regime. Whenever any society holds such a conviction, there is no ethical movement but downwards. For a country as flat as Holland, it is surprising how fast its citizens have managed to slither down the slippery slope of euthanasia.

True, the Dutch experience is somewhat different from ours in detail. For example, the Dutch have centred their stage 2 on voluntary euthanasia for competent patients, whereas ours, in the UK, has focussed on the non-voluntary killing of incompetent victims. But the outcomes will be no different. The Dutch have, with their new euthanasia law in 2001, already completed stage 3. We are lagging behind. But, there can be little doubt that in the UK we will witness an increase in the number of victims as well as a widening of the grounds for euthanasia within the next few years. On an economic basis alone, stage 4 will then become overwhelmingly attractive, and could mark the beginning of even involuntary euthanasia. After all, if it can be determined that you have a 'life not worthy to be lived' and that it would be in your 'best interests' to be dead, then none of us is safe.

There can be very few people who would seriously deny the existence of slippery slopes and their like—when they do, they often have some ulterior motive for their denial. Our concern should be not so much with proving the existence of such slopes, but rather with assessing their steepness and their slipperiness—that is, how fast and how far will we descend, and how can we halt or slow the slide? This whole topic exposes our enormous capacity for 'incremental adaptation'. That is, we are willing to accept change, little by little, whereas we are characteristically opposed to one large and sudden shift, even though the end result of both routes will be identical. This is important for us to recognize. If we compare our current bioethical practices with those of last year, or the last decade, we may not become too unnerved by the extent or speed of our descent. However, my contention is that we need a better comparator, a better standard, than mere past performance. This book is seriously suggesting that we should use the absolutes of the Word of God as our plumb line.

PART 5

Some Answers

'Truth is powerful when it is argued; it is even more powerful when it is exhibited.'

John Stott, (1990) *Issues Facing Christians Today*.

B ooks about bioethical issues will never be adequate if they simply present the topics in a theoretical, barren format. Of course, these edge-of-life issues require some discussion and some answers, but they also demand some action. These issues are not just for the floor of the rowdy debating chamber, or the comfort of the cosy chair by the crackling log fire. If modern medicine really has gone wrong, then it needs putting right.

Having examined topics like dying, death and euthanasia, it would be callous to leave the reader in the lurch, aware of the issues, but unsure what to do about them. The ethical rubber must hit the practical road. This Part seeks to provide down-to-earth, practical responses.

These responses have two major aspects—outward and inward, though they may often overlap. The former involve actions that are public and open, such as being salt and light in our neighbourhoods. The latter are private and secret, and include preparing for our own dying and death.

The backbone of the professional's proper response to dying, death and euthanasia is the hospice movement and palliative care. Two comforting chapters describe their benefits.

This book began with the issues of dying and death, and it ends with them too. This is the individual's response. None of us will escape the final stage of dying, or its aftermath. The two final chapters in this Part deal with them both. Preparation for death is a lost art that needs rediscovering. Considering our last days and hours will help us to live through them better. Coping with the repercussions of death, namely, bereavement, is the fitting topic for the final chapter.

So what must we do?

Dying, death and euthanasia are topics now dominated by a non-Christian worldview. Few people, Christian or otherwise, would demur from this analysis. We may not be able to articulate this position with great accuracy or lucidity, but our lack of articulation is less serious than our lack of extrication. In other words, as we have noted before, we need to beware that we are not caught up and carried along with this world's philosophical tides and outcomes, be they, secular humanism, or its cousins like, moral relativism, situation ethics, post-modernism, or the cult of self. The only safeguard that will prevent us 'going with the flow' in both thought and deed is summed up in that unassailable proposition— 'what you think determines what you do.' Thoughts and actions are inseparable. Reason like a secular humanist, and you will behave like one. Judge wrongly and you will act wrongly. Therefore, we must develop the Christian mind, in order to bring about some equally-matching Christian action.

Sadly, at times, there seems to be little difference in the attitudes and actions of Christians and pagans concerning edge-of-life issues. There jolly well should be. Christians seek to please God, live with eternity in view, have the mind of Christ, be guardians and purveyors of the Gospel, and strive to uphold the culture of life. By contrast, pagans seek to please themselves, live for today, think like brute men and women, have nothing substantial or lasting to recommend, and acquiesce to the culture of death. Can you feel the tension? Conflict between the two cultures is unavoidable. That does not mean that all day long we are at loggerheads with those around us. But scratch the surface, uncover the underlying mindset, and begin to plumb the depths of motivation, and the differences should be only too obvious.

Previous chapters have sought to stimulate thinking and Christian understanding concerning edge-of-life issues. If thinking begets action, then the thinking Christian must become involved. So what must we do? There are at least seven answers to this all-important question. Some of these have been previously outlined in *Responding to the Culture of*

Death—A Primer of Bioethical Issues, but because they are of such fundamental significance, they warrant some repetition, and addition, here.

22.1 We must pray

We can begin where King David once began, and millions since have followed, 'Hear, O LORD, and answer me, for I am poor and needy' (Psalm 86:1). Here is the link, the transcendent connection, between the Creator and the created. No wonder it is said that, 'The prayer of a righteous man is powerful and effective' (James 5:16). This is Christian life-support. God hears *and* he answers. He can, and he does, sovereignly change situations and people, meaning, yours and mine, and you and me. So prayer must be the prerequisite for that sought-after, longed-for, genuine change. Therefore, these edge-of-life issues ought to be a regular part of our prayer lives, both individual and corporate.

We should start with ourselves. We must pray for our own minds, that they may be biblically-informed, for our own hearts, that they would be biblically-motivated, for our own speech, that it would be biblically-fragrant, and for our own responses, that they would be biblically-correct. We must pray for those personally caught up, and sometimes trapped, in the distress of these issues—for the disabled, the elderly, the senile, and so on, including, of course, the dying and their families and carers. We must pray for those in the forefront of the battles—for doctors, hospital administrators, and especially for nurses. We must pray for believers engaged in these particular occupations that they would resist the culture of death and stand up for the culture of life. We must also pray for our rulers and decision-makers (1 Timothy 2:1–3). Accordingly, we must pray for the government and the opposition, for the police, trade union leaders, parents, schoolteachers, employers, magistrates, '... for kings and all those in authority ...'

22.2 We must educate

Again, we start with ourselves. There are no short cuts here—it will demand some sacrifice, discipline and application. If I knew of an easier way, I would certainly tell you. Hopefully, the preceding pages have helped. In addition, there are many first-rate leaflets, booklets, books, videos and websites—see the list of Resources beginning on p. 266. Read, mark and learn from some of them. The task is not overwhelming. You are not aiming to become a professor of moral philosophy, but rather, an informed, sensible and constructive person with a decent grasp of life issues at the edge.

We need to learn some truths. Truth number one must again be the reality of death—its awesomeness, inevitability and pervasiveness. And above all, the imminence of our own death should pervade our very being. We need to develop that theology of dying, which will help us live fully, but lightly, towards this world.

Then there are all those other facts. For example, did you know about the Anthony Bland case and its far-reaching implications? Had you ever heard of John Pearson? Did you understand the euthanasia situation in the Netherlands? Were you aware of the incidence of suicide in the UK?

Then we need to root out some myths. Euthanasia is not, as it is so often portrayed, 'progressive and enlightened'. Eugenics did not disappear with the Nazis in the 1940s. And, yes, infanticide does currently occur in our hospitals.

We may need to change the ways we think about and approach the physically and mentally disabled, the very young, the elderly and the senile—all those who are bearers of the *imago Dei*.

After educating ourselves, we must educate our families, encompassing the whole family tree, from great-grandparents to second cousins. And especially, we must educate our children. In the economy of God, parents are responsible for instructing their children in truth and righteousness— 'Train a child in the way he should go, and when he is old he will not turn from it' (Proverbs 22:6). If we ignore our responsibilities, then others will teach them claptrap, mythology and anti-Christian ideas. Parents must not abrogate their duties and hope that schoolteachers and others will do their work for them. Dying and death in the family are great tests and solemn teaching aids—do not tiptoe around the opportunities they present.

If we are parents, we can also check on our schools' education curricula. Did you know, for example, that euthanasia is now a topic within many of the syllabuses of GCSE religious education, as well as personal and social education (PSE)? How is this taught? Are, for example, euthanasia and suicide being implicitly approved of, or even recommended to our children? What about death itself, infanticide, eugenics, and all the other edge-of-life issues? Without doubt, some of these topics are being discussed in the classroom. It would be distressing if your children first learned about such subjects from an uncertain and confused, or worse still, an anti-life, teacher, rather than from you.

While on the subject of schools, there are now additional opportunities to become governors, who can, quite properly, influence the ethical ethos of a school—if you volunteer, you will almost certainly be accepted!

We can also help to educate our friends and neighbours by talking about these issues. From time to time, the opportunities arise, at funerals, over the garden fence, during illnesses, over a cup of coffee, throughout bereavements. Often a gentle word in season is all that is needed, not a bioethical lecture. At other times, you will be pleasantly surprised by the interest and reaction of friends to having a good, well-informed chew over these issues.

We must educate our churches. Christians were slow off the mark when the 1967 Abortion Act was passing through the Houses of Parliament— just where were those evangelical voices of opposition? Will we again be silent when euthanasia legislation is proposed in the near future? It is only in the last twenty years that growing numbers of evangelicals have begun to understand bioethical issues and have been prepared to stand up and be counted. Too many have previously pleaded some sort of neutrality, or pretended to adopt a middle-of-the-road, non-aligned status, thereby perjuring the truth.

Ministers, pastors and church leaders have a central educational role here. Theirs is the overwhelming responsibility to help people prepare to meet their Maker. We must not continue to fail our people by ignoring to teach them the Bible's foundations and responses to these edge-of-life issues. Too many are still confused about the ethics of, for instance, voluntary euthanasia and suicide, and too few congregations have developed that theology of living *and* of dying.

To this end, some churches have organized, either alone, or, better still, with others in their area, successful day or half-day conferences, or simple evening meetings dealing with various bioethical issues. What about planning one for your church, or your locality? There are knowledgeable, first-rate speakers who would be happy to be invited. Such gatherings, as well as being excellent educational exercises, can also be happy times of fellowship with others of like mind. The outcomes of such ventures can be better-educated Christians and the formulation of future collaborative pro-life efforts.

We need to remember that Christians are not immune to old age, or suicidal thoughts, or senility, or disabled children, and the like. There are currently over 1.2 million people in the UK with learning difficulties. One in three of us will suffer, sometime during our lifetime, from mental illness and the same proportion will develop cancer. And every member of our congregation will be dead before this century has come to an end. These are sobering thoughts that should focus our minds on life and death issues.

We need to take note of the media. We need to understand the times. We must not be unaware, or naive. For example, what is the VES? It is the Voluntary Euthanasia Society—it is certainly not a helpful organization because it runs a well-oiled pro-euthanasia public relations machine. And we need to learn to judge bias. We may think that British television and newspapers are fair and balanced—they are not. They are usually covertly anti-Christian in their personnel, outlook and output. Pro-euthanasia people can appear to be so attractive, articulate and convincing—do not let such qualities obscure the truth. Watch out for people like Peter Singer, Mary Warnock and Ludovic Kennedy—listen to them very, very carefully.

So, that is education all sown up! Do not let the number of the above options overwhelm you so that you become immobilized and do nothing. A little reading here, a little reflection there, and a little conversation here and there, is all that is required in the early days. You will be surprised how quickly you can master the foundational arguments—yes, you will! Then you will grow in knowledge and progress in understanding. But above all, please, please, please start the education process.

22.3 We must be salt and light

During the Sermon on the Mount, immediately after he had presented the incomparable Beatitudes, the Lord Jesus Christ declared his disciples to be salt and light (Matthew 5:13–16). What remarkable metaphors! Salt may initially be mistaken for sugar, but its purpose is quite different—Christians are never to be syrupy people with candyfloss ethics. Instead, we are to be salty people, with seasoned ethics. Salt has that remarkable ability to stop decay and rottenness, and so safeguard what is good and wholesomely preserve it. Its other property is to season and enhance the good, improve the better, and bring out the best. Therefore Christians, by their thinking, speaking and responses, are to make this world less spoiled and more palatable. But first, salt must be sprinkled on, or even better, rubbed in. Christians are to rub shoulders with the world—there is to be no Christian isolationism, no withdrawal from society (John 17:18). Instead, to stop the putrefaction, to sting the decay, to make society more pleasant, Christians must be mixed into society. We are also to be 'the light of the world'. Light illuminates. It dispels darkness, banishes confusion and chases away ignorance. It enables people to see themselves and their circumstances more clearly. And it exposes dirty tricks and grubby activities.

As salt and light, we are to resist evil and to struggle for Christian truth and values. And do you know what happens when we stop resisting and struggling, when Christians disengage from society and remain silent? Not nothing—there is no ethical vacuum. What happens is that the arguments and policies of secular humanism win the day. Non-Christian values flood in. In many ways, we get the ethical climate that we deserve. If we have lost our saltiness and hidden our lights under buckets, if we have become insipid and dull, then who is to blame? By contrast, seasoned and shining Christian disciples can deeply affect a neighbourhood and a society, and usher in both the regeneration and reformation that we long for and need.

There can be no doubt that the public debates and policy decisions about dying, death and euthanasia need both the Christian worldview and Christian action. They have much to say, and nothing but good to offer. Without firm Christian foundations, such deliberations will founder and such policies will misfire. Yet, so often we disenfranchise ourselves and fail to engage with either the public, or the relevant policy-makers, social practitioners and politicians.

The civic and political arenas are foreign places for most Christians. We have the democratic vote and, as good citizens, we should use it. Therefore, we are unlike the early Church, who had little, if any, political power. Of course, we should not give our vote automatically to the pro-life candidate—he or she may be dreadful in other areas of public and political life. But, at least, we should raise some of the great bioethical and edge-of-life issues during general and local election campaigns, when those prospective candidates speak at hustings, or come canvassing on our doorsteps.

We can also write to, and meet with, our Parliamentary, or Assembly, members. Have you ever met yours? I always recommend that you do so before you die, or better still, within the next year or two—it can be such an eye-opener! All political representatives hold regular 'surgeries', and your local library and newspapers will carry the details. Politicians cannot be well informed about all subjects, and many will actually welcome some reasoned input. The timid can form a little delegation. Some time ago, two of us visited our MP to discuss human embryo experimentation, however, at the meeting he was much more interested in the euthanasia issue, so we handed him some appropriate literature (always be prepared!), which he gratefully received, and later read. Such visits can do much good, not least in disabusing our leaders of the idea that to be bioethically concerned and pro-life is to be quirky! After all, who else will speak up for the vulnerable, the disabled, the weak and the senile?

When speaking or writing to those in authority there are some basic rules to bear in mind. Be polite. Be ready. Be winsome. And if you want to avoid the standard, photocopied answer, then make sure you ask a particular question, perhaps requesting some local information, or some precise, future voting intentions.

Remember, the key is communication. A number of Christians like to rant, and not a few will happily turn the dialogue into a monologue. Such strident presentations may salve the consciences of some Christians, but they communicate little, and they advance the cause of Christ, and the culture of life, even less. Rather, we should be courteous and gentle, yet straightforward and honest—no trickery, no threats. We are not point-scoring, rather we are trying to persuade a man, or a woman, that the Bible's teaching on a certain issue, and the ensuing Christian practical response, are both entirely reasonable and eminently workable, and that if followed, the outcome will be for the betterment of all. Our Christian proclamation needs to be set alongside an appeal to the hearts and minds of a secular society. Evangelical Christians are, by and large, not very good at this—that is not surprising—we lack the practice.

It may be that your MP, MA, or local politician is pro-life, and even a Christian. If so, then make the most of it, and support and encourage them in their stand. And do not forget that appreciative letter, or happy 'thank you'. We are not only men and women with grievances—Christians can be a cheery lot too. And those who have stood up and supported our bioethical stance, sometimes at considerable personal cost, deserve our admiration, and our gratitude, whatever their politics, religion, or failings.

Most politicians, together with the vast majority of the population, now have virtually no Christian knowledge or understanding—we should bear this in mind. How can we convey the magnitude of what is at stake, namely, the specialness and the dignity of all those made in the image of God? Christians have an onerous task here. Nevertheless, we have been entrusted with both the diagnosis and the cure. And the Christian worldview does possess robust answers to difficult questions. We do, or, at least, we should have, a first-rate understanding of edge-of-life questions. Because we have come to know ourselves and our God, the issues of life and death are our daily bread. We need not fear men, or women. Remember, a lisping, stammering tongue is not a sign of the weakness, or falsity, of our cause—it is certainly far more honourable than a silent tongue.

From time to time, government departments, like the Department of Health, or its agencies, like the Human Genetics Commission, ask for comment on particular bioethical issues. Sometime, in the near future, views on certain aspects of euthanasia will be solicited. Responding to these consultation papers can be a valuable exercise. First, not only do you have to clarify your own thinking, but second, it is imperative that the views of those representing the culture of life are communicated to those in authority.

We can check on the activities of the National Health Service, and our regional and local health authorities. What is your local hospital's policy on resuscitation of the elderly and infirm? Are there local guidelines on 'euthanasia' and living wills? This is not a call for Christians to be sneaks and snoops, but we all have a duty to exercise responsible citizenship.

If you are a trade union member, do you know your union's policies on these edge-of-life issues? They may be deliberately ambiguous and non-committal, but they may not be. Check them out.

You can write letters to local and national newspapers. Letters' pages are some of the most popular sections of newspapers, and short letters are the most read. You can meet with the editor of your local newspaper, give her some literature and tell her about concerns and action in your area—a short write-up, accompanied by a good photograph, will usually be gratefully received. So, get yourself in print. You can also contact national and local radio and television stations. Local stations often welcome comment on bioethical news stories and once you have proved yourself, they will contact you again, and again (often very early in the morning!). Of course, such activities are not for everyone, but a few readers could become serious media commentators. It is always refreshing to read letters or hear comments from the culture of life perspective. The authentic Christian voice is so rarely heard in the media these days—so, do not just complain about it, change it!

Being tasty, tangy salt and a bright, warm light is not easy—it will take some effort. Nevertheless, the possibilities open to us are myriad—we can pray, discuss, counsel, debate, entreat, leaflet, visit, broadcast, educate and write. They are enough. We will not have the time or energy for all of them, but if each of us could accomplish just one or two, what a difference that would make.

Finally, we need to settle the issue of co-belligerency, co-labouring. This scares some Christians. Out there are many, many people who agree with us that, for example, euthanasia is wrong, eugenics is appalling, and infanticide is hideous. They are the morally sensitive, and many of them are the nicest men and women you will ever meet. There is no compromise in working as co-belligerents with them. I have worked, for over twenty years, in the charity LIFE, with its mix of religious people, atheists and agnostics, and I have never once had to compromise my allegiance to Christ. We are fighting the same bioethical campaigns, the same edge-of-life battles. Of course, we may come to it from entirely different worldviews. Ecclesiastically, we may be poles apart. We may never agree on the primary doctrines of Christianity. But, I tell you, apart from some of these people, the pro-life flame would have been snuffed out in Britain long ago. We, as rather slothful, unaware, inexperienced and disengaged evangelicals, need to come to these issues with a certain amount of shame and humility—we should have been in the vanguard, but instead we have been the reluctant rearguard.

See, there is no room for apathy, or indolence. There is so much to do. You too can be a Christian agitator. You can bring salt and light to these issues and problems. You can act creatively, thoughtfully and effectively. Then you, and ten thousand like you, really will begin to make our society a more wholesome, less sinful place. May we yet prove that, 'Righteousness exalts a nation, but sin is a disgrace to any people' (Proverbs 14:34).

22.4 We must care

There is no credibility to anything we say, or do, or object to, unless we are prepared to care. Protesting at the killing of the young, ill and elderly is good, but never enough. We may rightly declare that, 'Infanticide is wrong', but that is insufficient. We forfeit all entitlements to condemn euthanasia, if we will not help those entangled in its snare, and care for the dying. We may pity from afar the troubled or bereaved family, yet more is required. Caring must permeate all we think and do. We must care for disabled children and their families, the elderly, the infirm, the senile, the vulnerable, and the dying, whoever. The Golden Rule (Matthew 7:12) is to be our rule.

You cannot read the Scriptures without being struck by the number of times we are pressed to care for others, to 'do good'. Evangelical Christians have often been guilty of disregarding, or, at least, relegating such injunctions. Historically, we have majored on personal salvation by faith alone and dismissed 'works' as having no part in that salvation. And, theologically, that is correct. But, to our discredit, we have gone too far, and minored on the place of 'good works' in our sanctification, which is where they belong, and centrally so.

A few passages of Scripture should redress the balance. For example, Titus 2:14 states that the Lord Jesus Christ wants, '... a people that are his very own, eager to do what is good.' Paul, when he bade farewell to the Ephesian elders, reminded them of his labours, 'In everything I did, I showed you that by this kind of hard work we must help the weak, remembering the words the Lord Jesus himself said: "It is more blessed to give than to receive"' (Acts 20:35). Or, what about Ephesians 2:10? 'For we are God's workmanship, created in Christ Jesus to do good works, which God prepared in advance for us to do.' And Philippians 2:4 reminds us that, 'Each of you should look not only to your own interests, but also to the interests of others.'

Therefore, we are to be full of good works. It is simply wrong-headed religion to think that the Christian life consists of nothing but witnessing and evangelism, and that it is for others, the less competent, somewhere in the background, to do 'the caring thing'. A look at the life of Christ will show us what a false a notion that is.

Caring is an assorted activity. It need not be heroic. The great eighteenth and nineteenth century preaching duo, John Wesley and Charles Spurgeon, may have founded and funded caring homes for orphans, but you are not necessarily expected to follow suit—they were extra-extraordinary men. Stuffing envelopes for an anti-euthanasia campaign is as caring as visiting the dying. Even giving a cup of cold water is to be regarded as a significant act of charity (Matthew 10:42). Think of some relevant, practical examples. How about visiting, reading and talking with some elderly man, or woman, even those within your family? Or, how about helping the parents of a disabled child or adult? Or, what about befriending the weak and the vulnerable? Such simple 'good works' are the fruit of recognizing their inherent preciousness, because they are made in the image of God. We should aim to initiate, develop and maintain human relationships. This may sound like corny, 'touchy-feely' talk, except that in our increasingly relationship-fractured age, such good works are all the more needed.

So, the call is loud and clear—care. Care we should, care we must. Therefore, we need to work on closing that yawning gulf that too often exists between our Christian declaration, which is relatively easy, and our Christian doing, which is relatively difficult. Already Christians are responding. Many are quietly developing their gifts within the local church and beyond. There are growing numbers of believers taking on leadership roles in pro-life organizations, at both the national and local level, as chairmen, treasurers, secretaries, counsellors and general helpers. The call, and the need, is not for formulaic answers and detached sympathy, but rather for rugged concern and straightforward practical help, rooted in Christian orthodoxy. This is that most excellent of responses, principled compassion.

22.5 We must join and give

There are big pro-life organizations throughout the land. There are little pro-life groups almost everywhere. And, if there is not one near you, then you know what to do—start one! Remember, once upon a time, every such group began with just a handful of founding members. Somebody had to make the first move—why not you?

We must give of ourselves, our time, our money and our energy. But, we are not to rub raw the consciences of other men and women. Some are already hard-pressed. But for many of us, if we could cut out just, say, one hour of television each week (women currently watch twenty-seven hours a week and men twenty-four), then we could write that letter, make that visit, phone that person. Similarly, many are not financially rich. Nevertheless, it is every charity's experience that it is the poor who are so often the most generous. We are all gifted—there is not one of us who cannot do something to advance the culture of life, and promote a proper understanding of edge-of-life issues. And such involvement can be so refreshing and life enhancing. There are latent talents to be discovered—you may be surprised how skilled you are at giving educational talks, producing a poster, organizing a fund-raising coffee morning, or writing to the local newspaper.

Women are often especially good at being directly involved, for example, in visiting the elderly, the dying and the bereaved. Men can decorate old people's homes, plan pro-life activities, and fetch and carry for fund-raising events. Every organization needs extra people for typing, phoning, counting, driving, reading, speaking, cleaning, opening and shutting, selling and buying, serving and clearing, and so forth—all first-class caring activities. There are always some good works to be done somewhere, and our joining and giving can become a genuine part of our Christian service.

We really must join the struggle. Of course, you can do a little on your own, especially locally—that is to be encouraged. But these issues are often of national, even international dimensions and, over the years, it has proved to be more productive to join one of the established organizations. They have the expertise, good literature, proper advice, and so on.

22.6 We must be groaners, not moaners

The final two sections of this chapter are directed, not to facing the vast bioethical issues, nor to the generality of people, but solely to death and the individual. Here the responses to the edge-of-life issues become intensely personal. Both sections focus on that greatest of all tasks, namely, preparing to die well, achieving your true euthanasia. They call for some self-examination, but not morbid introspection, or excessive selfishness. They summarize what you must do, not for others, but for yourself.

Dying well follows living well. 2 Corinthians 5:2 contains an important principle for living well, 'Meanwhile we groan, longing to be clothed with our heavenly dwelling ...' Therefore, when you survey your life and your future, you are to groan, not moan. You know how easy it is to gripe and grumble, and some of us are more prone than others to be moaning minnies. It is the sign of the ingrate. It is a mark of bitterness, wholly unattractive, and alas, highly contagious. Therefore, do not moan, instead, groan. Groan to be released from this sad, abnormal world. Groan to be in heaven. Then we will become members of that global groaning chorus, along with, '... the whole creation ...' (Romans 8:22). We should be eagerly looking forward to heaven, because it is our destiny and our destination, as 2 Corinthians 5:5 says, 'Now it is God who has made us for this very purpose ...' And, as if the prospect and the purpose were not enough, in the meantime, God '... has given us the Spirit as a deposit ...', as a down payment, '... guaranteeing what is to come.' Here is a divine pledge, a royal assurance. So, brush up on your eschatology. Do not moan about this world. Groan for the next! Groan 'to be clothed with our heavenly dwelling.' It is called living on earth, with heaven in mind.

22.7 Finally, we must be prepared

This chapter has asked that great question, So what must we do? The final, somewhat startling, answer can be summed up by Amos 4:12. It is, '... prepare to meet your God ...' It prompts that biggest of the big questions, initially asked in the opening pages of this book, 'Am I ready to die?' Unless and until you can answer that question in the affirmative, you will be neither content, nor of great help to others in this world. While we are restless and unsure about dying, we will remain distracted and diverted. Knowing that your future is safe and bright leads to contentment. Contentment is one the great marks of the mature Christian, who not only has a developed theology of living and dying, but holds the two in a biblical balance. 'But if we have food and clothing, we will be content with that' (1 Timothy 6:8), and 'Keep your lives free from the love of money and be content with what you have, because God has said, "Never will I leave you; never will I forsake you"' (Hebrews 13:5). Being content about your current situation, which is temporary, and knowing that your future, which is permanent, is settled and secure, are wonderful Christian consolations, about which the people of our busy, acquisitive world know very little. These are the unfeigned comforts of the Christian life, present and future. Foster them. It may sound contradictory, but strive to be content.

Some sections in the preceding chapters, and the whole of the following four chapters, encourage you to make prior preparations—to consider, plan and be happy about dying and death. There could be no sounder advice.

In the meantime, '... I urge you to live a life worthy of the calling you have received' (Ephesians 4:1). Live your earthly life to the full. Serve, eat, cry, meditate, enjoy, paint, worship, give, read, laugh, care. 'So whether you eat or drink or whatever you do, do it all for the glory of God' (1 Corinthians 10:31). Be blessed—go over those Beatitudes again in Matthew 5 and determine to make them yours. Then, when you are at the very edge of life, your life's work will be finished, and you will ready for that great day, prepared to meet your God.

These seven answers to the question, So what must we do?, are bound up in Christian duty. This is often described in Scripture as a simultaneous undertaking of two parts, such as, avoid and pursue, shrink from and hold on to, reject and adopt. Who said the Christian life was all negative? One of the clearest illustrations of this principle is found in Colossians 3, where we are told first, to put off sin and second, to put on righteousness. Its application in the realm of these edge-of-life issues is plain—we are to shun the culture of death and all its hideous thinking and practices, and at the same time, we are to embrace the culture of life, live well and prepare to die well. That is, we are to develop an ethic of avoidance *and* an ethic of engagement. Working out these seven answers will help us to perform our whole Christian duty much better.

The outcome of achieving these practical responses will be individuals, families and little communities of people, who still maintain the dignity and worth of all human life, whether pre-born, born, or approaching its natural end. We will be those people, who cherish the young and the old, and who respect the big and the small. And when our earthly end approaches, we will be ready to meet our God. May he give us all the wisdom and energy to accomplish all of this.

Hospices

When you are at the very edge of life, in whose hands do you want to be? It is a pertinent question because there are doctors, nurses and hospital administrators who are euthanasia sympathizers, some are even euthanasia advocates, and a few are euthanasia practitioners. They will not treat you well. Thankfully, there are also still plenty of healthcare workers who are not in favour of euthanasia, at least, not yet. And there is that ever-gallant band of Hippocratic-Christian medical personnel, who are resolutely determined never to become sullied by the likes of euthanasia.

23.1 Euthanasia advocates
The pro-euthanasia camp does seem to be inhabited by some pretty unpleasant people—they are Hippocratic hypocrites. They seem to be everywhere—North America, Europe, Australasia. We have already met two of them in section 5.10. For a start, there is that American, Dr Jack Kevorkian, also known as 'Dr Death'. What a doctor! When he was a pathologist, none of his patients ever got better, then, when he became a euthanasiast, nothing changed.

And, then there is that Australian, Dr Philip Nitschke, who devised his macabre 'death machine', which killed Bob Dent, the first person in the world to die under euthanasia legislation. Nitschke has plans to buy a ship, moor it off the coasts of various countries, and offer euthanasia packages, beyond the arm of the law.

Or, there is the Englishman, Derek Humphry, founder of the Hemlock Society and author of its 1991 best-selling handbook, *The Final Exit*, a d-i-y guide to suicide, or what he calls, 'the practicalities of self-deliverance'. Of the book, he has said, 'Follow my instructions for a perfect death, with no mess, and no post-mortem.' He helped his first wife, Jean, to die, and then promptly deserted his second, Ann, because she would not follow the suicidal advice in his book. He is now president of ERGO!, the Euthanasia Research & Guidance Organization, but still peddling his same old wares. Or, there is Jacques Attali, former aide to President Mitterrand of France, and president of the European Bank for Reconstruction and Development. He has said, 'As soon as he goes beyond sixty to sixty-five years of age, man lives longer than his capacity to produce, and he then costs society a lot of money ... Euthanasia will become one of the essential instruments of our future.' Or, there is Dr Bernard Kouchner, co-founder of Médecins sans Frontières, the international aid organization, and French minister of health. He has said, 'I have practised euthanasia on several occasions. I gave injections to people, never pills, injections with lots of morphine.' Or, there is Marshall Perron, the Chief Minister of the Australian Parliament, who masterminded the Northern Territory's euthanasia law. He has said, 'Encourage civil disobedience. Encourage doctors to "come out" and admit they help people to die.'

This is not a nice bunch of men. Keep them away from my deathbed—I will hide under the sheets if they come near me. Instead, when I am dying, put me in the hands of someone like Dame Cicely Saunders, the founder of the modern hospice movement. She says, '… it is important to live until you die.' She maintains that the 'last days' must not be 'lost days'. She considers that death is, '… a time to complete the unfinished business of our lives, to make amends, say the unsaid, write the unwritten, express the unexpressed. Time to pack your bags, and say goodbye, and sorry, and thank you.' Now, that's more like it—a proper doctor practising principled, compassionate medicine.

23.2 Hospices and Cicely Saunders

Hospices apparently date back to the fourth century BC, when an unnamed and unknown Roman nurse opened her house to needy strangers. Others, before her, had undoubtedly done the same, but every movement of history has to start sometime, somewhere, with someone. The Latin word, *hospes*, actually means 'stranger', though later it came to signify 'guest', and the place where these nurses and needy patients would meet was a *hospitium*. By the fourth century AD, such institutions were spreading across Europe, mostly motivated by the words of Matthew 25:40, 'The King will reply, "I tell you the truth, whatever you did for one of the least of these brothers of mine, you did for me."' During the Middle Ages, hospices ministered mainly to travellers, including those on religious pilgrimages, but they came to an abrupt end during the Reformation.

These early hospices were not solely, or even especially, for the dying. The first hospice exclusively for the care of the dying was opened in 1842 by Mme Jeanne Garnier in Lyons. A similar, but unconnected, hospice for incurable and dying patients was begun by the Irish Sisters of Charity in Dublin in 1879, and this was followed in 1904 by St Joseph's Hospice in East London. At about the same time, three Protestant hospices, all based in London, started to care for the dying. They were the Friedensheim Home of Rest in 1885, the Hostel of God in 1891, and St Luke's Home for the Dying Poor in 1893.

Then, almost two-and-a-half thousand years after their inception, Cicely Saunders began what was to develop into the modern hospice movement. She has been called, 'the woman who changed the face of death.' Not long ago, I met Dr Saunders at 'her' hospice and spent a happy afternoon, a few days before her eighty-third birthday, talking about her lifelong work and edge-of-life issues. She is a remarkable woman and hers is a most remarkable story—it deserves a place in this book.

In 1938, after leaving Roedean School, she started to read philosophy, politics and economics as a student at St Anne's, Oxford, but she came down after one term of study having decided, 'This was no place for a gal.' She then did some Red Cross work until 1940, when she entered St Thomas' Hospital, London to train as a wartime nurse, but it wrecked her back and she was forced to give up at the end of her third year. Instead, in 1944, she completed her PPE degree at St Anne's, and then returned to St Thomas' to become a lady almoner, a type of medical social worker. This was, she recalls, a crucial step in her life because it enabled her later, '… to see the whole patient as part of a whole family. It was also at that time that I came to appreciate the impact of patients dying in pain, and distressed families trying to cope at home, and the difficulty of getting patients into any of the few homes that did exist, and what it was going to be like when they got there.'

She remained both single and single-minded. 'And I'm so glad I didn't marry then,' she says, 'because I wouldn't have done any of this.' But she, as a Protestant Christian, did fall in love with one of her patients, a Polish waiter, who was an agnostic Jew, named David Tasma. He was dying of an inoperable cancer in the first ward she took over as a lady almoner in July 1947. She followed him up as an outpatient and when, in the following

January, he collapsed and was admitted to Middlesex County Hospital, she visited him there about twenty-five times in the two months as he was dying. When he died, aged forty, he left her £500, saying, 'I'll be a window in your home.' This was the seedcorn that launched her life's work, enabling people to die well, in comfort, and at peace.

From 1948 for the next three years, she continued as an almoner, but she began working once or twice a week as a volunteer nurse, caring for the terminally ill at St Luke's Hospital. She needed to know more about dying and death, and especially about pain. 'The surgeon I was working for, pushed me into reading medicine. He told me, "You'll only be frustrated if you don't do it properly, and they won't listen to you."' So, from 1951 to 1957, she enrolled as a medical student at St Thomas' and, eventually, at the age of thirty-nine, qualified as a doctor. A year later, she was awarded a clinical research fellowship at St Joseph's Hospice to study terminal pain and its relief. There she found, 'No drug charts, no patients' notes, no ward reports, drugs on demand, like everywhere else, and patients 'earning' their morphine by having their pain first.' During her years as a volunteer at St Luke's she had seen the regular giving of oral morphine and the resulting better pain control, so she introduced similar regimes at St Joseph's—'The nuns were delighted to have someone come and do something about pain and other symptoms.'

It was at this time, in 1957, that she produced her first research paper entitled, *The Care of the Dying*, and she more clearly envisaged what was to become St Christopher's Hospice. Two underlying features of her future work were also established at this time. First, she began serious medical research, such as, clinical trials comparing the efficacy of new and old analgesics, and second, she learned how to take time to listen to her patients. Her understanding of pain and its control was improving, and she was becoming more enthusiastic about her labours. Patients were already enjoying the fruits of both. The concept of 'total pain', as a complex of the physical, emotional, social and spiritual, was being formulated in her mind, as was the principal need to provide 'active total care' for the patient *and* the patient's family, both *before* and *after* death.

In 1967, the pioneering St Christopher's Hospice was opened in Sydenham, South London—the first ever teaching and research hospice. It cost £27,000 for the site and £500,000 for the buildings. It is now a thriving community of healthcare professionals, plus some nine hundred volunteers. In 1980, she married, Marian Bohusz-Szyszko, another Pole. He died fifteen years later, at 'her' hospice, aged ninety-two. As if to confirm the significance of his wife's vocation, he could declare, 'I've done what I had to do in my life and I'm ready to die.'

Cicely Saunders is adamant about many things. For a start, the dying patient, and the family, must have the priority—'Let the patient speak.' Accordingly, at St Christopher's they have, not just painkilling drugs, but also parties, aromatherapy and household pets. Second, she has always been resolute that the hospice should be at the forefront of pain research, otherwise it would become merely a 'long-stay nursing home.' Third, she has always been keen on innovation. A recent advance in her work is the development of the home-based care service. St Christopher's itself houses less than sixty patients, whereas it sends out a team of thirty nurses, who care for an additional 450 'at home' patients. Fourth, she is convinced that the spiritual needs of patients and their families must never be sidelined, 'A person is an indivisible entity, a physical and a spiritual being.' St Christopher's has a Christian foundation, '... of a very open character ...', though she remains staunch in her conviction that, 'We would not have been here if it was not for God's call.'

St Christopher's takes in mostly cancer victims, though patients with Aids, motor neurone disease, heart disease and chronic lung problems are also admitted. It simply cannot cope with Alzheimer's patients. 'We never said we would be a solution to the whole thing,' is Cicely Saunders' response. 'The fact that you can't do everything, doesn't mean you should stop doing something.' And who of us can gainsay that?

For a plain, but moving account of its work, read *St Christopher's in Celebration*, edited by Cicely Saunders (1988). And for those who would like a more detailed read on the subject of hospices and so forth, there is the hefty and comprehensive *Oxford Textbook of Palliative Medicine* by Doyle *et al.* (1999).

23.3 The modern hospice movement

The modern hospice movement's greatest achievements are, without doubt, symptom control, especially pain control, alongside its insistence on the centrality of the dying person. It is far more than just dispensing painkillers when the patient can no longer endure it. It is far more than just not shifting the dying to a distant side ward, or to the bed nearest the door, and waiting. Rather, it has brought together the best of tough clinical medicine and the best of principled compassion in order to serve the dying. That is what is now called palliative medicine. Long live hospice care!

Of course, the Voluntary Euthanasia Society, and its like, remain cynical. They consider that hospices offer nothing other than a slow form of euthanasia, 'increasing the doses of painkillers until people die.' But what do they know? Cicely Saunders says that, 'The actual doses of morphine used in hospices are uncommonly low, and for twenty per cent of patients they are actually decreased, as death approaches.'

Compared with hospice-type palliative care, euthanasia is extraordinarily cheap. Furthermore, it has always been less demanding to kill than to care. If we were to pursue a public policy of euthanasia, then there would be very few advances in palliative medicine. After all, what would be the motivation for helping and caring for those at the edge of life? In contrast, the hospice movement has shown the ethical way forward. To care genuinely for the patient as a whole person, to achieve symptom control, and to bring the family into the arena of dying and death, has to be a better way. It is the way to die well. Hands up, if you want this when you are dying. Yes, that looks unanimous!

Palliative care

Hippocratic and Christian-based medicine maintains that a doctor has two general responsibilities—to preserve life and to relieve suffering. When the patient is approaching the edge of life, these two can sometimes appear to be in conflict. However, this is an illusion, largely propagated by the practitioners of bad medicine and the supporters of euthanasia. When the patient is near to death, preserving life becomes increasingly unimportant, and instead, a doctor's responsibilities and efforts are directed towards relieving any suffering and preparing the patient to face death, and finally, to die well.

Contrary to the fears of many, suffering, and particularly pain, are not an inevitable part of dying. Nevertheless, if present, it is the doctor's duty to provide symptom control by measures that are without direct, intentional risk to the patient's life. This ethical relief of suffering, together with the provision of comfort, and reassurance for the dying patient, are at the heart of palliative care.

24.1 What is palliative care?

Palliative care is one of the grand spin-offs from the hospice movement. In 1990, the World Health Organization published a report entitled, *Cancer Pain Relief and Palliative Care*. It contained (p. 11) this definition, 'Palliative care is the active total care of patients whose disease is not responsive to curative treatment. Control of pain, of other symptoms, and of psychological, social and spiritual problems is paramount. The goal of palliative care is achievement of the best possible quality of life for patients and their families.' Dame Cicely Saunders would, I am sure, wholeheartedly agree with this.

Palliative care became officially recognized as a medical sub-specialty only in 1987, but, in many ways, it was nothing new. In days gone by, before the advent of antibiotics, complex surgery and advanced technology, palliative care was the major task of many within the medical profession. It was an essential part of the 'ordinary' care that was then given to those who were dying and close to death.

Nowadays, palliative care is an increasingly sophisticated and specialized enterprise, and it is comforting to know that more doctors are entering it than any other medical specialty. It is comforting because greater than ever numbers of us, worldwide, will be dying, not from the old-fashioned acute conditions, but from chronic and progressive illnesses—accordingly, more and more of us will be seeking the benefits of palliative care.

This shift in the causes of death, together with our increasingly elderly populations, mean that during the early decades of the twenty-first century, greater financial resources will need to be allocated to the sort of healthcare required at the end of patients' lives. Indeed, this has begun to happen, albeit, slowly. In the US, about a quarter of the Medicare budget is currently being spent on edge-of-life medicine. This is driven by the fact that during the last year of a patient's life almost three times more is spent on healthcare compared with that spent on a healthy person of a similar age. In the UK, almost a quarter of hospital bed capacity is occupied by patients in their last year of life. These facts and trends all emphasize the need for, and the growing importance of, palliative care.

It was the voluntary sector, especially through the hospice movement, that led the way in establishing and developing modern palliative care. Now, palliative care services are growing throughout the world, but fairly unevenly. In 1999, there were 6,560 hospices, or palliative care services, in eighty-four countries. Of these, 933 were in the UK, about 1,200 in the rest of Europe, 3,600 in North America and 350 in Australasia. But within these countries, the distribution of palliative care remains uneven. In some areas of the UK, as many as seventy per cent of patients with cancer are cared for by palliative care teams. On the other hand, patients with terminally-progressive diseases other than cancers are less well catered for—only about four per cent of patients who are referred to palliative care centres have non-cancer diagnoses. Furthermore, the actual palliative care services provided are not uniform. For a start, they may be funded by the National Health Service, the private, or the voluntary sectors. Then their palliative care teams may differ in their composition—a good team might consist of a doctor, a nurse, a social worker and a psychologist. Their staff:patient ratio, out-of-hours care, treatment protocols, and so on, will also vary. A high quality scheme would be one, such as the 'Hospital at Home' scheme, which runs in Cambridge. It offers up to two weeks of round-the-clock nursing care for patients approaching death. Such palliative care facilities should be part of all good hospital management schemes. They should provide individual rooms for dying patients, special diets, peaceful areas, specific nursing care, and so forth. In reality, we may be faced with lesser facilities. It cannot be denied that medical resources can be scarce, especially when it comes to caring, rather than curing.

Although the majority of people die in hospital—the proportion in England and Wales is currently about three-quarters—dying at home is, perhaps surprisingly, in our highly-medicalized society, becoming the choice of more and more. For instance, at least half of all terminally-ill patients would wish to die at home. In response to this trend, there has, in recent years, been a considerable increase in palliative care-at-home teams throughout the UK.

24.2 A false view of curing and caring

Our society has adopted a wrong view of modern medicine. We expect it to deliver therapies and cures for all ills and extend human life indefinitely, well, almost. What we have done is, overemphasize curing compared with, and often at the expense of, caring.

This is not some neat little piece of lexical trickery. We truly have confused ourselves about the difference between curing and caring. For instance, people can be profoundly shocked when modern medicine cannot cure their aged grandfather's heart condition, or even their sister's breast cancer. All our lives we have gone into hospitals, ill, and come out of them, cured. The thought of *not* coming out, of medicine failing to cure us, has become largely unthinkable. How absurd we have become, how slow we are to face the inevitability of death.

Whatever our misconceptions and false expectations of modern medicine are, they should never allow us to tolerate unnatural death at the hands of a doctor. Because medicine cannot cure, does not mean it should kill. Euthanasia is a total no-no. This is where hospices and palliative care come into their own. They are the rivals of euthanasia, the white knights who will deliver us from its threatening clutches. If there were hospices, or hospice-type care, more widely available, then euthanasia would hardly even be an issue. The hospice movement has challenged our utilitarian view of human life. It has begun to reclaim the 'good and happy death' motif, which has, for too long, been commandeered and twisted by the pro-euthanasia movement.

24.3 When should treatment stop?

Modern medicine can hoist itself on its own petard—its phenomenal success in some areas has led us to expect too much from it in others. We can be misled into thinking that it will always cure, always conquer. Therefore, some people will consider that aggressive, restorative treatment should never be stopped, at least, not until death is indisputably diagnosed. Such an attitude shows a deficient grasp of the issues of medicine, as well as those of life and death.

But when should treatment stop? When the prognosis is very poor, as it will become in all cases of terminal illness. Remember, this will not be an issue for everyone—treatment will never have been started for those who die gently of 'natural causes', or for the victims of sudden deaths, such as those caused by accidents, heart attacks, and so on. But for many, treatment will have been started, perhaps days, even years before. For these dying patients there comes a time of crossover. This is the move from curative treatment to palliative care. This is not a cop out. We have to face the inescapable fact that medicine cannot, and never will, defeat death. This may go against the grain of twenty-first century populist thinking, as well as the aspirations of triumphalist medical practitioners, but it is nonetheless true.

When does this crossover occur? The answer is, when treatment becomes futile. Futile treatment is treatment, which is of no benefit, or even a burden, to the patient. It should always be opposed and avoided. And let us also be entirely clear about one other issue—there is no single measurement, no precise indicator, no universal answer that will identify when treatment should be stopped. For most, it will be obvious—the final hours have arrived. Now and again, there are dilemmas to be faced by doctors. A typical one might be like this—a dying, old man's heart stops, should he be rushed to the operating theatre, should he be intubated to help his breathing, causing him additional pain, or should attempts be made to start his heart physically, thereby probably breaking some of his ribs? What treatment would you recommend for him? There are no standard answers to these questions. They are real life, catch-22 situations.

When I speak on this topic there is one frequently-asked question from the audience, of the type, 'Was it right to stop the treatment of my father when …?' And all I can say is, 'I don't know. I wasn't there. I cannot assess all the circumstances.' Such apparent failure on my part is often met with visible disappointment from the questioner. But let us try to be mature at this point. Sure, we all want answers to all our questions—the very purpose of this book is to supply many—but some questions are unanswerable, or at least, they are not subject to some pat, standardized answer, primarily because medical situations involving people are not standardized. Principles can be standardized, patients cannot.

Everyone's dying and death are unique. Around the deathbed is where we all need wisdom and a good dose of reality. When we are there, we need to be listening, asking questions, thinking and praying. We need to be closely in touch with the healthcare team and its decision-making. These times can be fraught with difficulties. But of one thing we can be sure—the patient will *not* get better, ever.

24.4 Asking the right questions

So how do you ensure that your loved one is getting the right quality of care, quality of life and quality of death? There are at least three areas where questions will arise—they should be asked, and they should be answered.

First, there are medical factors. What have been the patient's diagnosis and prognosis? What is the treatment and how successful has it been? Have there been complications, suffering, pain? Second, there are emotional factors. Does the patient feel contented? Does he consider that his life's work is complete? Is he competent or incompetent? Is the rest of the family involved, and do they accept the situation? Third, there are spiritual factors. Is the patient weary of this life and ready for the next? Does he have Christian faith? Does he have spiritual questions? These are but general guidelines and sample questions, but they should alert us to the dynamics of dying, something we can all too often try either to ignore, or to avoid. All such factors need wise and ongoing consideration by the family, medical team and other carers.

24.5 What about suffering and pain?

Human suffering is more than the experience of pain. For the dying patient, memories, loves and joys, loneliness, missed opportunities, regrets and much more, can all contribute to the sum of suffering. Yet suffering and pain are inextricably linked to, and inescapably part of, human living (Genesis 3:16–19; Ecclesiastes 2:22–23; 1 Peter 4:12–19). Furthermore, they can be heightened at the edge of life. Pain and suffering are a mix of the physical, psychological and spiritual—we recognize that from personal experience and biblical warrant. We know of the physical hurt from headaches, torn muscles, childbirth, and so on. Psychological and spiritual hurt can be more serious, and it may encompass grief and anguish (Job 2:11–13), the feeling of abandonment (Psalm 43:2, 5), and even forsaking, as ultimately described in Matthew 27:46.

Like so much at the edge of life, we can harbour a wrong view of pain and suffering. Many people fear them, like almost nothing else, even though they can be profitable (James 1:2–4). We try to escape them by evasion, or stoicism, or platitudes, or even faulty theology. Our medicalized world, gripped by this tyranny of cure, views pain and suffering, and finally death, as huge clinical failures. This is all quite wrong and unhelpful. Pain, suffering, dying and death are fundamental aspects of human life and the human experience. To view them as failures is to regard ourselves as omnipotent and to misunderstand creation, redemption, resurrection, and our God. Yet, the Christian worldview is not a masochist's charter. We need not endure the physical pain of toothache for want of a couple of aspirin tablets, nor the pain of some cancers for a lack of morphine. On the other hand, psychological and spiritual pain is usually not so easily faced and overcome. But we must remind ourselves, again, and again, and again that some pain and some suffering are an intimate, predictable and unavoidable part of living and dying. No one escapes them completely. Of course, we can use analgesics, sedatives, Scripture, prayer and other legitimate means to alleviate our symptoms, and we should be thankful for such palliatives. However, what we must scrupulously avoid is making irreversibly bad edge-of-life decisions in an attempt to circumvent all pain and all suffering.

One, if not the, major argument in favour of euthanasia ceases to be relevant when we understand that modern science has taken the greater part of pain out of dying. The problem of pain undeniably exists and it should never be minimized. Of course, it is not just the presence of pain, but rather its severity, that is the important factor. Nevertheless, pain, even at moderate intensity, can be all-consuming and unless it is controlled, the patient can think of, or achieve, little else.

Take cancer as an example. Worldwide, there are something like nine million new cases of cancer each year. For those people who will die of cancer, it is estimated that between thirty and forty per cent will experience pain in the early stages, but as the disease advances, this proportion increases to about seventy per cent and the pain will become moderate to severe.

So how much can be controlled? The conclusion (p. 14) of the World Health Organization's *Cancer Pain Relief* (1996) is, 'A relatively inexpensive yet effective method exists for relieving cancer pain in seventy to ninety per cent of patients.' In *Hospice and Palliative Care*, edited by Cicely Saunders, the assessment (p. 32) is that, 'Between five and ten per cent of cancer patients fail to obtain full pain relief.' This so-called 'intractable pain' is often associated with the complications of nerve destruction as well as 'emotional, family and spiritual problems'. According to Dr Saunders in 2001, 'Practically all of that can now be dealt with. A very small number of people you have to make sleepy. But there you are much more likely to be dealing with terminal restlessness rather than terminal pain.' And she adds, 'There is a lot of pain about, and there is still much to learn, but the thing to do is to kill the pain, not the patient.'

However, remember, not everybody who is dying suffers serious pain—it is not inevitable. Where it does occur, edge-of-life pain can most often be controlled by the expert use of analgesics—whether it is or not, is another matter. Hospice staff tend to be the most skilled in the relief of pain. It used to be accepted wisdom that pain control was better for patients in hospitals than at home, but now there is emerging evidence, especially since the introduction of hospice-type home care programmes, that home control can be just as good as, or even better than, that of hospitals.

24.6 Palliative care and pain

Let us be entirely clear—it is simply and utterly wrong to assume that terminal pain can be managed only by administering death to the patient. That is dishonest pro-euthanasia propaganda. Pain management within palliative care recognizes the uniqueness of each patient and his pain. The patient is listened to. He says, 'The pain frightens me, especially when I am alone at night.' The causes and symptoms are assessed and explained, and other factors, such as the pain's location, severity and timing are considered, so that a few days later the patient can say, 'Now I understand my pain, it seems to be much better.' Perhaps he then asks, 'But why do I vomit?' The palliative care team next discusses, 'Is it as a result of his chemotherapy, or his medications, or something else?' The cause is sought. Symptom control is then individualized—it is not a 'cookbook' prescribing of analgesics. There is a selective use and personal titration of painkillers—not all analgesics are the same, nor are all people's responses to them. Whether the cause of pain is benign or malignant, treatment, often by opioids, is tailored to the individual, reviewed, and titred. If necessary, the World Health Organization's three-step 'analgesic ladder' (*Cancer Pain Relief*, 1996, p. 9) may be used to match increasing pain with adequate control. Step one is the use of non-opioids, like paracetamol and non-steroidal anti-inflammatory drugs (NSAIDs), then step two progresses to weak opioids, like codeine and dihydrocodeine, then step three involves strong opioids, like morphine and fentanyl.

Acute episodes of pain can be treated with an emergency dose of so-called 'breakthrough' analgesics, followed by frequent review. Pain can still disturb an unconscious person because the cause is still present. If the patient has problems with swallowing, then the subcutaneous route for the delivery of drugs can be used. Diamorphine, is often the opioid of choice and because of its solubility, it can be delivered through a hypodermic syringe. Where, for example, the patient is experiencing bone pain, then a NSAID can be used. Similarly, a drug, like diazepam, can be effective in controlling muscular spasm. In addition, other forms of pain, like mouth dryness and pressure sores, require their own particular non-drug treatments. This is all part of symptom control, in this case, pain control, within proper palliative care. Good, isn't it?

The 1990 World Health Organization report, *Cancer Pain Relief and Palliative Care*, stated (p. 55) that, '… with the development of modern methods of palliative care, legalization of voluntary euthanasia is unnecessary. Now that a practical alternative to death in pain exists, there should be concentrated efforts to implement programmes of palliative care, rather than a yielding to pressure for legal euthanasia.' So, while the problem of pain exists and it must be recognized, the proper response does not lie in legislating for euthanasia, 'to put patients out of their misery', but rather, in committing additional resources to research and to caring for those who suffer pain.

24.7 Another benefit of palliative care

Palliative care has another positive spin-off—it can take away the argument for the legalization of euthanasia. Prior to its legalization in 2001, the practice of unauthorized euthanasia had become widespread in the Netherlands. Why? The Netherlands is backward when it comes to palliative care. Dutch doctors have had little training in palliative care and therefore they are unable to offer their dying patients anything much other than euthanasia. Another factor is that there are so few, as few as only seventy, specialist palliative care beds throughout the whole of Holland. As Dr Ben Zylicz, one of that rare breed of Dutch palliative care doctors has said, (*British Medical Journal*, 1998, 317:1613), 'If you accept euthanasia as a solution to difficult and unresolved problems in palliative care, you will never learn anything.' Twenty-five per cent of the patients admitted to his palliative care centre had originally requested euthanasia, but none have ultimately needed, or used it.

Similarly, the inadequate palliative care training and facilities in the US were highlighted by a 1996 survey (*Journal of American Medical Association* 275:919–925) of doctors in Washington State. It found that about a quarter of patients who sought their doctor's help in committing suicide were actually given a prescription for that purpose. Also about a quarter of patients requesting assisted euthanasia received their doctor's help. The American Medical Association (AMA) commented that the survey, '… strengthens the AMA's contention that considerable physician education is necessary to ensure quality, compassionate care for patients nearing death.' At the same time, the AMA reiterated its opposition to physician-assisted suicide. But these are no more than empty words unless, and until, it begins to prioritize that much-needed palliative care.

Dying well is far from impossible. For the vast, vast majority of Christians, it will be their happy lot. Christians should also be mindful that any suffering and pain associated with their dying and death will be the very last they ever experience. That must be good news! But what about others? If we want them to die well physically, mentally, socially and spiritually, then they too will need this principled compassion, this palliative care. The great need for them is not to have euthanasia legalized, or to provide immunity for doctors if they and their patients agree on medically-assisted suicide. The pressing need is to expand and apply programmes of palliative medicine and palliative care. Only these will reduce, if not eliminate, calls for euthanasia. Providing better standards of palliative, continuing and long-term care are the right responses to those who suffer. We must counter the idea that there are only two options— dying in pain, or euthanasia. Palliative medicine answers the first. The second is rebutted by the ethical truth that 'killing patients is always wrong'. Principled compassion, in the form of palliative care, is the very best medicine for the very edge of life.

The last days and hours

The close approach of death has been described in various ways, including, 'in the suburbs of heaven', 'the gate of death', and 'the honest hour'. These poetic labels should not be allowed to obscure the starkness of the reality. We will all have such an encounter, on one particular day, in one specific place. At that time-and-space juncture, we will indeed be at the very edge of life. In their detail, these last hours will be different for each of us, but some features will be common to most of us. These are presented here to help us all, the dying and their families, gain a better understanding of this most significant of all life's closing transactions.

25.1 The experience

Although a few of us will die unexpectedly and suddenly, nearly all of us will die unsurprisingly and comparatively slowly, over days, even weeks. This process of dying has often helpfully been divided into three stages of experience. During the initial stage, or what has been called 'facing the threat', the dying person may go through a spectrum of emotions, including fear, anger, shock, denial, humour and hope. The chronic stage, or 'being ill', may bring some understanding and resolution of those emotions experienced during the initial stage. And this phase is often characterized by a measure of depression. The final stage, or 'acceptance', may be marked by acknowledgement of the inevitable, but not necessarily so. These stages are not fixed points, but merely a generalized pattern— some of us will die with quite different experiences.

Besides these emotional aspects, there is also a commonly-recognized pattern of physical events. During the final days or hours, most people experience some increasing weakness in their bodies as well as a general immobility. They become disinterested in food and drink, they often have difficulty in swallowing, and they can become drowsy. The dying person may experience breathlessness, which can cause fear and anxiety for both the patient and family—it can be overcome by various treatments, ranging from the complexities of opioid administration, to oxygen therapy, to simply repositioning the patient. Restlessness and confusion can often be relieved by attending to the patient's environment—soft lights, familiar faces and quietness can all help. Drugs may also be required, but it may be that the patient is undergoing some emotional or spiritual anguish for which there is no drug alleviation. Nausea and vomiting are not common at this stage, but if they do occur, they should be treated with antiemetics.

Emergency situations can arise. It is important that appropriate and timely actions are taken, not only for the comfort of the patient, but also for that of the relatives and carers, who can be unduly alarmed by such events. Some emergencies are predictable, because of the patient's medical history, and some are preventable. Nevertheless, most emergencies in the last hours are irreversible and palliative treatment should be directed towards the urgent relief of distress.

For those who have suffered from a long-term incurable illness, these last stages of dying can often be predicted and therefore anticipated well in advance. For others, the end may be hastened by a more sudden and unexpected deterioration. Whatever the details, death is truly imminent—the patient is about to die, perhaps within a few days, or even hours. It is a time for other changes. For example, nursing care and the control of the patient's symptoms no longer rely on aggressive clinical investigations and treatments. It is that crossover time. What, a short while before, were considered to be essential drugs, such as antidepressants and corticosteroids, are often dispensed with, and other drugs, such as analgesics and sedatives, become the required medicines if pain and restlessness are present. Also, support for the family and carers assumes a new priority. This is the time when anxieties, stress and emotions run high for all concerned. The type and extent of care provided should be frequently reviewed.

These are some of the common experiences of dying. And these responses and treatments are the foundational patterns of good palliative care. An understanding of them will contribute to the patient dying well and the experience and memory of a good death by all the other people involved.

25.2 Support for the dying and the living

Involvement with dying people is not straightforward. It will, at first, perhaps make us feel uneasy and awkward. It is said that the British attitude towards the dying is six feet away and three feet above—in other words, remote and detached. But if we need to do it, and want to do it well, then reading a short book, like *Living with Dying—A Guide to Palliative Care*, by Cicely Saunders *et al.* (1993) should help us considerably.

One of the keys to dying well is the availability of support. This consists, needless to say, of support for the patient, but also for the family, and for the carers, both lay and professional. Because of a distorted view of death, these latter people can often resist it so strenuously that they can become exhausted. It is a time when relatives can also become especially fatigued, as well as perhaps perplexed and guilt-ridden. Carers need to be cared for too because they can become resentful, and cross at the lack of success of their efforts. In the midst of death, even doctors and nurses sometimes need to be told that it is not their fault that the patient is dying. These carers can already be doing a dozen and one things for the dying patient, and, as each day goes by, there are additional chores and duties. Tempers can be frayed and patience frazzled—such people really will need support. To be sure, at the very edge of life can be a time and place of tension.

Nowadays, dying and death have become largely private, somewhat embarrassing, and even sanitized, affairs. How different it was just a generation or two ago when a whole village or neighbourhood would be affected by the death of one of its residents. One mark of this change is the decline of the custom of the wake, a mix of lament and celebration attended by family, friends and the locals. Nowadays, it tends to be a 'family only' occasion.

The role of families in the dying and death of a person can be crucial. Yet they can differ enormously in their intra-familial relationships. Two extremes can be recognized. First, there is 'the patient *in* the family', which is typically a warm and caring environment. Second, there is 'the patient *and* the family', which is characterized by rather cold and distant relationships. 'You and yours' probably fit somewhere between these two ends of the range, but, hopefully, up towards the 'warmer' end.

Families are certainly assorted. Some are 'synchronous', that is, they function admirably as long as their daily routine is maintained. Alter it, such as when one member is dying, and that cohesive structure can come unstuck and so, unexpectedly, can their ability to cope with the edge-of-life experiences. For other families, dying and death can uncomfortably force them together and that can rekindle past animosities and serve to highlight their dysfunctional nature. Then again, some families, who are distant, both socially and geographically, can be reunited by the dying and death of one of their own relatives—thus, it can, even should, be a constructive, reconciliatory time. Incidentally, these vast opportunities for fostering personal maturity and family relationships are why hospice personnel are generally opposed to denying patients access to the truth about their condition, as well as any legislation that would encourage the hastening of their death. These can be difficult, but also precious, times.

At these times, clear communication must be high on the agenda, not only between family members, but also with doctors, carers and especially towards the patient. State-of-the-art medicine has made personal communication increasingly fragile. Therefore, encourage it. Become a brick, not in that toe-curling, bumptious manner, but as the Lord Jesus would do—gently, compassionately and genuinely. Our communication must be sincere and realistic, and it includes both speaking and listening. There must be questions and explanations about what is happening, what will probably happen, what medicines are being used, what support is available, and how the family can provide help for not only the carers but, above all, for the dying one. There should also, when and where appropriate, be prayer and Gospel communication from church leaders and others.

Such true communication is honest communication. There is some debate about whether the dying patient should be told the truth. Should information be withheld? The Christian rule must surely be, always tell the patient the truth about what is happening. Truth, whether spiritual or medical, does set you free. In twenty-first century parlance, this is empowerment, enabling patients to exercise their intrinsic dignity. Of course, care must be taken to tell the truth in a way that will not cause the patient undue apprehension—bad news is best broken in small pieces, rather than as a bombshell. The more frightened a person is, the less he is likely to talk about his doubts and fears. Whatever the prognosis, the patient can be assured that he is dying and that all is well—he can stop struggling and relax.

Practical support that is insufficient is the main reason why many patients have to leave their homes and be admitted to a hospital, or a hospice. For some this move can be problematic because it can be accompanied by a hastening deterioration, both physically and mentally. Or, at least, it can often seem that way. However, such declines were probably occurring anyway, and the new environment can simply make them more obvious. Now read carefully, and remember this—this person, your loved one, is *never* going to recover, he is dying, right? Perhaps he will live for just a day, or a week, or even surprisingly for a month or longer, but the end is now irreversibly in view. Such a move out of the family home is no disgrace—it is *not* a failure on your part, whether you are the spouse, or a member of the family, or caring team. Some dying people need 24/7 care, and no husband, or wife, son, or daughter can give that for more than a few days. So be sensible—there is already one patient, nobody wants two or more!

Nevertheless, whether the patient is spending his last hours at home, or in hospital, extra help is often needed. There is much that the Christian fellowship can do at this time. But, be sensitive. Do not arrive unannounced. Do not phone late at night. Do not outstay your welcome. Perhaps one or two people could coordinate this extra assistance. And do not forget that there will be a need to continue some aspects of this support once the family has been bereaved. What can best summarize this type of Christian response? Surely, it is the application of injunctions like those of 1 Timothy 6:18, 'Command them to do good, to be rich in good deeds, and to be generous and willing to share' and Romans 12:15, 'Rejoice with those who rejoice; mourn with those who mourn.'

25.3 Religious concerns

The elderly and the dying need to be assured of comfort, both physical and spiritual, and that their current life is neither meaningless, nor useless. As many will know, visiting the dying Christian can frequently result in the visitor receiving more counsel, spiritual and otherwise, than the visited. Even so, the dying can have religious concerns and fears—these too need to be addressed. Asking a minister to visit a dying person can have useful, therapeutic outcomes. It can also precipitate a 'crisis of faith'. This book is not the place to rehearse the duties and privileges of the Christian pastor or minister, but they should not be minimized. This is, after all, the last time for the dying, unbelieving person to accept Christ as Lord and Saviour. Can there ever be a more critical time of ministry?

There is the reality of the deathbed conversion, and we should never underplay it. Nor should we necessarily be downcast if we do not observe it. Who knows what occurs during the last hours of a person's life? Searching for God, recalling earlier-heard truths, memories of Christian teaching and testimony, who knows? The dying thief is our exemplar (Luke 23:43). But we should also beware of creating false hopes in ourselves and others. We do not always know how God works, except that it is forever in love, according to his purposes and sovereignly. Conversion is not our business, it is God's. It is he who has said, 'I will have mercy on whom I will have mercy, and I will have compassion on whom I will have compassion' (Exodus 33:19). Our task is to be true and faithful. Nevertheless, the death of someone with uncertain saving faith and undecided eternal destiny should cause us to, 'Seek the LORD while he may be found; call on him while he is near' (Isaiah 55:6) and prompt others to do the same. But can we doubt that we are going to be astonished by some we meet in heaven?

25.4 Earlier preparations

None of us can predict when, where, or how we will die. Some may want to go unannounced by way of a sudden and massive heart attack. Most of us probably want to go quickly. For what it is worth, I would like to go coherently, at home, with my family around my bed. I would like my last meal to be lobster followed by profiteroles, cooked by my wife, though I acknowledge it may have to be just lobster bisque and chocolate sauce! I would want my pastor to have read to us, my favourite Bible book, Colossians, and then prayed with us all. I would encourage my family to follow the Faith, and then say my farewells. Then I would go to sleep, die peacefully, and go to be with my Lord. Maybe it will, maybe it will not, be like that for me. But have you ever thought honestly about your great event? Have you thought about, or better still written, your obituary notice, and your funeral service, have you chosen the hymns and the Bible readings? How is it that we can spend long hours planning a holiday, or so meticulously prepare to redecorate the dining room, but think so little about making the arrangements for our last and most certain event of this life?

Think about those last days and hours—it will do you good. They lead to death and eternity. There are no subjects in the whole, wide world about which men and women ought to be more interested. None of us has had any previous, personal experience of it. In many ways, death is that great unknown. But, the wise will learn from those who have gone before. And, above all others, there is One to learn from. He is the One who has already experienced death. He is the One who has already conquered death and experienced resurrection, and has told us about them both. Is there an afterlife? Can you doubt it? Do you doubt it? Then, read John 14:1–4. The second person of the Trinity has promised to make a new home for all his people and to take us there. I cannot speak for you, but that promise is good enough for me.

And it was also good enough for many of our believing predecessors. They knew how to prepare for death. We have largely forgotten how to, and that is our loss. Most of us are too busy living to consider dying. Now, while we are in good health and strength, is the time to start preparing ourselves. Such a momentous event deserves extensive and thorough preparation. To wait until we are on our deathbeds would seem to be too late, almost like after the event.

Such preparation includes reading and contemplating. Pride of place must, of course, go to the greatest book on life and death, the Bible—it is peerless. There are other books too. One of the best is that nineteenth-century golden oldie, Archibald Alexander's *Thoughts on Religious Experience* (1967). Musing on Psalm 71, he so wisely wrote, (p. 250), 'Let the aged then tell to those that come after them, the works of divine grace which they have witnessed or which their fathers have told them. Let them be active as long as they can, and when bodily strength fails, let them wield the pen; or if unable to write for the edification of the church, let them exhibit consistent and shining example of the Christian temper, in kindness and good will to all; in uncomplaining patience; in contented poverty; in cheerful submission to painful providences; and in mute resignation to the loss of their dearest friends. And when death comes, let them not be afraid or dismayed; then will be the time to honour God by implicitly and confidently trusting in His promises. Let them "against hope believe in hope".'

Dying can be a difficult time. Yet the Christian has numerous consolations. Foremost among these must be one of Christ's promises, spoken, seemingly out of place, at the very end of the Great Commission. It is, 'And surely I will be with you always, to the very end of the age' (Matthew 28:20). He will be there—Christ will warm our deathbed—he will be our *amicus mortis*, our friend during dying, and then at death. It is like a ricochet from Psalm 23:4, 'Even though I walk through the valley of the shadow of death, I will fear no evil, for you are with me …' This is the God who has promised to be with and to comfort his people. This is the God who has said throughout the ages, from Deuteronomy 31:6 to Hebrews 13:5, 'Never will I leave you; never will I forsake you.' Whatever the distress, however strong the pain, despite the discomfort, God has promised to be with you. Can there be a greater Comforter, or better comfort? To go through dying with him, is going to be infinitely more comfortable than without him. And this divine comfort is not just for the dying. That in itself would be sufficient, and more than we deserve, but God's comfort also extends to those left behind. 'Blessed are those who mourn, for they will be comforted' (Matthew 5:4). Some will deride all this as 'pie in the sky'—I call it 'the blessings of God'.

25.5 The prospect of heaven

This should be the best and the richest section of the whole book, though I fear it will not be. The topic is beyond compare, and certainly beyond my literary capabilities. I know that I can never do it justice, however many times I rewrite these words. My consolation is that heaven will be far more astonishingly better than I can ever describe. To contemplate the aftermath of death for the Christian is like trying to explain to a blind man the brilliance of the stars, or a rainbow. Alexander does a much better job than I, when reflecting on the great transition (p. 187), '… from the state of imprisonment in this clay tenement to an unknown state of existence, would be overwhelming … That the scene will be new and sublime, beyond all conception, cannot be doubted; but what our susceptibilities and feelings will be, when separated from the body, we cannot tell.' But of this we can be sure—it will be excellent, at least as good as life was in the original Garden of Eden.

Such contemplations must not lead us to bicker about the minutiae of heaven—what will my body be like, what will I wear and eat, what language will I speak? Such questions are from the realm of idle curiosity and time-wasting speculation. The antidote to any such squabblings is 1 John 3:2, '... and what we will be has not yet been made known.' Such details are not given to us in the Bible, and anyway, we do not need to know these pleasures yet, they are, for the present time, unknowable. One day we will know, because we will see, hear, touch, smell and taste them. But of some things we can be certain. Again, let me borrow the words of Alexander (p. 253), '... one of the first feelings of the departed saint will be a lively sense of complete deliverance from all evil, natural and moral. The pains of death will be the last pangs ever experienced. When these are over, the soul will enjoy the feelings of complete salvation from ever distress. What a new and delightful sensation will it be, to feel safe from every future danger, as well as saved from all past trouble.'

And, above all, he will be there. He who rescued us while on earth, he who died in our place, he who transferred us from the dominion of darkness into the kingdom of light. Now, it can hardly be imagined, then, it will be the real thing. Though we are blessed now, then we will know newer, better, greater heights. Therefore, now, while here on earth, we should be living in happy expectation of such an eternal life. Corruption, tears, pain, dishonour and weakness will give way to incorruption, smiles, joy, honour and strength. Ah! How wonderful!

Finally, think about dying, death, resurrection and heaven in one of the ways that the Bible does. It employs the analogy of seeds. 1 Corinthians 15:37 states, 'When you sow, you do not plant the body that will be, but just a seed, perhaps of wheat or of something else.' No gardener can fail to be amazed at the transformation when she surveys the wizened, brown seeds in the palm of her hand, and then a couple of months later, the glorious, multicoloured flowers, or the succulent vegetables. This encapsulates the Christian hope. 'So will it be with the resurrection of the dead. The body that is sown is perishable, it is raised imperishable; it is sown in dishonour, it is raised in glory; it is sown in weakness, it is raised in power; it is sown a natural body, it is raised a spiritual body' (1 Corinthians 15:42–44).

The big question is, are you ready? Ready for your last days and hours? Ready for your last journey? Here are your three-fold biblical travel instructions. First, make sure that your place is confirmed, 'Therefore, my brothers, be all the more eager to make your calling and election sure' (2 Peter 1:10). Second, think about your destination, 'Let us fix our eyes on Jesus, the author and perfecter of our faith … sat down at the right hand of the throne of God' (Hebrews 12:2). Third, prepare to emigrate, '… I desire to depart and be with Christ, which is better by far …' (Philippians 1:23).

Loss and bereavement

Losses are a function of human life—we are all acquainted with them. Everyone has already lost yesterday, our childhood has also long gone, and by now, many of life's opportunities have vanished. But do not let this sort of introspection make you miserable. Come on—we still have today, we have put away childish things, and new prospects and horizons are before us. Those notwithstanding, we must admit that growing old brings with it a unique set of losses. They may be work-related, such as fading job satisfaction. They may be due to retirement and therefore include losses of a working role, the social aspects of employment, income, and so forth. They may also be due to declining health, like sensory losses, mental losses, physical incapacities, losses of independence, and the like.

26.1 Loss as bereavement

And decisively, there is the loss associated with death—bereavement. This experience is common to all men, women and children, Christian and non-Christian. If you have not experienced it yet, you will. It can be potentially dangerous to our health—as many as a third of bereaved people develop a depressive illness, albeit, mostly of a temporary nature. However, bereavement need not be such a feared and damaging experience because there is good evidence that it can also bring about maturity and wisdom. And, because of its universality, bereavement, like death, can, and should, be anticipated and prepared for.

26.2 Expressing and coping with grief

The death of a loved one, even when expected, is a time of emotional turmoil for the bereaved. The Christian must show self-control (Galatians 5:23), and is not '... to grieve like the rest of men, who have no hope' (1 Thessalonians 4:13). Nevertheless, grief is a Christian emotion. After all, 'Godly men buried Stephen and *mourned deeply* for him' (Acts 8:2), and 'Jesus wept' at the tomb of his friend, Lazarus (John 11:35). Sorrow and mourning at the death of a Christian are real and to be expressed, though they are to be mingled with hope and joy because, 'Blessed are the dead who die in the Lord from now on' (Revelation 14:13). Many of us have experienced that warm blend of solid joy and genuine sorrow at a believer's funeral.

On the other hand, many of us have felt dejected and despondent when it is an unbeliever who is being buried. The sorrow and mourning at the death of a non-Christian may also be genuine, but they cannot be mingled with hope and joy. Family and close friends who continue to reject Christ will cause us to have, '… great sorrow and unceasing anguish …' (Romans 9:2). Yet, usually, we can never be entirely sure that such rejection has persisted until death—there is that hope of the deathbed conversion.

So, like dying and death, bereavement can be a tough time—Christians and non-Christians alike can go through the emotional mangle. The bereaved want to cry, look back, and search for what has been lost. Of all the emotions that accompany bereavement, grief is the chief. Typically, the bereaved pass through three phases of grieving. The first phase is the distress that occurs around the actual time of death. This is often suppressed, and a period of numbness, lasting for hours, or even days, can follow. Second, there are usually intense feelings of pining for the dead person, often coupled with severe anxiety. Appetites are lost, daily routines go awry, mental concentration is short, and the person can become irritable and depressed. Then the third phase of grieving occurs, when disorganization, and misery, and gloom can become established.

The expression of these phases of grief, which are usually jumbled up with additional emotions like shock, disbelief, relief and denial, can be vastly variable. They do not automatically occur in a strict order, nor are they necessarily passed through only once. For example, while it can be quite normal for a widow to weep every day over the loss of her husband, if this continues for more than a year, there may be cause for concern. On the other hand, some people express little or no emotion, and that can be equally undesirable.

Physical changes can also be apparent. For example, body weight often fluctuates—during the first four months of bereavement, it is lost, then it returns, then, by perhaps month six, overweight can set in. Thereafter, good signs usually begin to gather momentum. There is a slow return to caring for personal appearance, the renewal of social contacts, and, usually within two years, most bereaved people will recognize that they are recovering.

The vast majority of people do readjust, move on, and re-engage with society. However, for a few, the trauma of bereavement can prove to be too much. As Alvin Toffler observed (p. 299), long ago in his rather sensationalist book, *Future Shock,* (Pan Books, 1970), 'If the death of one's spouse is rated as one hundred points, then moving to a new home is rated by most people as worth only twenty points, a vacation thirteen. The death of a spouse ... is almost universally regarded as the single most impactful change that can befall a person in the normal course of his life.' Furthermore, Toffler noted (p. 303), '... that death rates among widows and widowers, during the first year after the loss of a spouse, are higher than normal ... the shock of widowhood weakens resistance to illness and tends to accelerate ageing.' A generation later, Toffler's remarks are still true.

26.3 Helping the bereaved

However, such losses can be minimized, if not eventually overcome, and that will happen sooner and better, if the appropriate help is at hand. Principled compassion is the great need of bereaved people. For the elderly, especially the confused, careful explanations, perhaps seeing the body, attending the funeral service, and visits to the grave, can help settle the often-repeated questions. Simple tokens can be profoundly beneficial—a phone call, a written note, or an apple pie can be so effective. An appropriate touch or hug can sometimes be more helpful than many, or any, words. The bereaved should be reassured that their emotional experiences are nothing other than normal. Accurate and honest answers should be given to questions. These are the proper ways forward. The first anniversary of a death can be an especially difficult time. Some bereaved people need to know that their obligations to the dead loved one have been completed and that they have permission, and the opportunity, to move on with their lives. Though the typically-observed, initial episodes of intense grief will lessen with time, they may never entirely disappear because events, such as anniversaries and family gatherings, can easily trigger deep and fond memories of the absent loved one.

All this can be a hard time for the Christian, as well as the non-Christian, for none is immune to the effects of bereavement. Christian faith will be tested and previously-held beliefs may well be questioned. Of course, prayer, fellowship, worship, and the reading of Scripture are the great comforts for the Christian. This is undoubtedly a 'time of need', so Hebrews 4:16 must be applied, '... so that we may receive mercy and find grace to help us ...' Pity the poor non-Christians with no such comforts—they need help.

We should be careful not to dismiss the emotions of the bereaved as 'perfectly understandable' and thereby miss the real opportunity to help them. Nor should we adopt, or recommend, the stiff-upper lip approach. This is stoicism and it is not the Christian way. Upon hearing of the death of his friend, Lazarus, the Lord Jesus Christ '... was deeply moved in spirit and troubled' (John 11:33). The result was that 'Jesus wept' (John 11:35)—the shortest verse in the Bible, but also one of its most tender.

26.4 Children and bereavement

It is not only the elderly who die, nor is it only adults who are bereaved—children also die, and they too are bereaved. About 3,000 babies and youngsters die each year in the UK. The death of a child is one of the most painful and heart-rending preludes to bereavement, especially for the parents and siblings. Parental death also affects something like 40,000 under-nineteen-year-old children each year in the UK. And, of course, children's grandparents, aunts, uncles and more distant family relatives, also die. Children should never be excluded from the actualities of death—it can only make bereavement harder for them to bear. If Mum or Dad is dying, they should be told—they should never be lied to.

The death of a sibling or a parent can be especially difficult for a child to bear. The child may feel anger and frustration towards the one who has died, and then guilt for even entertaining such emotions. Children should certainly not be dismissed as 'resilient' and therefore 'best left out' of these matters. Children, as young as two or three years old, can have some understanding of death, and between the ages of five and eight their understanding can be well-informed. Explanations and some forewarning of the imminence and inevitability of the death of a family member can help children prepare for bereavement. Attending a funeral service can also be advantageous, but they should be protected from excessive public expressions of grief that can sometimes occur on such occasions.

Bereavement can be a good time for parents to explain the veracities of life and death, heaven and hell to their children. Above all, it is a time to be sensitive to their dear offspring. Similarly, for teenagers, bereavement can precipitate huge personal and spiritual turmoil, but also personal development. It is here that the Christian parent or close relative can shine in displaying care and compassion. In the providence of God, these are great pastoral opportunities—we should make the most of them.

This was never intended to be the definitive guide to bereavement. There are good books to read and, hopefully, there are good people within your own circle to talk to and enquire about specific information. They will also enable you to cope with both the simple and the complicated situation. The concern here has been to provide some general outline of what we might expect to happen during the common course of bereavement. After all, we are all going to experience it, probably several times within our own life span. And the best recoveries are seen among those who are best prepared to face it.

PART 6

And Finally

'Advice is seldom welcome; and those who want it the most, always like it the least.'

Lord Chesterfield, (29 January 1748) *Letter to his son.*

This book concludes with a look to the future. It is not a very bright prospect. Edge-of-life issues have corrupted our lives, our medicine, and therefore our future. What is more, they seem to be on the increase. Yet, there is some hope—not everyone is in the pro-euthanasia camp, all are not pleased to be living within a culture of death. If morally-sensitive men and women, and even children, including above all, Christians, would grasp what is at stake, understand the damage caused by these issues, and seize the day, the future could be quite different. Therein lies a major challenge of this book.

Finally, there is again that ultimate end-of-life issue—death itself. For some this is an unwelcome prospect, and the advice given here will not be welcomed by all, even though it is of the utmost urgency.

The future

O ne of the opening themes of this book described the philosophical and practical linkage between the three great and nasty bioethical issues—abortion, infanticide and euthanasia. Most people are not particularly in favour of them. But, we live in a social climate where we are not encouraged to speak disapprovingly of anything—'open-mindedness' and 'toleration' are its watchwords. Therefore, we often prefer not to discuss such issues, and thus we avoid assessing or criticizing some of the more shadowy aspects of the world of medical ethics and practice. Such a situation is disastrous. Not only does it stop us thinking and questioning, but it also means that we carelessly agree with the opinions and ideas of the secular humanistic powerful few. Though we consider ourselves to be principled, responsible and uncompromising, really we have become substantially less. From now on, refuse to be. Instead, become a radical Christian. Now there is not a new idea—is there any other sort?

27.1 Is there some hope?

Most of us have now tolerated abortion, infanticide and euthanasia for over a generation. That is too long. This book has rehearsed some of the damage these practices have done, and will continue to do, if not checked. But times, issues and people's thinking can change. For instance, nowadays women have ultrasound images of their unborn offspring—these tinies are unquestionably alive and kicking. They are destined to become the pictures on page one of their parents' baby albums. Such pictures were not available a generation ago. They cause women to think. Compared with their mothers, some of today's women are beginning to feel differently about abortion. The generation brought up with abortion is starting to reject it. For instance, today's doctors, especially women doctors, are increasingly refusing to perform abortions, much to the annoyance of the founding sisters of the feminist movement, not to mention the medical old guard. Abortion-on-demand is now not available in ninety per cent of the counties across the USA, mostly because of a distaste for the procedure among the younger medical professionals. While it is emphatically not on the way out, could it be that the wheels are starting to fall off the abortion juggernaut? In other words, is there hope, albeit a distant hope, that we will yet come to our bioethical senses?

If killing for convenience at the beginning of life is being increasingly questioned, could it be that killing at the other end of the life spectrum, namely euthanasia, will also be a phase through which we have to pass, before we reject it? The history of bioethics is curious. Rather than being resolute and steadfastly rejecting an unthinkable practice, it seems that we first have to sniff it, then taste it, and swallow it, before we finally regurgitate it.

Such rejection does occur. The widespread enslavement of men, women and children during the eighteenth century and the eventual passing of the 1833 Abolition of Slavery Act, is our great precedent. The toppling of that horror took many years and the efforts of many people, most notably the evangelicals of the 'Clapham sect' under William Wilberforce, to achieve. We are a similarly long way away from rejecting abortion. At the beginning of the twenty-first century, our society has certainly not yet given up on either the idea, or the practice, of abortion and what is more, we are on the verge of embracing euthanasia. Meanwhile, the scandal of infanticide, the go-between of abortion and euthanasia, continues.

27.2 The problems ahead

With abortion, we are fighting a rearguard action—both the law and practice are firmly in place. With euthanasia, including the neonatal variety, infanticide, we are fighting a largely unknown enemy—so far, there is no comprehensive law, but already furtive practices are taking place.

How will this develop? Laws can be prohibitive as well as permissive. For example, the 1957 Homicide Act is prohibitive, yet, also protective of human life. The 1967 Abortion Act is certainly permissive, and also destructive of human life. The 2008 (or whenever) Euthanasia Act must be prohibitive and protective. Already, politicians and others are arguing that the legalization of even limited euthanasia, 'for a few deserving cases', would be too complicated and unworkable. OK, then ban it. Maintain the current prohibition. If a new legal strengthening is needed to assuage the threat of widespread euthanasia, then ensure that the 2008 Act is proscriptively beefy. Those who say, 'But you can't make such hard and fast rules', must not be allowed to win the day. Their position is a dodge and based on nothing other than arbitrariness. They are the cause of the slippery slope. Christians should always reject such an approach. The Christian approach must be based on the stringent, non-negotiable principles, as laid out in chapter 2.

Can this Christian approach work? Of course it can! And for at least three reasons. First, it has a long history of ethical goodness. Where did family life, marriage, the work ethic, personal dignity and value, and much more, come from? Second, it has a long history of social goodness. Where did wholesome hospitals, hospices, education, democratic freedoms, and much more, come from? Third, Christianity changes men, women and children. It does not tinker with the peripherals—it goes straight to the heart. It transforms men—the abortionist becomes the pro-life campaigner. It changes women—the footloose becomes the champion of the dying. And all surrounding men and women are affected and enhanced by the presence of their salt and light. The question is not, 'Will it work?', but, 'When will it be tried?'

What values should we apply to future medicine? Why not Hippocratic and Judaeo-Christian ones? After all, they have proved themselves once. They transformed the early pagan, abusing, dangerous medicine into a culture of life. Look at their enduring and fruitful influences. They can do it again. Opposition to a return to Hippocratic-Christian medicine will come from many quarters. Those blithely led by the elite of secular humanism will want to maintain their illusory autonomy, freedom, rights and choice. Healthcare professionals can be unusually hostile towards any attempts to instruct and correct them. Too many politicians remain duty-bound by party loyalties rather than truth. The media will be jealous to retain their hard-won control of the nation's intellect. And almost everyone else just could not care less.

None of this is going to change very quickly, is it? We are in for the long haul. But, if our laws are wrong, if our understanding of human life is deficient, if our medical practice is sub-standard, if secular humanism is forging our false ethics, if the wrong people are making the wrong decisions, then they need changing. We must admit that we are currently in deep, deep trouble, but we must not admit defeat. This is where Christians must interface. Otherwise, what is the purpose of ever being salt and light? Is our rich heritage of effective social action, as nothing? Are our lifelong concerns about the welfare of others, not sufficient? Is our understanding of the issues of life and death, unsatisfactory? Here is that recurring challenge of this book—we must no longer simply sit on our hands and bemoan the unethical practices and shabby principles of our society, and particularly of modern medicine. We must think truth, speak truth, and act truth.

27.3 Is it too late?

This book has argued that much of medicine has failed the test. Its grand old ethical foundations have been largely abandoned, so that now medicine is practised upon an unstable philosophical base, and within an environment that can best be described as a culture of death. The disciplines of obstetrics and gynaecology, paediatrics and geriatrics are at the forefront of this crumbling medicine. Yet, these are the very aspects of medicine that deal with the primary edge-of-life issues, the subject of this book. Is it too late for these once admirable medical specialties to reform? I fear it might be. The rot is now so deeply entrenched. This situation is compounded by the fact that many of our best young people—Christians and the morally sensitive—now no longer feel able to enter professions that are as ethically-bankrupt as doctoring and nursing. The future certainly can look dreary.

27.4 What we really need

At many points in human history, personal and public, the best way forward has been to start again. Christians who trace their religious heritage via, for example, Nonconformity and the Reformation will be only too well aware of this. A crisis can produce a crossroads. I think that we might be at a bioethical crossroads. Can we wait and try to reform medicine from the inside, or do we opt out and create what others have called a 'pro-life counter-culture'? Is it now time to forsake the culture of death and instead concentrate on creating a culture of life? To begin to re-establish God-honouring, Hippocratic-type medicine in our land we would have to set up new healthcare centres, clinics, and maybe even hospitals. These would all proclaim themselves to be abortion-free, infanticide-free and euthanasia-free zones. This is extreme stuff. But in many ways the hospice movement, initiated, and still largely maintained, by the voluntary sector, has pointed the way. The need for such admirable facilities, in which we can feel, and be, safe, receiving pro-life treatment from the hands of pro-life doctors and nurses, is becoming more and more pressing.

Would it be feasible? It would be difficult. But there are several initiatives that can serve as prototypes and encouragements. Here are just two. Prospects is a Christian charity serving people with physical and mental disabilities. It started in 1976, after three families, each with disabled children, realized the need for long-term, Christian-based provision for their children when they became too old to care for them, or died. Now it provides residential care in almost forty UK locations, plus day care services for a total of about 150 people. The other is Zoë's Place, situated at the LIFE Health Centre in Liverpool. It was the first neonatal hospice in the UK, probably the world. At any one time its staff can care for up to six babies, from birth to age four, who have life-limiting illnesses, and multiple special needs. Of course, both initiatives are but drops in a bucket of need. Yet the alternative is to do what—nothing? Prospects and Zoë's are models of what can be done—everything else is so negative.

Is this a cop-out? Is it counter to the tenor of this book, namely, that we are to live as salt and light among an unbelieving and perverse generation? No, no, no. We are not opting out of this world and its problems. Rather, we would be showing the world how it can, and should, be done. Medicine practised within the culture of life is sweet and attractive. Is this the pro-life challenge of the century? Will the world, one day, beat a path to the doors of pro-life medical centres and hospitals, as it has done with the hospice movement, and ask, 'Please show us how to do it'?

No one can forecast the state of medical ethics and practice in ten, or even five, years. According to current trends, it will be worse than at present. But remaining in our current bioethical rut is not compulsory. It is possible to bring about change. It could be done, if we had the will—I do not know if we have. But this I do know, if you and I, as ordinary citizens, turn our backs on these edge-of-life issues, and shrug our shoulders, and say they are nothing to do with us, then the future will be bleak indeed. If, on the other hand, you and I, and a million others grasp the issues, denounce what is wrong, and determine to provide positive alternatives, then ..... Attentive readers will recall that this is just about where we came in. The question on page 27 was, how should Christians think, speak, and act in the face of the edge-of-life issues? Now you know!

'Let me die the death of the righteous, and may my end be like theirs!'

Numbers 23:10.

Dear Reader,

This book has been written from a Christian perspective, primarily, but not exclusively, for a Christian readership. All its hopes and certainties are Christian hope and certainty. Death has been its central theme. For Christians, death is the way to heaven—it is their happy expectation, and it will be their joy. For the non-Christian, there are no such consolations.

The Bible talks about hell as much as it talks about heaven. The Lord Jesus Christ gave details of both, many, many times. All human life is lived on just two roads, entered through one of only two gateways. You are on the one, or the other. There is no middle road, no third way. There is the narrow road that leads to heaven, and there is the broad road that leads to hell. There is a heaven to be won, and a hell to be shunned. Therefore, as the Lord Jesus Christ said,

'Enter through the narrow gate. For wide is the gate and broad is the road that leads to destruction, and many enter through it. But small is the gate and narrow the road that leads to life, and only a few find it.'
Matthew 7:13–14.

Therefore,

'Make every effort to enter through the narrow door, because many, I tell you, will try to enter and will not be able to.'
Luke 13:24.

and finally,

'... prepare to meet your God ...'
Amos 4:12.

Resources

There is an almost endless, and ever-growing, list of edge-of-life resources. Here are just a few, which can be used to extend some of the topics covered within this book. But beware, they are not all from the culture of life—some have their origins firmly in the culture of death. Happy hunting, and profitable (and discerning) reading!

Books

Alexander, Archibald (1967). *Thoughts on Religious Experience*. Banner of Truth Trust, London.

Beauchamp, Thomas L & James F Childress (1979). *Principles of Biomedical Ethics*. Oxford University Press, New York.

Burleigh, Michael (1995). *Death and Deliverance. 'Euthanasia' in Germany 1900–1945*. Cambridge University Press, Cambridge.

Doyle, Derek, Geoffrey W C Hanks & Neil McDonald (1999). *Oxford Textbook of Palliative Medicine*. Oxford University Press, Oxford.

Gert, Bernard, Charles M Culver & K Danner Clouser (1997). *Bioethics: A Return to Fundamentals*. Oxford University Press, Oxford.

Glover, Jonathan (1977). *Causing Death and Saving Lives*. Penguin Books, London.

Harris, John (1985). *The Value of Life*. Routledge & Kegan Paul, London.

House of Lords (1994). *Report of the Select Committee on Medical Ethics*. HMSO, London.

Keown, John (1995). *Euthanasia Examined*. Cambridge University Press, Cambridge.

Kuhse, Helga & Peter Singer (1985). *Should the Baby Live? The Problem of Handicapped Infants*. Oxford University Press, Oxford.

Lecky, William E H (1913). *History of European Morals from Augustine to Charlemagne*. Longmans, Green and Co, London.

Ling, John R (2001). *Responding to the Culture of Death—A Primer of Bioethical Issues*. Day One Publications, Epsom.

Phillips, Melanie & John Dawson (1985). *Doctors' Dilemmas. Medical Ethics and Contemporary Science*. Harvester Press, Brighton.

Porter, Roy (1997). *The Greatest Benefit to Mankind. A Medical History of Humanity from Antiquity to the Present*. Fontana Press, London.

Rachels, James (1986). *The End of Life—Euthanasia and Morality*. Oxford University Press, Oxford.

Saunders, Cicely (1988). *St Christopher's in Celebration—Twenty-One Years of Britain's First Modern Hospice*. Hodder and Stoughton, London.

Saunders, Cicely (1990). *Hospice and Palliative Care: An Interdisciplinary Approach*. Edward Arnold, London.

Saunders, Cicely, Mary Baines & Robert Dunlop (1993). *Living with Dying—A Guide to Palliative Care*. Oxford University Press, Oxford.

Schaeffer, Francis A & C Everett Koop (1979). *Whatever Happened to the Human Race?* British edition. Marshall, Morgan & Scott, London. (1983) Revised US edition. Crossway Books, Wheaton.

Singer, Peter (1995). *Rethinking Life and Death*. Oxford University Press, Oxford.

Tassano, Fabian (1995). *The Power of Life or Death. A Critique of Medical Tyranny*. Duckworth, London.

Tada, Joni E (1992). *When is it Right to Die? Suicide, Euthanasia, Suffering, Mercy*. Zondervan Publishing House, Grand Rapids.

Tooley, Michael (1983). *Abortion and Infanticide*. Clarendon Press, Oxford.

Warnock, Mary (1998). *An Intelligent Person's Guide to Ethics*. Duckworth, London.

World Health Organization (1990). *Cancer Pain Relief and Palliative Care*. Technical Report Series 804. World Health Organization, Geneva.

World Health Organization (1996). *Cancer Pain Relief: With a Guide to Opioid Availability*. World Health Organization, Geneva.

Worldwide web sites

This is a source of millions of articles and comments, but it must be said that the vast majority are pretty poor and unsuitable. However, there are some excellent websites, like that of the *British Medical Journal*, which is fully searchable. Relevant and useful sites which cover bioethical issues include:

American Medical Association, www.ama-assn.org/ethic

- the official site for US medical thinking and practice.

British Medical Journal, www.bmj.com

- one of the best searchable, authoritative sites available.

Resources

Center for Bioethics and Human Dignity, www.cbhd.org
- a daily up-dated US site with good essays on key issues.

Christian Action, Research and Education (CARE), www.care.org.uk
- Christian perspective on bioethical issues and much, much more.

Christian Institute, www.christian.org.uk
- bioethical campaigning and educating information, plus useful links.

Fellowship of Independent Evangelical Churches (FIEC), www.fiec.org.uk/citizenship.htm
- these pages contain information of bioethical interest.

Human Genetics Commission (HGC), www.hgc.gov.uk
- news and views on genetics from the government's advisory body.

International Anti-Euthanasia Task Force, www.iaetf.org
- updates on euthanasia, assisted suicide, advance directives, etc.

LIFE, www.lifeuk.org
- pro-life articles, press releases, facts and figures.

Voluntary Euthanasia Society, www.ves.org.uk
- read what 'the enemy' is thinking and saying.

Useful addresses

Age Concern, 1268 London Road, London SW16 4ER.
CARE, 53 Romney Street, London SW1P 3RF.
Christian Institute, 26 Jesmond Street, Newcastle upon Tyne NE2 4PQ.
House of Commons, London SW1A 0AA.
House of Lords, London SW1A 0PW.
LIFE, LIFE House, Newbold Terrace, Leamington Spa CV32 4AE.
LIFE Health Centre, Yew Tree Lane, West Derby, Liverpool L12 9HH.
Prospects, PO Box 351, Reading RG1 7AL.

Index

D

Dawson, John 52
Death 15, 40, 62, 64, 197
Death on Request 146
Deathbed 237, 248
Demography 175
Dent, Bob 93
Devine, Andrew 132
Disabled 43, 86, 102, 139, 155, 170
Do not resuscitate 202
Dockery, Gary 131
Dominoes 19, 205
Double effect 192
Down's syndrome 53, 101, 108, 140, 168, 170, 207
Duff, Raymond 108
Dying 40, 62, 224, 243

E

Education 213
Emery, John 109
Eugenics 134
Euthanasia 17, 21, 79, 208, 259
Evangelical churches 80, 215
Evangelicals for LIFE 14
Extraordinary means 196

F

Fall 65
Families 20, 95, 179, 214, 229, 245, 256
Farquharson, Mr Justice 168
Fertilization 37

Financial resources 21, 140, 155, 223
Fourteen-day rule 207
Franklin, Benjamin 18
Freedom 184

G

Galton, Francis 135
Gene therapy 141
Genetic screening 102, 139
Geothe, Johann 115
Glover, Jonathan 107
Golden Rule 48, 221
Good works 221
Grief 253
Groaning 224

H

Haeckel, Ernst 154
Handicap 43, 86, 102, 139, 155, 170
Hard cases 19, 23, 42, 98, 205
Hardy-Weinberg principle 137
Harris, John 86, 92
Healthy living 176
Heaven 250
Hemlock Society 148, 227
Hippocratic oath 29, 47
Hoche, Alfred 154
Holland 100, 109, 140, 144, 209, 241
Hospices 227, 234, 263
House of Lords' Report 144

Index

By the same author

RESPONDING TO THE CULTURE OF DEATH

John R Ling

128 pages A5 PB   £5.99

1 903087 26 0

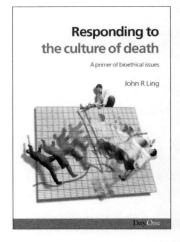

Most people are confused about 'new' bioethical issues such as human cloning and genetic engineering. Many have not even thought through the 'old' bioethical issues like, abortion and euthanasia.

The author's conviction is that we now live in a culture of death. Much of modern medicine has gone seriously wrong, and now it has become a threat to all men, women, and children.

This book does not seek to give trite, comfortable answers. Rather it develops a rugged bioethical framework, based on principles derived from the Bible, and supported by analyses of recent trends in medicine and science. But this book is not simply about cosy, fireside casuistry. It wants you out of your armchair and doing—it calls for a response of 'principled compassion' to overcome this culture of death and gain the culture of life.

REFERENCE: RCD

'This excellent book provides a clear Christian analysis of recent trends in medicine and science.' **THE CHRISTIAN INSTITUTE**

'… highly readable, lucid and up-to-date, this is a 'must' for anyone wanting to find out how to put prolife issues in a Biblical perspective…' **LIFE NEWS**

'This is an excellent book, eminently readable and presented in a well-reasoned, sensitive way. Warmly recommended!' **EVANGELICAL TIMES**

'…the book is well worth reading and is sure to be thought-provoking.' **GRACE MAGAZINE**